JAMAICA
& THE CAYMAN ISLANDS

Cadogan Books plc
London House, Parkgate Road,
London SW11 4NQ, UK
guides@cadogan.demon.co.uk

Distributed in the USA by
The Globe Pequot Press
6 Business Park Road, PO Box 833, Old Saybrook,
Connecticut 06475–0833

Copyright © James Henderson 1996
Illustrations © Dominique Salm 1996
Cover illustrations by Horacio Monteverde

Book and cover design by Animage
Maps © Cadogan Guides, drawn by Map Creation Ltd

Series editors: Rachel Fielding and Vicki Ingle
Editor: Katrina Burroughs
Proof-reading: Lorna Horsfield
Indexing: Dorothy Frame
Production: Book Production Services
Output, printed and bound in the UK by Redwood Books Ltd, Trowbridge

ISBN 1–86011–021–5
A catalogue record for this book is available from the British Library

The author and publishers have made every effort to ensure the accuracy of the information in the book at the time of going to press. However, they cannot accept any responsibility for any loss, injury or inconvenience resulting from the use of information contained in this guide.

About the author

James Henderson has been travelling to Jamaica for the last ten years and calls it work. He has stayed in all the most luxurious and the most charming hotels, eaten the finest Jamaican fare and tested out the sand and watersports on the all the best beaches. He has braved the atten-tions of machete-flourishing coconut vendors, robots, Scotch bonnet pepper, duppies and igle jubies and sketelles. He loves Jamaican music and spends as much time as possible 'winding up and skinning out' (dancing with a wide-eyed grin). He lives in hope of actually seeing the Green Flash from the cliffs in Negril.

Acknowledgements

My thanks go to all the Jamaicans, native and adop-tive, who turn dreary fact collection into an adventure with their endless hospitality and eccen-tricity: by offering lifts, beers, beds for the night (often in the most charming hotels), advice and directions (requested or otherwise), their general thoughts on life and, above all, their time, of which there is always plenty in Jamaica of course.

In particular, I am indebted to Pat Hannan for getting things moving in Jamaica and to Dawn Smith for keeping up the momentum in the face of tropical inertia. Around the island there were many tourist board officials and knowledgeable individuals who gave their time: Marguerite Gauron and Caroline Low in Port Antonio, Suzanne McManus, the elusive Mr Brown and, in Kingston, Olive Lewin. Also in Kingston, for sitting up straight during a barrage of terminally boring questioning, thanks to Emmogene and Allison. And, once again, I am grateful to Barry Matthis for being an ice-cool guide and a fount of knowledge.

Thanks to all those who took me in while on my tour of the island—Hugh Dunphy of the Bolivar Gallery, Peter and Annabella Proudlock at Harmony Hall and to Willie Fielding and Jonathan Routh. A big thank you to the crowd at Orange Valley—Alex H. and Heather and Ricki, Nicky and David and Linville—and especially to Nigel and the Kennedys, who included me in a family Christmas and a whole lot else besides. In the Caymans, many thanks to Barbara Currie Dailey.

Back at home, thanks go to all those who put up with the traveller returned as the book slowly took shape: to Katrina for making sense of it all; and finally, for comment, company and assis-tance in the Cayman Islands, to Celia.

Please help us to keep this guide up to date

Despite the valiant efforts of the author and publishers to keep the guide up to date, standards in restaurants and practical details such as prices are liable to change. We would be delighted to receive any comments concerning existing entries or indeed any suggestions for inclusion in future editions or companion volumes. Significant contributions will be acknowledged in the next edition, and authors of the best letters (or e-mails) will receive a copy of the Cadogan Guide of their choice.

Contents

Introduction

There is nothing like music to evoke a sense of place. In Jamaica life is lived to a semi-permanent soundtrack of reggae music. As the island reveals itself to you in a nexus of impressions—the warmth of the tropical sun, the glistening of leaves after the rain, the magnificent gardens of the plantation houses, the languor of the palms and beaches, the hedonistic haze induced by rum, sun and reefers—these sensations are inextricably interlaced with the easy pulse of reggae. Hear the music again at home and memories will flood back.

The turtle shape of Jamaica lies in the Caribbean Sea to the south of Cuba and to the west of Haiti, about five hundred miles south of Florida. The third largest of the Greater Antilles, the island has an area of 4411 square miles (11,424 square kilometres), about half the size of Wales. From east to west Jamaica measures 146 miles (243km) and it is 51 miles (81km) from north to south.

Physically Jamaica is spectacular. Greenery bursts into life everywhere, tended in the canefields and plantations, uncontrollable around the mountain valleys. The island is so fertile that you could almost expect a pencil to take root. And the scenery is fantastic: within a few hundred yards of the sea you can be at 1000ft (about two-fifths of the island is above this elevation). Parts of the Blue Mountains and the weird eggbox-hillocks of the Cockpit Country are so sheer and rough that they are barely accessible.

Jamaica became independent from Britain on 6 August 1962, but traces of three centuries of British colonial rule are still evident in the churches and Georgian great houses constructed by the planters, and the town clocks that chime as they do in Britain. And some British institutions remain in creolized form, including the Westminster model of democracy and the belts, peaked caps and serge trousers of uniformed policemen. However this colonial façade fails to mask a very strong African heritage. Jamaican marching bands may wear scarlet tunics with trimmings of gold braid, but their movements are not the clipped and formal procession of the British, they have the rhythmic swagger of the Jamaican. Cricket is still played in whites, but it has developed its own, typically West Indian, expression and is now thrown back at the English with a vengeance. The steadily increasing influence of the US is displayed in every sports bar and burger joint.

On a map Jamaica may look as though it languishes like a turtle, but its two and a half million inhabitants are energetic, lively, noisy and sometimes tricky. Life in Jamaica can be electric, even daunting, for a visitor. The Jamaicans are very forward: some stop you to give advice or to say hello, others to hustle you. Take time to enjoy the 'theatre of the street'. Markets, from downtown Kingston to groups of three or four people selling fruit at the roadside in the country, are mayhem as the vendors and busmen shout and quip with one another. As you travel around the towns and country roads, posses of schoolchildren race by—their uniforms changing colour, school by school. The Jamaicans do not suffer regulation or formality gladly and the quaint old convention of queueing died soon after the British left.

It is to their credit that a small country like Jamaica has made such an impression on the world. Three of the fastest eight men in the world in the 100-metre final in the Seoul Olympics were Jamaican born: Linford Christie (who ran for the UK), Raymond Stewart (Jamaica) and Ben Johnson (Canada—though he failed the drugs test).

But Jamaica's most famous export is music, brought to the world by the likes of Third World, Peter Tosh and of course Bob Marley. Jamaica just sounds wonderful, particularly at the moment. Until recently, the island was dominated by the monotonous and nigh inde-cipherable rat-a-tat rap of dancehall music; but now you will hear more 'culture reggae', a slower and softer beat with more melody, which sounds more like the traditional seventies reggae bands.

For the visitor, Jamaica has the most romantic allure of all the Caribbean islands. Neglected stone gateposts and decaying walls of abandoned plantation houses bear witness to the centuries when the island was the focus of British dreams, and source of fortunes for the planters. In the 20th century, too, Jamaica has exercised the same irresistible attraction; Noël Coward, Winston Churchill, Ian Fleming and Errol Flynn all fell in love with the place. And now package tours make it possible for almost everyone to carry on the love affair. Jamaica has a large tourism industry (in places the coastline is overdeveloped with ranks of hotels), and there is something for everyone here: tucked between the humming resorts that specialize in sun, sea and sand vacations are some extremely elegant locations, and in the hills you will find hideaways on the plantations, which preserve a glorious air of old Jamaica.

Jamaica has something of a reputation as a destination fraught with unpleasant hustling. One solution to the problem is never to leave the compound of your hotel; if you want nothing but a beach then this is a passable plan, but you will miss out on the best of Jamaica. Being hustled can be a bit tough, but reports that the island is unsafe are vastly overstated—just take as much care as you would in any poor country; do not go to certain places after dark and do not expose yourself to unnecessary risks.

Jamaica repays the adventurous, and of course there is simply nothing like sitting in a rickety Jamaican beach bar, Red Stripe in hand, surrounded by sand, palms and a warm sea, with the island's heartbeat of reggae playing in the background.

Suggested Itinerary

You can make this tour of Jamaica, following the coastline clockwise, in a couple of weeks. It will give you time in the tourist resorts as well as a look at something more Jamaican: the magnificent interior of the island and maybe Kingston.

Whether you fly in to Kingston or Montego Bay, your first stop will probably be one of the tourist areas on the **north coast**, between Negril and Ocho Rios. This is where the beaches and the main facilities are, and the liveliest crowds. If you are not booked in to a hotel then there are plenty of smaller, less expensive places to stay and you can hop from one to the next. If you know you are looking for a quieter resort, then go straight on to Port Antonio or to the south coast.

Port Antonio is a charming, laid-back town in the far east, the lushest and most strikingly fertile part of the island. From here you can go up into the **Blue Mountains**, the quietest, most idyllic region of Jamaica. If you have time, **Kingston** is well worth a visit, though it is not the most relaxing experience. The capital will show you the Jamaicans' Jamaica—check out the markets downtown and take a ferry over to **Port Royal**. From here you should head west to the sleepy towns of **Treasure Beach** and **Black River**, where the Jamaicans take their holidays.

Finally, leave enough time for a last stop in **Negril**, a tourist town with a difference. It has all the facilities of the major resorts, without their frantic atmosphere. It is great for a few days' hanging out, watching for the sunset and waiting for the flight home.

Resort Report

Blue Mountains: Some of the most natural and spectacularly beautiful parts of Jamaica are here, just a short drive from Kingston. Relax in the mountain villages, in accommodation from camping to high luxury. Excellent walking and wildlife and a gentle atmosphere.

Montego Bay: The hotel heartland and airport hub of the tourist industry. Large and busy, with plenty of beaches and watersports for the daytime, some 'sights' and activities in the interior, and restaurants and bars for the evening. High hustle factor around Gloucester Avenue and downtown.

Negril: Building continues apace wherever there is space left on the beach, and the atmosphere becomes steadily more upbeat, but still a relaxed place to indulge in the time-honoured Jamaican pursuit of watching the sunset. Some excellent retreats and millions of bars. Water is sometimes a problem in Negril, especially along the cliffs, where the pressure drops. The hustle factor is about as bad as ever.

Ocho Rios: Soulless as always, but trying to get its infrastructure in order—a bypass has recently been built, with huge difficulties and plenty of scandal. Some outstanding hotels amid the majority of mid-range lacklustre properties. Plenty of bars and restaurants and also many 'sights' to visit during the days. Runaway Bay and Discovery Bay are two small clusters of tourist hotels between the main resorts of Montego Bay and Ocho Rios, without the infrastructure but within visiting range of the larger towns. Limited restaurants and bars.

Port Antonio: Dozy town set in the loveliest, most rugged corner of Jamaica. Quieter, more friendly atmosphere than the main resorts, with some good hotels in all categories. Excellent beaches, just a few restaurants and bars.

Treasure Beach: Although Treasure Beach is often referred to as a resort, it's a remote, sleepy town, with just a few small guest houses and hotels (most of them modern) among the Jamaican houses.

Note: among the recommended places to stay, the author's favourites are highlighted with a palm symbol

Travel

Getting There By Air

Jamaica is well served by both scheduled and charter flights. There are two international airports on the island. The Sangster International Airport in Montego Bay serves the north coast and its resort towns of Negril, Montego Bay, Runaway Bay and Ocho Rios. If you are going to Kingston or travelling on to Port Antonio, you should fly to the Norman Manley International Airport just outside Kingston itself. Long-haul scheduled flights often make a stop at both airports. Charters tend to fly only into Montego Bay. If flight timings are not convenient, flying via Miami is an option. Jamaica is about an hour and a half from Miami.

From the UK

The only direct scheduled flights to Jamaica are from London, on **British Airways**, ✆ 0345 222111, three times a week, and **Air Jamaica**, ✆ 0181 570 9171, also three times a week.

The scheduled airlines issue standard open tickets at a very expensive year-round fare, though these are discounted with a variety of apex fares (booked 21 days in advance) which vary on a monthly and even weekly basis. The most expensive times to travel, when there are fewest apex tickets on offer, are: June, July and August, and in the weeks around Christmas. The standard scheduled return fare from the UK to Jamaica bought through the airlines is around £1000, not usually discounted to much below £700. It is almost invariably cheaper to go through the many travel agents, who are able to offer reductions; a restricted number of these tickets are released by the airlines, and only for certain dates of travel.

A number of charter airlines fly from Brtain to Jamaica and it is now possible to get a seat-only ticket on these flights (availability depends on the time of year and how booked up they are). Charter seats to Jamaica are usually for two weeks, but most offer a one-week or three/four week stay for a supplement. Charter companies include **Caledonian**, **Britannia** and **Airtours**. However, tickets cannot be bought direct from the charter companies; they must be bought through a travel agent.

Fares on a charter airline vary enormously across the year and you can pay anything between £300 and £600. Christmas and Easter are expensive times, as is the high summer, July–September. Low season, the best time for discounted fares, is May and November–December, not a good period to travel to Jamaica, because it is the rainy season. However, there is some discounting in January and February, one of the best times to travel weather-wise, so it is worth scouting around then. Bear in mind, though, the tourist hotels are charging their high rates at this time.

Specialist ticket shops in the UK, selling flights to Jamaica and other Caribbean islands, include: **Caribbean Travel**, 367 Portobello Rd, London W10 5SG,

✆ 0181 969 6230; **Calypso Gold**, Equerry House, 1 Kingston Lane, Teddington, Middelsex TW11 9HL, ✆ 0181 943 0070; **New Look Travel**, 11 High Street, Harlesden, London NW10 4TR, ✆ 0181 965 9657; **Newmont Travel**, 85 Balls Pond Road, London N1 4BL, ✆ 0171 254 6546; **Stoke Newington Travel**, 168 Stoke Newington Road, London N16 7UY, ✆ 0171 254 0136. The **Caribbean Reunion Club** (yearly membership £5) also offers cut price flights and a knowledgeable operator to the Eastern Caribbean is **Transatlantic Wings**, 70 Pembroke Road, London W8 6NX, ✆ 0171 602 4021.

In Birmingham, contact **Uncle Sam Travel**, 295 Soho Road, Handsworth, Birmingham B21 9SA, ✆ 0121 523 3141, and **Diamond Travel**, 178 Dudley Road, Edgebaston, N18 7QX and in Manchester try **Miss Eena's Travel**, 18 Upper Charlton Road, Old Trafford, Manchester M16 7RN, ✆ 0161 232 9979. Some of these companies will also be able to book inexpensive accommodation for you.

From Europe

Airlines offering scheduled flights from Europe to Jamaica include **Martinair** (Amsterdam ✆ 20 60 11 310, which makes a weekly trip from Amsterdam to Montego Bay. Charter operators include **Condor**, ✆ 61 07 75 50, which flies weekly from Frankfurt to Montego Bay.

From the USA

There are direct scheduled flights to Montego Bay (and often to Kingston) on either **Air Jamaica** or **American Airlines** from Atlanta (daily), Baltimore (twice daily), Dallas (daily), Detroit (daily on Northwest Airlines), Fort Lauderdale (daily), Kansas City (daily), Los Angeles (twice weekly), Miami (plenty each day), New York (several flights daily), Orlando (five times weekly), Philadelphia (daily) and Tampa (daily on Northwest Airlines). Kingston is well served from Miami and New York, for the returning Jamaican market. Charter operators include **Apple Vacations**, **Funjet Vacations** and **Sunburst Holidays**, and tickets on these flights are available through travel agents.

The price of tickets depends on the season (it is high in the summer and at important dates such as Thanksgiving and at Christmas and New Year), on the length of the stay (a week's ticket is cheaper than a three-day fare) and on whether you travel at the weekend. To get the best deal you will need to book in advance.

For a return ticket to Jamaica you can expect to pay around $250 from Miami, about $350 from the northeast, $400 from the mid-west and from the west coast about $450.

From Canada

The only direct scheduled flights from Canada to Jamaica are from Toronto, daily on both **Air Jamaica** and **Air Canada**, ℅ 800 268 7240, to Kingston and five times a week to Montego Bay; so if you are flying from elsewhere in Canada you can change in Toronto or in a convenient city in the USA. There are a number of charter flights that also fly into Montego Bay (from Toronto year-round and from Vancouver in the winter) and seat-only tickets are available through travel agents.

The fare will vary according to the season, to the length of the stay and to the time of travel (it's cheaper mid-week). For an apex ticket, you can expect to pay anything from C$450.

From other Caribbean Islands

These tend to fly into Kingston rather than Montego Bay because they serve local businesspeople rather than tourists. There is not really any seasonal discounting but it may well be worth investigating some of the many hopper tickets offered by the Caribbean airlines.

There are flights most days from Grand Cayman on either Air Jamaica or Cayman Airways (some also stop at Montego Bay), and two weekly flights to Nassau in the Bahamas and three a week to Havana in Cuba on Cubana (there are also three flights each week from Montego Bay to Cuba). There are direct flights on BWIA (the Trinidadian airline) to several destinations in the eastern Caribbean: to Sint Maarten (twice weekly), Antigua (five times) and Barbados (daily). Port of Spain in Trinidad is served daily as well. BWIA has a ticket called the Intra-Carib Airpass, which allows you to link with other islands in the eastern Caribbean with certain restriction and regulations (no back-tracking, 30 day validity), price US$356. South of Jamaica, Curaçao is served twice weekly from Kingston on ALM, who offer a 'System Pass' between Jamaica and the Dutch Antillean islands.

Connections from South America are usually made in Miami, from where there are plenty of flights each day, but it is possible to change in Panama, from where there are three flights a week. There are no direct flights from the Caribbean cities of Port au Prince in Haiti or Santo Domingo in the Dominican Republic and there are no direct links to San Juan in Puerto Rico.

Specialist Tour Operators

If you decide to take a package holiday, you will probably buy it from a brochure produced by a tour operator. The package will usually include flights (from the UK you can often choose whether to fly with a scheduled or a charter airline), airport transfer to your hotel, and accommodation. There are endless different prices (for the different meal plans, weekend travel supplements, etc.). Some tour operators will tailor-make holidays for you (and many will send hotel brochures if you request them), but this is quite expensive. Many offer two-centre holidays, usually with Florida. As a general rule, the tour operators tend not to discount their packages, but occasionally there are deals, in May and September (from the UK and Europe), when the charter flight operators are looking to fill seats and the hotels are in their low season.

Tour Operators in the UK

BA Holidays, Astral Towers, Betts Way, London Road, Crawley RH10 2XA, ✆ 01293 723161, ✉ 01293 722650, books a variety of the leading all-inclusives and mid- to upper-range hotels.

Caribbean Connection, Concorde House, Forest Street, Chester CH1 1QR, ✆ 01244 329671, ✉ 01244 310255, offers a number of the top hotels, has a brochure covering the all-inclusives, and will tailor-make holidays.

Caribtours, 161 Fulham Road, London SW3 6SN, ✆ 0171 581 3517, ✉ 0171 225 2491. A wide range of top-notch and less expensive hotels; good prices.

Harlequin Worldwide, 2 North Road, South Ockendon, Essex RM 15 6QJ, ✆ 01708 852780, ✉ 01708 814184. Offers only a few of the best hotels, but will tailor-make to places that most companies do not cover. Some diving and nature packages.

Elegant Resorts, the Old Palace, Chester CH1 1RB, ✆ 01244 897999, ✉ 01244 897990. Some of the top hotels and some villas.

Thomas Cook, PO Box 36, Thorpe Wood, Peterborough, Cambridgeshire PE3, ✆ 01733 332255, ✉ 01733 505784. Mid- to upper-range properties.

Airtours, Wavell House, Holcombe Road, Helmshore, Rossendale, Lancs BB4 4NB, ✆ 01706 260000, offers a wide variety of mid- to lower-range accommodation, all-inclusives and self-catering properties.

A number of the flights specialists also offer limited accommodation around the island, usually in the less expensive hotels that are not covered by the large tour operators. The **Caribbean Centre**, ✆ 0181 940 3399, has arrangements with a number of the smaller hotels and can get you started if you are travelling around the island. Alternatively, try **Just Jamaica**, ✆ 0800 27 26 25; London ✆ 0171 436 9292; Birmingham ✆ 0121 523 4288.

Villa specialists include **International Chapters**, 102 St John's Wood Terrace, London NW8 6PL, ✆ 0171 722 0722, ✉ 0171 722 9140, and **Palmer and Parker Holidays**, The Beacon, Penn, Buckingham HP10 8ND, ✆ 01494 815411, ✆ 01494 814184. Villas can be rented with staff and sometimes with cars (check with the company for the exact arrangements). You will need to arrange your own flights. You can also book villas accommodation through **JAVA**, Suite 607, Langham House, 302–8 Regent Street, London W1 5AL, ✆ 0800 272625, ✉ 0171 580 7220.

Tour Operators in the USA

A good travel agent should be able sort through the stacks of wholesalers' and tour company brochures and come up with the ideal place for you to stay. If you wish to stay in one of Jamaica's smarter hotels, then you can book direct through the reservation numbers in the States (listed in the 'Where to Stay' sections in the gazetteer chapters), or your travel agent can arrange the booking, flights and the transfers.

Wholesalers cover the hotels in a broad price range. They include **Go-Go Tours**, which has offices all over the country: head office, ✆ 201 934 3500; in New York, toll free ✆ 1 800 526 0405. **Travel Impressions** also has offices around the country, toll free ✆ 1 800 284 0044. A smaller operator is **Caribbean Concepts**, based in Syosset, ✆ 516 496 9800, ✉ 516 496 9880, toll free ✆ 1 800 423 4433; they cover mainly the all-inclusive properties. For villas, **JAVA**'s main US address is in Chicago: 1501 West Fullerton Avenue, Chicago, IL 60614, ✆ 312 883 3485, ✉ 312 883 5140, toll free ✆ 1 800 VILLAS6.

Specialist tour operators include **Reggaejam Tours** of Tampa, Florida, ✆ 813 965 7944, ✉ 813 989 0200, toll free ✆ 1 800 U REGGAE, who arrange special music tours of Jamaica at the time of the major concerts and festivals, and **Dreamscape Dive Tours**, based in Fort Lauderdale, ✆ 954 572 2850, ✉ 954 572 2975, who will fix a diving holiday for you.

Tour Operators in Canada

Tour operators in Canada tend to cover the mass market and so if you wish to stay in the most expensive hotels in Jamaica you should book through your travel agent. Package operators include **Sunquest**, ✆ 1416 485 1700, and **Signature** ✆ 1416 967 1510. You can also try **Air Canada Vacations**, ✆ 1604 606 1425.

Entry Formalities

British visitors and all others from the EC must show a passport, but no visa is required. US and Canadian citizens must show proof of citizenship, either in the form of a passport or voter registration card and driving licence; no visa is required. Japanese visitors need a passport and must have a visa for a stay of more than 30 days. Some residents of South American countries do need visas to enter Jamaica.

All visitors must present an onward or return ticket to get into the country. There is a departure tax of J$500 (approximately £8 or $12).

Visitors are permitted to enter the country with two litres of alchohol and with a carton of cigarettes. On returing home, UK visitors are permitted the same allowances as from any other country—200 cigarettes or 50 cigars and a litre of spirits. US visitors are allowed two litres of spirits if one litre is Jamaican and, once they have stayed 48 hours, they are allowed $400 worth of goods.

For all Jamaica's easy image, the customs officials do not take a lenient line on illegal drugs and if you are caught with some you will be charged.

Getting Around

By Air

If you need to make a transfer to an international flight and would prefer not to risk the mountainous Jamaican roads, the main Jamaican towns are linked by air, with flights scheduled on **Air Jamaica Express**. The airline was revamped in 1996 but it is now flying to all the major airports around Jamaica.

In Kingston you fly from Tinson Pen Airport (airport code KTP, ✆ 923 8680). From here you can catch one of the eight daily flights to Montego Bay (MBJ, ✆ 952 5401), which take about 30 minutes; four flights daily go to Negril (NEG, ✆ 957 4251), taking about 40 minutes; Ocho Rios is served twice daily (OCJ, ✆ 975 3254); as is Port Antonio (POT, ✆ 993 2405), 15 minutes from Kingston.

If there are enough of you, then you might charter a plane. Contact the companies listed in the gazetteer section. You can take a sight-seeing flight over the Cockpit Country from Sangster International airport in Montego Bay and in Ocho Rios you can even go sight-seeing by helicopter: contact **Helitours**, ✆ 974 2265, a couple of days in advance.

By Bus

The Jamaicans tend to laugh when a visitor announces an intention to catch a bus. Jamaican buses are noisy (only sometimes because of the stereo systems, which have been banned), and they are usually hot and crowded. They do, however, give you an excellent exposure to Jamaican life. If you are sitting, you may well find that a 'standee' hands you their luggage to hold—fine when it's a satchel or a briefcase, but a little odd when a baby is thrust into your arms. Although you can get pretty well anywhere in Jamaica on a bus, they are often quite slow and uncomfortable. Within the large towns there always seem to be hundreds of buses (usually minibuses) running in every direction, but never quite enough of them. For the bus stations and routings between towns, *see* the separate chapters in the gazetteer section.

Between the main towns, the limited number of government coaches is supplemented by endless private minivans. There are no official schedules, but buses seem to run on every road on the island. It is best to travel in the morning, but they run until dusk and later on the main routes. It is also a good idea to check the fare as you get on, though you may not actually hand over the money until later in the journey. In the country, flag buses down from the side of the road with a frantic wave.

Buses to towns on the north coast leave from downtown Kingston, west along Beckford Street from the Parade. For Spanish Town and Mandeville go to the station at HalfWay Tree. In Montego Bay the main terminus is on Barnett Street just south of the downtown area, in Negril at the roundabout, in Ocho Rios at the roundabout and in Port Antonio on Foreshore Road on the eastern harbour.

On a long journey you will find that the drivers take a break midway through the journey, giving the passengers a chance to stretch their legs and get a drink or something to eat. The different rest stops en route from the capital are known for their different snacks. At Old Harbour (going west from Kingston) there is fry fish and bammy, at Melrose Hill (near Mandeville) the popular meal is roast yam and salt fish, at Fates Pen (Kingston to Ocho Rios) you will find a variety of snacks and at Friendship Gap the popular snack is fry chicken.

Mini-buses run in networks from the main towns to smaller settlements outside and these can usually be caught at the main termini. There is also a parallel system of share-taxis; whatever their make, they are referred to as Ladas. They charge a little more than the buses and come in for as much abuse as the buses themselves. There is a current joke about a man who left his private car (a Lada as it happens) with its engine running outside a shop while he raced in for a delivery, only to find it full of people waiting to be driven out of town when he re-emerged. Ladas are also known as robot taxis, because by general consent they are driven as if by automatons: at high speed, with no regard for other road-users, from morning till night—to be fair, many of the drivers have to drive most of the day to make enough money to cover the hire of the vehicle, before they actually make any money for themselves. To signal to a driver point repeatedly and rapidly at the ground and shout.

Hitch-hiking in Jamaica is not really to be recommended. If a car stops, it is probably a taxi anyway.

By Car

The Jamaicans joke that car hire in Jamaica is so expensive that really you buy the car each time you hire one.

However, if you can afford it, it is well worth having one to explore the remarkably beautiful mountain roads and the headlands and bays along the coastline. There are plenty of hire cars available, but it is still a good idea to arrange it a few days ahead in season.

The Jamaicans are pretty awful drivers and the roads are notorious for being pot-holed, causing people to weave all over the road just when you would like them to move over to let you pass. The system works, after a fashion, though to a new-comer it may seem pretty chaotic and a little alarming. In town, the Jamaicans perform some remarkable manœuvres in their constant hurry. Driving on the high roads is correspondingly more dangerous, as all the same manoeuvres are per-formed at high speed. People seem to pass in some quite surprising (not to say dangerous) places, and then solemnly cut you up in order to get back into the left-hand lane. You are expected to give ground quickly if a truck comes around the corner. Often you will find that drivers do not dip their headlights at night—but if you try the same trick they will often do so. Avoid driving in downtown Kingston except for sport (although unfortunately the traffic is so slow there at the moment that even this is gone). Finally, if you hear the distant but steadily approaching wail of a fog-horn, you should begin to panic—it warns that a juggernaut is travelling as fast as it can towards you, and that the driver is not intending to give way to anyone. Be ready to get off the road in a hurry.

Although it is friendly and a good way to discover things about the country, giving lifts to people is ill-advised. Perhaps restrict it to ladies dressed in crinolines on Sundays, when they need a lift on the way to church. Another word of warning: a traffic accident that involves a death in Jamaica can develop quickly into a nasty sit-uation. Bus drivers have been lynched for crashes due to irresponsible driving. A senior police officer advised a British friend that if he was involved in a traffic acci-dent he should not stop, but rather drive straight to the nearest police station to report it.

The country is not that well sign-posted, so take a good map (available from the hire companies and the Tourist Board). Jamaica has recently converted to kilo-metres. Driving happens mainly on the left; watch out for goats and cows. A driving licence from home is acceptable, minimum age 25. Take a credit card for the hefty security deposit. There are many hire companies, with a variety of dif-ferent contracts—read yours. The Jamaica U-Drive Association represents a number of car-hire companies who share a standard code of business; a list is obtainable at the Tourist Board offices. Reckon on rental of at least US$60 plus charges for the smallest car for a single day. There are other smaller, local enter-prises which offer lower rates, though you are advised to read the small print of the insurance form carefully. If you are fearful of driving in Jamaica, cars with drivers are available at a little extra cost (and the security deposit is waived). Most compa-nies have free airport and hotel drop-off but will charge an inter-city delivery fee.

Taxis are readily available in the tourist towns in Jamaica. If it is raining or for some reason you cannot find one, then you can book them through any hotel lobby and through taxi stands (*see* under appropriate towns). Steel yourself to run the gauntlet of drivers touting for business as you emerge from the airport. The Tourist Board sets a standard fare, posted in **JUTA** taxis and quoted in both US and Jamaican dollars. With the others, bargain. Taxis are not usually metered in Jamaica and so you are advised to settle the fare before you set off. All licensed taxis have the red PPV plates. Some restaurants will send a car to pick you up and return you to your hotel.

Many of the taxi drivers double as tour guides if you wish to take a ride to the local sights or up into the hills. Any hotel lobby will find a driver for you and the price is usually reasonable when divided between four.

Practical A–Z

Beaches

There are plenty of good beaches around Jamaica, and many of them have the superb white sand, gin-clear water and fringe of palm trees that make picture-postcard perfection. There are beaches to suit everyone's taste: from the seemingly endless strand at Negril with its fantastic view of the sunset and non-stop watersports, to the narrow bays in the east around Port Antonio, where the mountains tumble into the sea, enclosing a small, idyllic cave. There are lively beaches, with watersports outfits and bars, and secluded, very quiet ones.

Most of the best beaches are along the north shore, where the sand is usually bright white because of the reef just out to sea. The southern shore tends to have greyer sand, and the water there is often a little murkier. You should remember that not every hotel in Jamaica is on the beach and that not every hotel beach in Jamaica is that nice. If the beach is the most vital component of your holiday, you should go into the details of its nature and facilities with your tour operator. Most hotels of any size on a beach will have some watersports. Again, check to see what they offer.

Many of the best stretches of sand in Jamaica are effectively private. Legally speaking, all beaches in Jamaica are public up to the high water mark, but if there is no access over the land, unless you are prepared to swim in, they are unreachable. Some hotels allow non-residents on their beaches, usually for a small fee (ask around in your area). All-inclusive hotels, which make up a high proportion of the hotels in Jamaica now, will demand an expensive day fee, which entitles you to use of all their facilities and food and drink.

There are, however, public beaches, at least one in each of the major resort towns, some free, some charging a small fee. These are usually lively, particularly at weekends, when the Jamaicans themselves use them, and they will often have watersports concessions. Most have at least one snack and drinks bar.

The Jamaicans are far too modest (in public, about their bodies at any rate) to go nude on the beaches. Nudity is officially illegal, but it is also frowned upon by the locals, so there are very few public places in Jamaica where even toplessness is acceptable. However, several of the resorts do have designated nude beaches. Again, ask.

Bookshops

In the UK, the following London bookshops have a wide selection of travel books including a section on Jamaica.

Daunt's Bookshop, 83 Marylebone High Street, London W1M 4DE,
Ⓒ 0171 224 2295, will send you a list of their material.

The Travel Bookshop, 13 Blenheim Crescent, London W11 2EE,
✆ 0171 229 5260.

Stanford's have a number of outlets around London. Their shop at 12–14
Longacre, London WC2E 9LP, ✆ 0171 836 1321, is also a specialist
map shop.

In the USA, try:

British Travel Books, 40 West 57th Street, New York, NY 10019,
✆ 212 765 0898.

Rand McNally Map Travel, 444 North Michigan Avenue, Chicago, IL 60611.

The Complete Traveller, 4038 Westheimer, Houston, TX 77027.

Traveller's Bookstore, 22 West 52nd Street, New York, NY 10019,
✆ 212 664 0995.

Travel Logs, 222 West 83rd Street, New York, NY 10024, ✆ 212 799 8761.

Travel Merchandise, 1425 K Street NW, Washington, DC 20005,
✆ 202 371 6656.

For bookshops in Jamaica itself, *see* under specific towns.

Calendar of Events

January

The **Maroon Festival** takes place on 7 January in Accompong, in honour
of the Treaty signed with the British authorities, a day of official celebrations and announcements while fête-like games go on all around, followed
by an evening of concerts and dances. The Jamaican National Gallery in
Kingston holds the **Annual National Exhibition** of Jamaican artists. The
Negril Sprint Triathlon (swim, cycle and 10-km run) is in late January.
The Little Theatre, Kingston holds the **Jamaica School of Dance**
concert season.

February

On 6 February is the **Bob Marley Birthday Bash**: contact Tuff Gong
Studios in Kingston, ✆ 927 9152. The **Red Stripe Cricket Competition** is
held; some matches are played in Sabina Park against teams such as
Barbados, Trinidad, the Leeward Islands, the Windward Islands and
Guyana. **Miami to Montego Bay Yacht Race. UWI Carnival Revelries**
are staged by the University of the West Indies, along the lines of most
Caribbean carnivals, with street parades and dancing.

Miss Jamaica Caribbean Beauty Pageant, ✆ 938 2510.

Jamaica Carnival is held in Kingston, with smaller parades around other towns. **South Coast Fishing Tournament**, Black River. **Harmony Hall Easter Craft Fair** in Ocho Rios.

Negril Carnival, with street parades and dancing.

National Dance Theatre Company **Season of Dance**, in Little Theatre, Kingston.

The **Independence Day Celebrations** are staged on the first Monday of the month, held mainly in Kingston, with parades and marching bands in the National Stadium in Kingston. **Reggae Sumfest**, Montego Bay; **Reggae Sunsplash**, St Ann's.

Montego Bay hosts several **fishing tournaments**.

There's a **fishing tournament** at Ocho Rios, and the **International Blue Marlin Tournament** at Port Antonio, ✆ 923 8724. **James Bond Festival**, Ocho Rios.

The **LTM Pantomime** starts on Boxing Day and continues into spring.

The Jamaica Tourist Board publishes a twice-yearly list of festivals, giving the exact dates of forthcoming events.

Children

Despite its reputation as a couples' and honeymooners' destination, Jamaica offers a good holiday for children; the Jamaicans are friendly and indulgent towards them; they might even be invited to join one of the screaming small-persons' posses that chase around the countryside and beaches. And many of the 'sights' are fairly child-friendly: Dunn's River and other waterfalls, and some of the plantation tours, on which they can try out the different tropical fruits.

Most hotels have limited facilities to entertain children (board games, etc.), but they will all be able to arrange a babysitter for the evening. A few hotels at the top of the range have a policy of not admitting children under a certain age, usually in the winter season. But a couple of hotels actually specialize in children's holidays—the better of the two is **Boscobel Beach** in Ocho Rios (*see* p.163); otherwise try **FDR** in Runaway Bay (*see* p.171). Some others, including **Half Moon** in Montego Bay (*see* p.114), have extra children's facilities.

Alternatively, the best way to handle a family holiday might be to take one of the island's many villas—and with these it's quite easy to arrange a child-minder for evening and daytime too. The only disadvantage is that sports are often not laid on or even accessible nearby. A middle way is to choose a villa hotel or a suite hotel with its rooms arranged so that the family can take adjoining rooms, giving you a living area and your own bedrooms, but still enabling you to use the hotel facilities.

Climate

The Jamaican climate is impeccable. It is warm and sunny year-round and temperatures stay pretty well constant. It is much cooler in summer than Florida and yet in the winter months it never sees anything approaching a frost. The days vary a little in length between winter and summer: sunset is at about 6pm in December and at about 7pm in June. The Jamaicans do not adjust their clocks for daylight saving time. The temperature varies considerably because of the difference in altitude. At sea level the average is 27°C, but in the Blue Mountains it is much cooler, around 13°C.

The best time to visit Jamaica is probably January, February and March, when the climate is mildest. This is, of course, when the weather is most miserable in the north, and so it is also the most expensive time to visit. Another consideration worth bearing in mind when planning a visit is the rainy season.Officially the climate is tropical maritime: each year there are two rainy seasons, in May and then in October and November. In between, rainfall is still fairly common (particularly in the mountains), and it tends to arrive in sharp, heavy downpours. However, the sun comes out and dries it all up in a few minutes.

The sun in Jamaica will burn unprotected skin in minutes. You should be careful to take precautions as sunburn can ruin your holiday.

Eating Out

There are limitless places to eat, from top-notch dining rooms on the waterfront to easygoing clifftop bars in Negril, and busy local eateries in the main towns.

Unfortunately hotel food in the British Caribbean has always been a problem; the British did not leave much of a tradition of cuisine and, with the majority of tourists coming from America, fast food has been the main contemporary culinary influence. Hotel food, even in some of the more expensive resorts, can be dreary. It tends to be in a rather unadventurous 'international' style, often using ingredients imported from the US.

Things have improved a bit recently: some hotel and restaurant chefs make imaginative use of local ingredients and continental techniques, and the results can be excellent—fresh local lobster served in lime butter or red snapper *en papillotte*. Jamaican beef is excellent, but steak is often imported because the local supply is not large or reliable enough; it is also expensive, as is lobster and king prawn. Chicken and fish are the most popular dishes, often served with rice.

Tropical vegetables are quite heavy and starchy and restaurants often serve the more familiar carrots and beans. Salads are widely available. With so many tropical fruits on the island, there are some great desserts; the ice creams are particularly good. Many restaurants will offer you Jamaica's own Blue Mountain coffee, considered to be the finest coffee in the world.

For all the exotic creations in the more adventurous kitchens, you will find that the majority of restaurants also offer burgers and chips and pizzas. Quite a lot of hotels, particularly the all-inclusives, serve their meals as buffets; in the most expensive places, these have now become remarkably good.

Since many people stay in all-inclusives, with meals as part of the package, outside the hotels there are not that many really good restaurants. Each town has just a few places where you can expect to eat well in a fine setting. For the pick of the bunch, *see* the listings in the separate gazetteer chapters. A word of warning: Jamaican restaurants and dining rooms can be extremely frustrating because the service is so bad that it is almost surreal. There is little you can do except put on a 'philosopical' head and bear it or leave. Complaints rarely make any difference. Rest assured, however, that the Jamaicans themselves would never put up with such treatment.

Only in the larger tourist restaurants are credit cards accepted. Elsewhere you should expect to pay cash. If a restaurant charges in Jamaican dollars you are advised to pay in Jamaican because you will probably be offered a very low exchange rate if you present US dollars. There is a General Consumption Tax of 15 per cent (sometimes included), and most restaurants also add a service charge.

Under the 'Eating Out' sections in this book, restaurants are divided into three price categories, according to the price of a main dish—specifically a fish, chicken, goat or a vegetarian dish (steak, prawn and lobster dishes come at a further, variable premium of at least 20 per cent):

expensive	J$400 and above
moderate	J$200–$400
cheap	J$200 and below

Plenty of Jamaicans eat at the **jerk centres** (*see* p.60), but they also cater to the tourists. If you are travelling around the island then it is easiest to do as the Jamaicans do, and grab a bite from one of the local stalls, perhaps a box lunch (usually a simple box of fish or chicken and chips) or a pattie (*see* below). Two of the most popular chains for patties are **Tastee Patties** and **Juici Beef Patties**.

There are many **snack stops** around the island (collections of stalls on the main roads). Some along the north coast are designed specifically for tour buses and so they sell bags of crisps and are hideously expensive; the simpler Jamaican ones are all over the island, particularly around Kingston.

Jamaican Food

The Jamaican 'national dish' is **ackee and saltfish**, which was once the staple diet of the plantation slaves. Ackee is the yellow fruit of the ackee tree from Africa, which looks and even tastes a little like scrambled egg, and the salt fish is salted cod. Originally this was imported from Canada as the cheapest available source of protein, but now it is quite expensive.

Most typical dishes are made with meat on the bone simply cooked (**fry chicken** and **fry fish**), or cooked in a stew or with a thick sauce (**curry goat** and **brown stew** of chicken or fish). Other dishes are **fricassees**, served with rice, and fish **escoveitches**, cooked with a marinade of peppers and onions. A '**run down**' is a stew in which meat and vegetables are cooked slowly in coconut milk.

There are some rather alarming-sounding soups and 'souses' on offer in local Jamaican restaurants, such as **bullfoot** and **cowfoot soup**, but other equally exotic and more accessible soups include **callaloo**, which is made from greens and flavoured with crab or sometimes meat. **Okra** is often included, which gives it a slightly velvety and slick character. Jamaican **pumpkin soup** is excellent. A very local dish is **mannish water**, made from the innards and the head of a beast boiled with green banana and hot peppers. As the name and concoction might suggest, it is supposedly a cure for impotence and frigidity.

Caribbean vegetables are abundant, and you will often find your plate loaded with a mountain of **sweet potato**, **breadfruit**, **plantain** or **green banana** and the many root vegetables such as **yam**. You will sometimes be served with **dumplings and bammy** (cakes made with cassava). **Rice'n'peas** (really beans rather than peas) is a very popular accompaniment, excellent when cooked in coconut milk. **Coleslaw** is another popular side-dish. Vegetables are often well cooked; the Jamaicans seem to like them that way.

Many traditional Jamaican snacks are available from roadside stalls throughout the island. A **pattie** is a circle of cornmeal pastry folded over and crimped, traditionally with a beef filling (now with some more exotic fillings such as shrimp, fish, vegetable or even lobster). The traditional school-children's meal is a pattie wrapped in **coco-bread**, a roll with melted butter. Other hand-held snacks are **loafs**, a bread-like exterior with a meat, callaloo, or sometimes an ackee filling. There are also sweet versions: **plantain tarts** (the same shape as a pattie but with a crispy finish) and **gizzardas** (made with coconut). There is usually a proliferation of **coconut-breads** and **rock-cakes** on offer, to fill any remaining gap.

Other deserts include rather heavy **bread-puddings**, but Jamaica's many splendid fruits—**soursop, sweetsop, coconut, mango, pawpaw** and **pineapple**—make excellent ice-creams, which offer a light alternative.

Electricity

The standard electrical system in Jamaica is 110 volts at 50 cycles, but 220 volts is available at some of the hotels.

Embassies and Consulates

All the diplomatic representation is in the capital, Kingston; most of the embassies and high commissions (for British Commonwealth countries) are to be be found in the New Kingston area:

British High Commission: 26 Trafalgar Road, Kingston 10, ℂ 926 9050–4

Canadian High Commission: 30 Knutsford Boulevard, Kingston 5, ℂ 926 1500–7. Canada also has a consulate in Gloucester Avenue, Montego Bay.

French Embassy: 13 Hillcrest Avenue, Kingston 6, ℂ 927 7430

German Embassy: 6 St Lucia Avenue, Kingston 5, ℂ 926 6728

Japanese Embassy: 32 Trafalgar Road, Kingston 10, ℂ 929 7534

Netherlands Embassy: 53 Knutsford Boulevard, Kingston 5, ℂ 926 2026

United States Embassy: 2 Oxford Road, Kingston 5, ℂ 929 4850. The USA also has consular representation in Gloucester Avenue, Montego Bay.

Entertainment and Nightlife

Entertainment is often laid on for you in the hotels; it can be as packaged as the holiday that gets you there, and in some places it owes nothing to Jamaica—an endless round of wet T-shirt competitions, pot-belly contests, pool volleyball and other sorts of daytime 'vacational training' and then, in the evening, fire-eating shows, and limbo competitions. In the more sophisticated hotels, you be serenaded at dinner by some quite good combos, or there will be a piano bar. There are some good discotheques in some of the larger hotels. And it is worth considering an evening pass to one of the all-inclusives, where there is often a lively crowd. There are no casinos in Jamaica for the gamblers, but there are slot machines in many of the hotels.

To get the best of Jamaica you must be prepared to go beyond the confines of the hotel complex. The Jamaicans enjoy **cinema** much as the rest of the world and you will find cinemas in the main towns. For 'high' culture (theatre, chamber orchestras) you really have to go to Kingston. The **NDTC** (National Dance Theatre Company) stages dance performances twice-yearly. The **pantomime**, in the Ward Theatre in downtown Kingston (on the Parade), running from Boxing Day until the spring, is ever popular with Jamaican families.

Bars

The typical Caribbean activity is chilling out in bars. There are limitless options around Jamaica, from the elegant Ivor Guest House, in the hillside setting of a plantation house hotel, with a view of the Kingston lights, to the local rum shops in the Blue Mountain settlements, and the clifftop and beachside bars of Negril, where the crowds gather to watch the sunset with almost religious adoration. A number of bars have jazz bands once a week, which pull a local crowd. In some areas there is a 'circuit' where different bars are popular with the locals on different nights. Just ask around and you will be steered to the current favourites.

The clubs are well worth a visit to see the Jamaicans themselves at play, though you should be slightly wary in some areas of Montego Bay and Kingston about going in alone—you can always get a Jamaican to go with you. There are plenty of venues for concerts around the island; keep an eye on the papers because sometimes world-famous reggae bands will play a gig in a small club. Gogo dancing clubs are very popular with (some) Jamaican men, where they drink while watching women perform mind-boggling routines of X-rated dancing.

Drink

Much of what is on offer is imported. All the regular soft drinks are there—Coke, Pepsi, Sprite, etc. But the local fruits also make excellent juices, ideal for keeping you hydrated in the sun. Lime is probably the most thirst-quenching, but **lemon** and **orange** work pretty well; look out for other exotic fruit juices such as **soursop** and **June plum**. On the other hand, you might want to avoid **sea moss**, a concoction made with milk and seaweed.

The best restaurants do serve wine with their meals but, as it does not really travel that well with the heat, it is not used as much as you might expect. Besides, local food does not really require it—instead, people often drink beer. The national brew of Jamaica is **Red Stripe**, though you will also find many imported beers. A number of **malts** are available in local shops, but they tend to be a bit thick and heavy for the tropical weather.

Appleton is the best known **rum** on the island. The smoothest of its creations is Appleton Gold, but the most popular among the Jamaicans themselves is Appleton Overproof, a white rum which is also known as John Crow Batty because of its fearsome strength (over 100 per cent proof). Other brands include Wray and Nephew's Gold Label and Myers Rums (the company Wray and Nephew actually owns Appleton and Myers). Malibu is a Jamaican rum and you may well come across Sangster's rums, which are flavoured to make liqueurs. Jamaican rum is exported to put in chocolates all over the world. **Tia Maria**, a coffee liqueur, is also a Jamaican product.

Health

For early travellers, Jamaica was a dangerous and unhealthy place. Settlers died like flies from yellow fever and malaria, and there was a general fear of 'fevers, agues, fluxes and dropsies'. Soldiers were billetted high up in the mountains (in Newcastle and Gordon Town) because it was thought to be healthier there and people took their holidays in hill-stations rather than on the beach. Modern medicine cleared up most of these diseases a century or so ago; now Jamaica is generally benign and you need suffer nothing more uncomfortable than a mosquito bite.

You should give yourself general cover as you would anywhere (for tetanus and polio), but there is no reason to take any malarial or hepatitis precaution and there is no problem with yellow fever or typhoid. All common medicines are available on the island, but if you have a special prescription you will need to equip yourself in advance.

A doctor is on call in the larger hotels, for **medical emergencies**. If not, the hospitals and some of the clinics listed in the gazetteer sections will have accident and emergency rooms.

In Jamaica the **sun** can burn you in minutes, so use high-protection suntan cream, especially if your skin is sensitive. Keep sunbathing to short stints of 15–20 minutes, particularly during the first few days, or avoid baring your skin altogether during the hottest part of the day, 11am–3pm. Be particularly careful if you go snorkelling, because the combination of the sun and the cooling water is lethal.

Tap water is drinkable all around Jamaica, but bottled water is available pretty well everywhere, if you prefer it.

Inland Bathing

Some of the best bathing in Jamaica is in the river rockpools and waterfalls, where the water is always cool but never really cold and surrounded by the prettiest Jamaican greenery. Some rivers disappear into limestone cave systems and flow underground, emerging in a pool ideal for swimming. Ask around, because the locals will know where the best spots are; they are often quite difficult to find. Most of these places charge a small entry fee. It is better not to swim after rain because the mud will have been stirred up.

In the far east, inland from Manchioneal, are **Reach Falls**. You start at a stunning 25-ft waterfall, and walk up to a series of pools for a couple of miles. **Somerset Falls** at Hope Bay (just west of Port Antonio) are a little tame, but there is an interesting, sheer-sided chasm along which you can swim until you reach the falls themselves. If you go into the John Crow Mountains to Ginger House south of Port Antonio, there is a cascade and rockpool called **Jupiter**. At Upton above Ocho Rios (ask around), you will find good swimming at **Spanish Bridge** and there is a good place to spend the day at **Irie Beach**, not a beach in the conventional seaside sense, but a charming gulley where they have a bar and deck chairs and an excellent river to swim in.

In St Elizabeth Parish is a spot called **YS Falls**, an extremely impressive series of seven waterfalls with rockpools and a spacious garden; numerous tourists, but supremely beautiful. Nearby are some superb falls, off the beaten track near Apple Valley where the Black River flows through the **Apple Valley Gorge**. And **Mayfield Falls** is lost in dramatic countryside to the west of here, inland from Lucea: 22 pools large enough to bathe in over a couple of miles of charming river-bed.

Language

The official language of Jamaica is English, which will be understood anywhere in the island. However, between themselves the Jamaicans speak patois, which is a mixture of English and other languages from Africa. Most of the words are of English origin, but they have been shortened, changed around and elided, and are generally pronounced in a way different from either American or English English. Patois is quite difficult to understand, particularly to begin with (nigh impossible if you are trying to understand dancehall lyrics), but the Jamaicans will happily switch register a little to help you understand. Other languages spoken in the tourist areas of Jamaica include German, Italian and Japanese.

Living and Working in Jamaica

Chucking it all in and flying off to Jamaica to work in a cocktail bar might seem like a dream life, but it is not possible. In Jamaica there is a big enough unemployment problem already without allowing outsiders to compete for the scarce jobs. Only a limited number of skilled and professional people are given work permits.

It is easy to fall in love with Jamaica, but before you rush home to sell up, be warned: on further acquaintance, as the rose-tinted view of a quick first-time visit recedes, the country begins to change. Jamaica has the same sort of problems as everywhere else, made worse by the fact that it is a small island which creates a certain pressure-cooker effect. There are practical difficulties that might not seem much of an issue from outside, but are distressing for permanent residents. When the loo breaks, plumbers just never seem to come; what was quaint begins to look shambolic. Service in general is a problem—you may experience this in some restaurants and bars around the island. There are also some less visible social problems.

It takes a special sort of person to stay in love with Jamaica, one who is capable of laughing off the undoubted frustrations of life in the island. If you think you might be sanguine enough, then take it slowly. Rent a house there for a while, see whether you like the life, and don't be in a hurry to cut your roots with home.

Maps and Publications

The best map of Jamaica is an excellent road map, produced by the Jamaica Tourist Board; it's easily obtained in Jamaica itself, or through the tourist board's offices around the world. It covers all the metalled roads (and a few that are now really more like tracks) and marks the public beaches, and has some very good town plans too. You will also find small, advertising-led, town maps, which are of limited use.

In the proliferation of magazines and brochures generated by the tourist industry you will find a few useful publications. Most of the resort towns have at least one booklet or magazine which give a run-down of facilities and sometimes a calendar of coming events. These too are advertising led and so they tend not to give recommendations, but list everything on offer. You will also find endless brochures of the different tours, restaurants and bars. The best information is by word of mouth, but you often have to probe a little in Jamaica to make sure that you are not just being told about the usual tourist spots, which the locals assume everyone enjoys.

There is usually a good supply of entertaining booklets that take a humorous look at Jamaican life—anything from *The How to be Jamaican Handbook* to *The Official Dancehall Dictionary*, and books of Jamaican proverbs and expressions.

Press

The principal Jamaican newspaper is the *Daily Gleaner*, released in the morning. The same company, a formidable Jamaican institution, puts out *The Star* in the afternoon between Monday and Saturday. Other papers include two dailies: *The Herald* and *The Observer*.

Radio Stations

There are a number of good radio stations in Jamaica. The best one for reggae music is **Irie FM** which plays day-long culture reggae (not dancehall), but the other stations are worth tuning in to as they also play a good variety of Jamaican and Caribbean music. Jamaican radio is known for a number of hard-hitting commentators and talk-show hosts. Listen out for Mutti Perkins. Phone-in shows are particularly popular with the Jamaicans and amusing to tune in to.

A typically Caribbean institution that you may come across on Jamaican radio is the obituaries or 'deads', in which people are remembered on the radio to a background of funereal music. It is a hangover from centuries past, in which a sort of town crier would ride around the country villages announcing the names of those who had died.

The Main Stations and Some of the Popular DJs

RJR (Radio Jamaica Rediffusion): FM 94.5 and 104.5; Richie B hosts *The Beat*; also the *Good Morning Man* show.

Irie FM: 105.5 and 107.7 FM; day-long reggae, cultural not dancehall.

Power 106: 106FM; listen out for Barry G (Gordon).

KLAS: 89.9FM; *My Place* with Michael Cuff; *Straight Talk* with Wilmott (called Mutti) Perkins.

There are a number of religious radio stations, including **Love 101** on 101FM.

Money

The currency of Jamaica is the Jamaican dollar (J$), which fluctuates on the international exchange. At the time of writing the rate was about US$1 = J$38–40 or about £1 = J$55–60. It is legal to use US$ in Jamaica; they are accepted by companies and people who work in the tourist trade.

Pricing in the tourist trade tends to be linked with the US dollar (which holds steady while the Jamaican dollar moves) and so hotel, restaurant, hire-car and shopping bills (in the tourist areas) can be paid with US dollars. Credits cards are widely accepted, as are traveller's cheques. Personal cheques are not usually accepted. In restaurants and bars where the prices are listed in Jamaican dollars, it is better not to use US dollars, because you will be offered a very unfavourable rate of exchange.

You will certainly need some Jamaican dollars for getting about on the buses and for a pattie and a skyjuice at the roadside. There are foreign exchange desks in most hotels, at airports and in many banks. Keep your exchange receipts if you want to change Jamaican dollars back into another currency on departure.

Banks are open Mon–Thurs 9–2, and Fri 9–noon and 2.30–4 or 5pm. They are usually rather slow. You will also find **cambios** around the island, some of which are open on Saturdays. These are specifically for foreign exchange and generally they offer a slightly better rate of exchange than the banks.

Exchange outside the banks and cambios is illegal; there is not much of a **black market** in Jamaica and if you find a source the exchange rate will be only a little better. Be careful if you are changing money in the street. If you are in a part of Jamaica where there are not many tourists, you might try a supermarket to exchange your dollars.

Tipping is welcome in Jamaica, but it is not usually expected. Most restaurants will add a service charge, either 10 or 15 per cent, to your bill; in bars 10 per cent is quite normal. Elsewhere the code is undefined: baggage handlers at the airports definitely expect it, and they will brow-beat you a little to get your custom. Hotel porters, on the other hand, merely live in hope.

Most of the all-inclusive hotels do not permit tipping, so you do not need to carry any cash with you at any time. If the hotel bar or nightclub is crowded and busy, though, it might just encourage the barman to look after you that little bit better if you give him a sub at the beginning of the evening.

Opening Times

The museums, plantation houses (and their farms), sugar factories, botanical gardens and waterfalls around Jamaica keep standard opening times and the vast majority are open 9–5, some continuing until dusk (make sure you are in the system an hour before it gets dark). A few have specific tour times, which are mentioned in the text, but in most cases you can simply arrive and join in the next available tour. In the tourist areas of the north coast all the sights are open on Saturdays and Sundays.

Packing

With such a pleasant climate and informal atmosphere, you can take a minimalist approach to packing for a holiday in Jamaica; the most important items are sunglasses and a swimming costume. You should take suncream and you might also consider a sunhat, but these can be bought on arrival. During the daytime shorts or a skirt with a light shirt or T-shirt are adequate and in the evening you might need a longer skirt or trousers, particularly if you eat out in a fairly smart restaurant. It is only on winter evenings or in the mountains that you will need a thin jersey. Jeans are too warm in the summer months and cotton trousers are a good alternative.

If there is a general rule in restaurants, then it is that men wear long trousers and a shirt with a collar. There are only a couple of restaurants and hotel dining rooms on the island which require even a jacket for men (and some of these will actually lend you one). Most hotels will provide irons and hair-driers if they are not already in your room. Shops in Jamaica, particularly those on the tourist trail, are well stocked with anything you need in the way of batteries and simple medicines, clothes and photographic film. Montego Bay is the best supplied of the tourist towns, but if you need any advanced electronic or computer gear you will need to go to Kingston.

Photography

The poor old Jamaicans have had tourists poking cameras in their faces long enough to have decided that they don't really like it and so when you do pull out your camera it tends to elicit screams of horror and remonstrations. Photographing people in Jamaica is quite difficult and you will find that if they allow it at all, many Jamaicans expect you to pay (if you are actually prepared to pay, it is much easier to work out a fee before the event than afterwards).

Landscapes are often very satisfying subjects and don't usually charge (although hustlers have actually been known to come up and demand a fee for the privilege of photographing their country). Jamaican plants are very bright and colourful and particularly striking after rain. In the middle of the day you will find that the brightness of the sun bleaches most of the colour out of the landscape and so the best time to take photographs is in the late afternoon or early morning, when there is a stunning depth of reds, golds and greens.

Post

International postage can take anything from five days to three months, so don't depend on it! If you want to be sure of delivery from Kingston within a certain time you can use **DHL** at 54 Duke Street, Kingston, ✆ 922 7333, or **Federal Express**, 75 Knutsford Boulevard, Kingston 5, ✆ 926 1456.

Shopping

Everywhere you go on the Jamaican tourist trail you will find craft markets and duty-free shops. The towns are full of them and every tourist attraction has a little cluster where you will be hustled as you pass. Much of what they sell is not really very exciting—mostly 'Jamaica Me Crazy' T-shirts, clocks in the shape of the island and wooden machetes carved with the island's name. However, there are some good wood-carvers and some original artists on the island.

Duty-free shopping for Blue Mountain Coffee, perfume, alchohol and electrical goods and yet more T-shirts, if you haven't got enough already, is made very easy for visitors. There are shops around the main towns which will deliver your purchases to the airport or your cruise ship, and some beyond the customs barrier where you can use up the last of your Jamaican dollars. You will have to show your air-ticket when you make a duty-free purchase.

Shopping hours in Jamaica are generally weekdays 8–4, and Sat 8–1, but the hotel boutiques and in-bond warehouses extend their hours for tourists.

Sports

Watersports

Jamaica caters well for sports-minded holidaymakers. The full range of watersports is on offer on the island, from a ride in a stately pedalo or on a trusty wetbike to a high-speed ride on an inflated sausage or an evening cruise to catch the sunset. Negril offers the most operators along the beach, but every area has its public beach and hotels where you can hire equipment.

Facilities will vary from hotel to hotel—typically hotels will have a couple of small sailing dinghies and a windsurfer or two, but they may not have a motorized boat for waterskiing or scuba diving (though these things can usually be arranged fairly easily with someone from outside). If watersports are important to you, you should check what a hotel offers before you make a booking. Independent travellers can sometimes hire equipment from the hotels, or they can go to the watersports shops on the larger public beaches.

Windsurfers are available all over the island, but connoisseurs say the best beach for the sport is Burwood Beach, a public beach beyond Trelawny Beach just outside Falmouth. Small sailing **dinghies** are all available through the general operators, as is **waterskiing** (try any public beach). On the major beaches in Montego Bay, Negril and Ocho Rios you can also get a **jetski**, a **pedalo** or a ride strung beneath a **parasailer** or on a **bouncy banana**.

Day and half-day **yachting trips,** usually taking in some **snorkelling** and a picnic stop, are very popular and are available through all the hotels in the major resort areas. You will also find a number of silly, mock-piratical excursions on offer: if you are in the mood for an afternoon of rum-soaked fun and tee-ree-ree, you can fix these through any hotel or tour operator.

Deep-sea fishing is best off Port Antonio in the east. There is an annual fishing tournament for all fish held there in March and there are marlin fishing tournaments held in Montego Bay and Ocho Rios in September and early October, before all the fishermen return to Port Antonio for the year's major event in mid-October, ✆ 993 3209.

Jamaica is surrounded by offshore reefs, furred with sponges and corals, where tropical fish play and barracuda stalk their lunch—an ideal place for **scuba diving.** The reefs have been stripped for their corals in the past, but there is some protection now and there are still enough spots around the north coast resorts to keep divers occupied. The majority of operators of the Jamaica Association of Diver Operators work under PADI specifications (you must show your certification), and most can provide instruction. Underwater photographic equipment is for hire at the bigger rental companies. A single tank dive costs from US$45. **Glass-bottomed boats** are available on most beaches too for a trip to a nearby reef.

River rafting is a classic Jamaican tourist activity, but one that is nonetheless genuinely good fun, is river-rafting. You sit on a bamboo raft and cruise down through magnificent overhanging greenery, through canefields and fruit plantations. The water is always warm. Rafting is possible on several rivers: the Martha Brae near Falmouth and the Great River at Lethe near Montego Bay, the White River, ✆ 974 2527, just out of Ocho Rios and, best of all, the Rio Grande near Port Antonio, winding up at Rafter's Rest, ✆ 993 2778. Wear a bathing suit because when you have finished your rum punch you'll be expected to dive in. Some companies offer torch-lit night-time cruises.

Land Sports

There are **tennis** courts at most of the hotels around the island, or a public court can easily be booked through your hotel front desk. There are many **golf** courses in Jamaica, and each of the main resort towns (except Port Antonio) has at least one course where you can play. Montego Bay has four but there are others in Runaway Bay, Ocho Rios and Negril. There are also two courses in Kingston. Green fees vary considerably around the island and if a course is attached to a hotel, the guests have priority with teeing-off times.

If you wish to go **horse-riding,** for anything from a beach canter at dawn to a day-long trek into the Jamaican highlands, there are stables in all the main towns.

Riding costs roughly J$250 per hour. You are advised to call a day in advance to book the horses. **Polo** is quite big in Jamaica, and you can even hire polo ponies at **Chukka Cove Farm**, © 972 2506, near Ocho Rios, or get a refresher course if you haven't hit a nearside forehand for a while. If a nag seems a bit much, you can take a **cycling** tour of the Blue Mountains from Port Antonio instead. It sounds like quite hard work, but this is a specifically downhill tour (*see* p.180).

Horse racing is a popular spectator sport in Jamaica and you will find details of coming meetings in the local press. The main stadium, to the west of Kingston, is Caymanas Park and meeting are held there on weekends and Bank Holidays.

There are excellent possibilities for walkers in Jamaica, but very few organizations arrange anything remotely adventurous. *See* 'Tours' below.

Streetwise Jamaica

As a new arrival, you are likely to find yourself accosted by taxi-drivers, higglers (street vendors), hustlers and the occasional rent-a-dread on the streets and beaches of the main tourist towns. Sometimes their requests are innocent enough, but often they will launch into a whole inventory of services that they would like to set up for you—anything from collecting some fruit for you in the market to selling you ganja. It can be quite tedious (particularly when you are forced into a protracted conversation every hundred yards or so), and even a little threatening at times. Until you get a tan or learn to 'give them the eye', they will be persistent.

While travelling in Jamaica, take the same precautions you would in the cities of any foreign country, and be wary. Do not flash a full wallet around or hang an arm adorned with a bracelet out of a bus window. You are advised not to walk around downtown Kingston alone after dark. If you wish to go to an area you think might be dodgy, you can always get a Jamaican to go with you.

The Jamaican authorities strongly disapprove of illegal drugs and they do nobble offenders from time to time. In practice, you will be offered almost anything by the beach hustlers, from a single spliff to a hundred-weight of cullyweed, or cocaine, dropped in en route from South America. There are quite a few foreigners serving time in Jamaican prisons for drug possession.

Telephones and Time Zones

The IDD code for Jamaica is 1 809, followed by a 7-digit number.

On-island, you should prefix a zero if you are dialling long-distance; for local calls simply dial the 7 digits. There are an increasing number of mobile phones in Jamaica (numbers beginning 0991, 0995, etc.) and these are always dialled with a zero up front.

Public telephones in Jamaica now work exclusively with phone-cards rather than coins. Cards come in units of 20, 50, 100 and 200 Jamaican dollars and are sold in newsagents and other shops. The public phones themselves are fairly reliable, with about two-thirds to three-quarters working at any one time.

Jamaica is five hours behind GMT, on Eastern Standard Time. The island does not change its clocks during the summer months. This means that in the winter it is five hours behind UK time and six hours behind Central European time. In the summer this is reduced to four hours and five respectively. In the summer Jamaica will be an hour behind the eastern seaboard of the States.

Tours Around Jamaica

Jamaica is very well served with organized tours, and there is endless information on them in the hotel lobbies. There are tours to most of the tourist attractions mentioned in the gazetteer chapters (*see* appropriate chapters for major operators) and if you do not have transport they offer an easy way to get around and see the island. Most tour companies take you around in minibuses and typically they will include a couple of sights, lunch and a shopping stop.

Many of these tours, however, are a little tame. A few organizations are able to tailor-make some more adventurous excursions—anything from a twitching trip to see some of Jamaica's 250-odd species of birds to a jam-session in a Trenchtown yard, or even a tour of famous Jamaicans' gravestones. It is worth taking advice from these operators, both because of their knowledge of the country, but also because through personal contacts they have access to places on private land where you are not permitted to go.

SENSE Adventures, PO Box 216, Kingston 7, © 927 2097, @ 929 6967, have a flexible programme of outdoor activities with a slant towards eco-sensitive tourism. Based at Maya Lodge in Jack's Hill above Kingston, they can tailor-make walking tours into the Blue Mountains and elsewhere around Jamaica (including one to a remote waterfall on the Spanish River that drops an extraordinary 1100ft), and river-canoeing trips through white water or mangroves. If you are one for naturist recreation they can give you information on that as well. The **Touring Society of Jamaica**, Boscobel Post Office, St Mary, ©/@ 975 7158, has a number of day tours from the major resort towns (including picnics trips into the Cockpit Country and to remote waterfalls) and some speciality tours, for example a Jamaican Art Tour (with views of public and private collections) and a Plantation House and Gingerbread Tour of Jamaican architecture across the ages. **Countrystyle**, PO Box 60, Mandeville, Manchester Parish, © 962 3725, @ 962 1461, gives advice and assistance about the Mandeville area.

In Jamaica

In Jamaica itself the main tourist board offices are in **Kingston**: the Tourism Centre is in New Kingston, at 2 St Lucia Avenue, PO Box 360, Kingston 5, ℂ 929 9200, ℱ 929 9375, and there is an information desk at the airport, ℂ 924 8024.

In **Montego Bay** the office is in the north of the town, near Cornwall Beach, PO Box 67, ℂ 952 4425, with a desk in Sangster airport, ℂ 952 2462, before you pass Customs and Immigration. In **Negril** the office is in Jackson (formerly Adrija) Plaza, ℂ 957 4243.

In **Ocho Rios** there is an office at the Ocean Village Shopping Centre close to Turtle Beach, ℂ 974 2570, in **Port Antonio** at the City Centre Plaza, ℂ 993 3051, and in **Black River** on the High Street, ℂ 965 2074.

You will also find a number of small octagonal information booths dotted around the main tourist towns, with helpful and usually well-informed staff.

Abroad

The Jamaica Tourist Board has offices in:

UK: 1–2 Prince Consort Place, London SW7 4BZ, ℂ 071 224 0505, ℱ 071 224 0551.

Canada: 1 Eglington Avenue East, Suite 616 Toronto, Ontario M4P 3A1, ℂ 416 482 7850, ℱ 416 482 1730.

France: 32 rue de Pont Thierry, 4th floor, 75008 Paris, ℂ 145 61 90 58, ℱ 142 25 66 40.

Germany: Falkstraße 72–74, 6000 Frankfurt 90, ℂ 069 70 74 065, ℱ 069 70 10 07.

Italy: c/o Sergat Italia, Piazza dei Cenci 7A, 00186 Rome, ℂ 06 686 9112.

USA: 500 North Michigan Avenue, Suite 1030, **Chicago**, Illinois 60611, ℂ 312 527 1296, ℱ 312 527 1472; 1320 South Dixie Highway, Suite 1100, **Coral Gables**, Florida 33146, ℂ 305 665 0557, ℱ 305 666 7239; 3440 Wilshire Boulevard, Suite 1207, **Los Angeles**, CA 90010, ℂ 213 384 1123, ℱ 213 384 1780; 801 Second Avenue, 20th Floor, **New York**, NY 10017, ℂ 212 688 7650, ℱ 212 856 9730.

Don't be put off if your accommodation does not have air-conditioning. Jamaica's climate is not usually too hot, and anyway the heat is tempered by sea breezes. It is only in the height of summer when the heat indoors becomes uncomfortable without some sort of ventilation, and even then only modern concrete buildings, which tend to trap the heat, are affected.

Many Jamaican hotels use the old techniques for ventilation: louvred windows and ceiling fans, which together encourage a through-flow of air from outside. It is a more natural and altogether more pleasant way to live—air-conditioning involves closing off the room and making an artificial environment.

Where to Stay

Jamaica has a superb, wide range of hotels, set on the island's dramatic coastline or within its luxuriant interior, some of them among the finest of their type in the world. Of course there are the chic, extremely expensive hideaways and the splendid, secluded plantation house hotels in the countryside, but there is something for everyone in Jamaica, and you will also find small retreats with just a few rooms and friendly management and classic laid-back beachfront spots tucked in between the larger resorts. There are also many large and active hotels designed to make it easy to do nothing, where you can spend a week practising your windsurfing and concentrating on your tan.

How best to book them is a fundamental question. Most of the larger and better-known hotels are booked most easily and cheaply on a package from your home country—you will find them in the holiday brochures. Tour operators are able to get large discounts on published hotel-room and airline prices by block-booking, and so it usually cheapest to go with them.

However, not all of the nicest hotels in Jamaica can be booked through package tour operators; many of them are too small to have an arrangement with them, and so you have to book direct. It is also possible to hop from one hotel to the next as the whim takes you, if you prefer to travel around the island, arranging an itinerary as you go. Hotels and guest houses will usually have space for unexpected guests to book in for a couple of nights, except possibly in high season.

If you are travelling around the island, you should really have one night's accommodation arranged before you arrive—you will be required to put an address down on your immigration card on arrival. For help, contact the **Jamaica Reservation Service**, 1320 South Dixie Highway, Suite 1180, Coral Gables, FL 33146 (in USA ✆ toll free 1 800 JAMAICA and in Canada ✆ 800 432 7559. On the island you can get assistance through **Caribbean Travel and Tours Ltd**, 2A Lady Musgrave Road, Kingston, ✆ 927 6975, ✉ 927 6976.

There are a number of hotel organizations in Jamaica. The **Elegant Resorts of Jamaica** is a collection of top-of-the-range hotels; its guests can arrange to dine (and sometimes sleep, space permitting) at several hotels in the group. The Elegant Resorts include Round Hill, Tryall, Half Moon, Coyaba, Jamaica Inn and Trident Villas. These hotels offer a variety of plans, from room-only rates to the Full American Plan (all meals). It's cheapest to book the Elegant Resorts through tour operators, but reservations can be made through the booking agents listed under the appropriate 'Where to Stay' sections of the gazetteer chapters.

The all-inclusive hotels offer an even fuller package than the Full American Plan. 'All-inclusive' means that you get absolutely everything within the initial price (usually paid before you leave home): all your meals, all your drinks, and use of facilities for watersports. The idea is that you should not have to take out your wallet during your holiday unless you arrange to do something outside the hotel. The all-inclusives specialize in action-packed activity holidays but facilities vary. The usual watersports will certainly be on offer, but some places will have a fuller range than others; some may throw in an excursion. All-inclusives share a certain atmosphere: most thrive on being upbeat and lively and, as they work on scales of economy, they are almost all quite large (usually above 100 rooms). On the whole, if you are after a quiet retreat, then the all-inclusives are not really the place for you, although recently the odd all-inclusive has taken itself upmarket by offering à la carte dining.

There are two big chains of all-inclusives in Jamaica: **Superclubs** (UK and Europe reservations © 01749 677200; US and Canada © 1 800 859 SUPER), with a number of hotels in different styles to appeal to different age and price brackets (including a chain of mid-range resorts which calls itself Breezes); and **Sandals** (UK reservations © 0800 742742, US and Canada © 1 800 SANDALS, who have a half-dozen or so places scattered around the major resorts. The UK reservations offices do not arrange flights for either company, so you may find it cheaper to book through a tour operator.

Jamaica has a good selection of small independent hotels (some of them too small to work with tour operators). At the top of the range they include some of the Elegant Resorts, but they range in price down to $50 or $60 a night. Typically they have between 10 and 30 rooms, a small dining room and a bar, but limited, if any, watersports. The offer little in the way of nightlife and daytime activity; their beauty is in the quiet and seclusion and their personable management. Many of these places are set in magnificent old plantation-style houses. If you are an independent traveller, they offer the best of Jamaica, usually on an affordable budget. *See* the separate listings in the gazetteer chapters for the best examples.

A little farther down the scale you will find guest houses. These range in price up to about US$50 per night. They are set in a modern concrete villas (often built for members of a returning family and let out to paying guests) and decorated much in the style of a Jamaican home. Guest houses are also useful stopovers for independent travellers making a tour around the island. Again *see* the listings in the gazetteer chapters.

The hotels in Jamaica offer a number of different meal plans. In the smaller independent hotels you are likely to be offered bed alone, EP (European Plan); or bed and breakfast, CP (Continental Plan). MAP (Modified American Plan) is bed, breakfast and one other meal; and FAP (Full American Plan) includes bed and all meals. All inclusive means what it says (that everything is included in the one price).

Hotel room rates are usually quoted in US dollars; you can pay with credit cards and traveller's cheques in all hotels. A General Consumption Tax of 15% is levied on all purchases and hotel bills. It is worth noting that most hotels also charge service at 10%, so the bills can mount up rather suddenly. Price categories, based on the rate for a double room in high season (or the equivalent in the case of all-inclusives), are as follows:

luxury:	US$350 and above
very expensive:	$200-350
expensive:	$120-200
moderate:	$60-120
inexpensive:	$30-60
cheap:	$30 and below.

An alternative to staying in a hotel is to hire a villa. Most villas come with a maid who will cook for you as well as clean, or you can cater for yourself and go out to restaurants when you feel like it. A villa is also an ideal choice for two or three couples travelling together and, of course, for a family. Houses on offer vary from modern, purpose-built villas on the clifftops and beaches to restored 18th-century great houses. There are some villa hotels on the island, which offer self-containment but still provide some central facilities like a restaurant and watersports.

Individual villa rental, with anything from a studio to seven bedrooms on offer, can be arranged through **JAVA**, the Jamaica Association of Villas and Apartments, based in Ocho Rios, PO Box 298, Pineapple Place, ✆ 974 2508, ✆ 974 2967. They can be contacted in the USA at 1501 West Fullerton Avenue, Chicago, Ill 60614. Listings for villas can also be found in the Caribbean magazines and newspapers. *See also* the villa operators in **Travel**, p.5.

Note: among the recommended places to stay, the author's favourites are highlighted with a palm symbol

Women

Jamaican men are quite macho by nature and a women tourists can expect a fair amount of public attention: often a sharp hiss between the teeth or a 'Hey, White girl!' Advances of this sort are usually laughed off or ridiculed slightly by local women and visitors can do the same; they are often quite public and loud, but not usually persistent and they are verbal rather than physical. Trust a man like this as much as you would trust anyone trying to pick you up in the street at home.

Something of a tradition of sex has grown up in the tourist resorts to round off the sun, sea and sand vacation and not surprisingly the local studs like to encourage it. If they are anything like as good at seduction as they are at hustling (and the two are not unconnected in many cases), then they'll be pretty persuasive. Male staff in some really quite smart hotels will make a pass at a single woman, or one whose man appears to be absent.

The Jamaicans are quite modest, when it comes to showing their bodies in public at least, and topless bathing is not encouraged (it is actually illegal) outside the designated nudist areas in certain hotels. Women are also expected to wear more than a swimsuit when going into town or to any public place. Perhaps take a cotton wrap.

Nature

doctor bird

A surveyor sent to Jamaica in 1660 wrote:

> *It is something to making an oval Forme, being from east to west about 170 miles in length; from north to south about 70 miles and narrow at both the extreme ends; then at the middle having a ridge of lofti and raggie mountains running from east to west which are full of springs whence flow these main rivers that so plentifully water the island. The country is very hilly and mountainous, everywhere covered with tall and large savannas, and intermixt with the hills and woods.*

Jamaica is not really that large an island—only 146 miles from end to end by 51 at its widest point—but it seems far larger. The reason is that it is so mountainous. To get from one deep, steep-sided valley into the next, just a few miles away as the crow flies, can often take hours. Around two-fifths of Jamaica is at an altitude of more than 1000ft—sometimes this is within just a few hundred yards of the coastline.

It always seems to be raining somewhere in the eastern mountains and the island is plentifully watered: the rivers in Jamaica are worthy of continents. And it is certainly forested: around a quarter of the island is covered with woodland. There is an amazing variety of terrain within the island: rainforests and cloudforests and, not that far off, plains, which are hot and (relatively) dry, with scrubby vegetation and even cacti. This variety brings an astonishing array of natural life and animals, particularly birds.

The island of Jamaica is actually one of the peaks of a submarine mountain range, which runs along the northern edge of the Caribbean tectonic plate (the range runs through Puerto Rico, Hispaniola, Jamaica and then beyond to Honduras in Central America). Jamaica is tilting a couple of centimetres each year, rising in the north.

Jamaica's highest mountains are in the east, forming a barrier to the prevailing weather, the tradewinds, which rise in the Atlantic and head southwest towards the equator. These are moisture laden and when they hit first the John Crow Mountains (highest point 3750ft) and then the Blue Mountains (its highest point, the Blue Mountain Peak, tops 7402ft), they dump a massive amount of rainfall, about 300ins each year. The Blue Mountains, the highest range in the island, stand right behind Kingston and are immensely rugged and steep. You can expect it to rain every day in this area.

Heading north and west of Kingston you come to the Central Range, the backbone of the island, a limestone plateau that runs down to the north coast, where it forms a ridge a few miles inland. In the west, it culminates in the Cockpit Country south of Falmouth and descends to Montego Bay. The Cockpit Country is an area of curious karst formations, where a collection of conical peaks stand side by side a bit like the compartments of an egg-box. The Western Range runs on from here to the western end of the island and Dolphin Head (an 1800ft outcrop named for its shape when seen from the sea). On the south side of the island you will find other smaller ranges, still 2–3000ft, with stunning views.

The island has a mixed geological heritage; there are both volcanic areas (in the Blue Mountains, volcanoes long since inactive) and limestone areas, which are derived from periods of submersion in the sea and cover two-thirds of the island. As limestone is porous and eventually dissolves in water, the island is laced with caves and underground rivers, particularly around the Cockpit Country.

Limestone is a good building material and you will see it used in the older buildings for faced stone (cut so that it gives a smooth wall with a regular pattern), and cut stone (irregular broken lumps which give a crazy-paving effect), and for steps. In the rural parishes, there are numerous limestone walls, and the stone is also used as marl, the basis of much of Jamaica's road-building. In the past limestone was also used as a purifier for drinking water in the form of 'dripstones', large square or conical lumps of stone with a bowl cut in the top into which the water was poured. It would then drip through the stone and collect in another container beneath, cool and purified. The ladle to spoon it out was sometimes given a jagged edge to prevent people from drinking directly from it. Dripstones are only really seen in museums now, but they were once used all over the Caribbean.

The climate of Jamaica, like that of the rest of the Caribbean, is pretty well perfect (*see* also p.15). Unless you are unlucky, you can expect huge, bright blue skies where large, cumulo-nimbus clouds hang like massive stacks of cotton wool. However, the island is sometimes affected by the climate in the continental USA. If there is a storm to the north, Jamaica may be hit by the tail of the cyclone. In the winter this can bring a grey weather front—not cold, but grey and disappointing if you are trying to get a tan.

The prevailing weather comes from the Atlantic and varies with the tilt of the earth, coming from the east or northeast. The evaporation at the Equator creates an area of low pressure which sucks in air from the north, skewed because of the turning of the earth. These are called the tradewinds, not because they were used by trading ships to get to the Caribbean, but because they have a constant direction ('tread' in old English meant direction). There are also island breezes in coastal areas of Jamaica—onshore by day and offshore by night—created by the cooling and heating of the landmass as the sea remains at a constant temperature. These are also known locally as the the 'doctor's breeze' and the 'undertaker's breeze'.

The scourge of this otherwise benign climate are the hurricanes, which on their occasional visits leave the overwhelmingly green island looking like a wasted grey moonscape. Deluges of rain accompany winds near 200mph, which rip out telegraph poles, throw ships half a mile inland and can disturb coral life down to 200ft below sea level. Hurricane Gilbert was the worst to hit Jamaica recently; it carved through the eastern end of the island in 1988, causing untold damage. Planes (confiscated ganja-runners parked along the runway at Kingston airport) were simply plucked up and thrown into the trees. Hurricanes rise in the Atlantic off the coast of Africa: moisture evaporates from the sea, rises, cools and then falls and eventually begins to spiral. They gather in strength and intensity, move off to the west and then get a couple of thousand miles run-up before they sweep through the islands. Hurricanes turn anti-clockwise in the northern hemisphere (typhoons, their southern-hemisphere equivalents, turn clockwise), spinning around a central vortex, called the 'eye', which is eerily calm. Many of these storms set off each year but relatively few turn into hurricanes. As long as they are over the sea they will keep going, but once they reach land they peter out. Once the winds reach a sustained speed of 73mph, they are classified as a hurricane and named. The names are fixed alphabetically in a pre-determined sequence, boy, girl, boy, girl. Hurricanes can reach constant speeds of 140mph and gust at nearer 200mph.

Flora

Jamaica is amazingly fertile. The tight, steep-sided valleys in the mountains are a magnificent sight: all around you is an onward march of rampant, clambering plantlife which smothers the hillside in a million colours of green, marked in places by the straight lines of human activity in buildings and cultivation. Where it is left to itself it quickly becomes out of control. Whole trees are blanketed with vines and fences instantly become hedges; telephone poles are like climbing-frames and even the lines themselves become choked up as fuzzy little air-plants balance on the wires like little balls of grass. It used to be known as Green Hell.

On the south coast, in the 'rain-shadow' of the mountains, the land becomes drier and the vegetation quite scrubby. There are plains with open savanna-like grassland and there are wetlands or swamps where mangroves and grasses grow along the riverside. The soil is also immensely fertile—you can almost expect a pencil to sprout if you plant it. In the centre of the island you will see the distinctive rich red soil that produces bauxite. This geographical variety gives a huge diversity of landscape, climate and vegetation, providing habitats for many different birds and animals.

There are around 3000 plants on the island of which about 780 are unique to Jamaica. In the Blue Mountains alone there are known to be about 250 plants unique to Jamaica. Of course the island looks very different from when the Europeans first arrived because so many new plants were introduced by them. The Spaniards brought quite a few and then, in the late 18th century, ships sailed back and forth across the oceans redistributing plants all around the world, particularly those that could be used for food either as starch or as spices. Captain Bligh's *Bounty* was on such a mission, sent by the Society of West Indian Planters to carry a cargo of breadfruit saplings from the South Seas to the West Indies. Apparently, part of the reason for the famous mutiny was that the captain denied fresh water to his crew to keep the plants well watered. His first attempt to fulfill his commission failed but in 1793, a few years later, Bligh successfully delivered his breadfruit to Jamaica, where it was planted in Bath Botanical Garden. It was soon distributed all around the island and you will recognize it by the distinctive breadfruits themselves, which look like bright green cannonballs and hit the ground with an alarming thud, and by the shiny dark green leaves shaped like splayed fingers.

Many other plants were successfully introduced. Sugar-cane was brought by the Spaniards from Santo Domingo and by the mid-1700s the whole island was blanketed with it as the British turned Jamaica into a massive sugar factory. You can visit sugar-works at Appleton and at Hampden Estate, both near Montego Bay.

Cocoa is another foreigner that thrived in Jamaica; it was indigenous to the New World, where it was used as a drink by the American Indians. The cocoa tree grows 30–40ft high and its fruit, a yellow-brown and sometimes purple pod, sprouts indiscriminately from trunk and branches. Inside the pod are beans, which sit in a sticky-sweet mush—you can buy cocoa pods at the roadside and suck the beans. Cocoa itself is processed by fermenting the mush and then drying the beans on a *boucan*. The oily product of the beans is then rolled into sticks or balls which are grated into boiling water to give 'cocoa tea' (most hot drinks in Jamaica are referred to as 'tea'—one of the popular Jamaican singers has even taken the name Cocoa T).

Tea was never grown commercially in Jamaica, though the plant itself flourishes there. However, one of the most profitable crops in Jamaica at the moment is coffee; the bush, with its dark green leaves, grows 10 or 12ft high. Although coffee is grown all over the island, Jamaican Blue Mountain coffee, which grows above 2000ft in the Blue Mountains, is particularly well thought of. At £25 per pound, Blue Mountain commands a price four or five times higher than all other pure arabica coffees on the world market. In Japan (where most of the product goes) people pay US$10 for an average cup. It is well worth visiting the Blue Mountain coffee-processing factory at Mavis Bank (*see* p.222).

The ackee tree, which originated in Africa, was a source of reliable and familiar sustenance to the transplanted slaves. The tree grows to 50ft and it fruits with yellow and red pods. When these are ripe they open to reveal yellow flesh with a shiny black seed. If processed incorrectly ackee is poisonous and so it should be prepared and cooked carefully. The ackee was also transported by Captain Bligh and this is reflected in its botanical name, *Blighia sapida*. Ackee and salt-fish (an old slave food, then the cheapest available, but now quite expensive) has become something of a Jamaican national dish. The ackee often tastes and looks remarkably similar to a salty scrambled egg; its fruit is also used as a soap. Avocado, a small tree with large leaves native to Central America, grows happily in Jamaica, where it is referred to as a 'pear'. There are a number of different varieties, distinguished by their smooth green or nobbly purple and black skins. The harvest season is August –December.

In such fertile earth you will always find a number of trees that bear spices. Cinnamon is processed from the bark of the cinnamon tree, and the nutmeg tree produces two spices: nutmeg itself and mace, used in confectionery. Pimento is indigenous to the island and very popular in Jamaica; it is also known as allspice (because it is supposed to taste like a combination of cinnamon, clove, nutmeg and pepper). The pimento tree is small and the spice comes from the dried berries, which look very similar to black pepper. Pimento is almost always an ingredient in Jamaica's various jerk sauces; the wood itself has been used for the jerk barbecue, but it is expensive and scarce. The West Indians are famed for their hot pepper sauces, and Jamaicans use the particularly fiery Scotch bonnet pepper. Other spices grown in Jamaica include camphor and clove, both of which grow on trees, and ginger, which is garnered from a root. Tamarind is an extremely bitter additive which is derived from the brown pulp inside the pods of the tamarind tree.

And Jamaica is home to some fascinating oddities of the plant world. Quick-stick is used as a hedge or a barrier at the roadside—cuttings simply have to be placed in the ground and they will take. It grows into a tree with pink blooms that overhang the road. 'Scots attorney' is a large-leaved creeping vine that smothers the trunks of trees and sometimes even throttles them. It is so named because many of the lawyers and overseers employed by English absentee landlords to run sugar plantations were Scotsmen; they often did well for themselves to the detriment of their employers. The sensitive plant or mimosa grass is known as 'shame-a-lady' because its series of symmetrical leaves close up at the gentlest of touches, like a lady clapping her hands to her face at seeing something embarrassing.

Fruits

In the markets of Jamaica, there is an abundance of diverse fruits. It is well worth buying a box of fruits in season—but take a Jamaican with you to ensure a reasonable price. Jamaican farmers also export a number of fruits, including banana, pawpaw and mango, by air.

A number of different varieties of banana are grown on the island. The best is the honey or sweet banana, which is shorter and fatter than the cavendish and tastes sweet and delicious. Pawpaw (also called papaya) grows on a very robust stem (it is not quite a tree) and the fruit seem to drip down it from a crown of leaves on stalks. When ripe, pawpaw has an orange flesh, tasting not unlike a melon, but green pawpaw can be cooked as a vegetable. Meat is wrapped in pawpaw leaves before cooking to tenderize it.

HMS *Flora* brought the mango tree to the island in 1782 and it was soon flourishing throughout the island. Mangoes grow on beautiful, bushy and shady trees that fruit in July and August; as they ripen, the profuse green fruits flush to yellow with a pink tinge. The most popular mangoes are the Julie and the Bombay and the most common is the Number 11. Pineapples are native to the New World, brought to Jamaica by the Spaniards, where they still thrive in their numerous varieties on farms around the main towns. The pineapple bush stands low and has a crown of spiky cactus-like leaves, in the middle of which appears the pineapple itself. The fruit, which appears on the Jamaican coat of arms, was a symbol of welcome in 17th-century Europe, so it is also on the gateposts of many country houses.

There are endless citrus fruits—limes, lemons, oranges, grapefruits—and also a number of oddities that have been invented on the island through cross-breeding. The ortanique is a hybrid of the orange and tangerine and its name is finished off with the -ique of unique. The ugli fruit is a cross between a grapefruit and a tangerine, and strikingly true to its name: a squat fruit with a nobbled, warty skin, but with pleasant juicy flesh.

Less familiar fruits on Jamaica include the soursop, which grows on a low tree. The fruit itself, green and irregularly shaped with dark hooks on the skin and a white flesh, tastes both sweet and tart, a cross between citrus and banana flavour. It can be made into excellent ice cream. Sweetsop, also known as sugar apple, is shaped like a green pinecone and has a very sweet flesh. Pear-shaped otaheite apples ripen to a rich red, but inside their perfumed, snow-white flesh is crisp and pulpy. Guava has a hard rind of different colours which contains a bittersweet mushy pulp, with lots of pips. It can be eaten as a fruit, but it is often made into a jelly. Guineps, a little smaller than a squash ball, have a hard green exterior and a large inner stone around which is a sweet white pulp. The jackfruit is a huge starchy fruit related to the breadfruit which grows up to 30 or 40lbs.

A number of nuts are grown in Jamaica including peanuts and macadamia, but the best loved is the cashew, which originated in the Americas. Cashew nuts are expensive because they are labour-intensive to produce, but they are readily available at stalls around the island. Finally, the coconut, one of the most familiar tropical fruits, thrives on the island. One variety was indigenous to Jamaica but this has been almost wiped out through yellowing disease. It has been virtually replaced by a smaller coconut palm which gives the green and yellow nut that you see around the island now. The coconut is incredibly versatile: the juice or milk can be drunk (it's sold at the roadside) and used in cooking. The flesh can be eaten or dried to make coconut chips, or used as oil for candles or soap. The fronds of the coconut plam are often used for making roof thatch.

Ground provisions are the staples of old Jamaican country life and you will see them, still covered in earth and mud, on the stands at the markets. Yam is a tuber that originated in Africa and has become one of Jamaica's most popular vegetables. The vine grows up a stick, twining around it and looking like shaggy heads of hair, but the food itself is in the roots, which are long and thin. Cassava, also called yuca, was a staple of the American Indians. It grows as the root of the cassava plant, and must be processed carefully because some varieties have a poisonous juice. Cassava is used to make bammy. Also a native of the the Americas, the sweet potato is a sweet, starchy vegetable which grows in the same way as a normal potato. Calaloo is a bush; its leaves are eaten as spinach and in soup and in pepperpot. The cho-cho is a green, pear-shaped vegetable which grows on a vine. It has a crisp, light-coloured flesh which softens on cooking and has a fairly bland taste.

There are a number of vegetables related to the banana: plantains are often cooked unripe, before they sweeten, and then mashed and eaten with butter, as are hog bananas, which are fat and green or purple. The breadnut is a relation to the bread-fruit tree: it looks like it and crops in a similar way except that the cannonball fruit has sections with nut-like protrusions.

Bush Medicine

In Jamaica the 'bush doctor' is often the first call for someone with an illness. He or she is a recognized figure in most Jamaican communities, who will give advice on what herbs to use to cure illnesses and, if also expert in obeah (see p.54), on a number of other non-medical complaints. Most remedies are made up as a 'tea', from leaves added to boiling water or stewed, but some are prepared as poultices.

Fever grass, or lemon grass, is used against fever and colds and peppermint is used against colds and headaches. The leaves and fruit of the soursop tree are used as an antidote for worms, against hypertension and as a tranquilliser, and the leaves and bark of the lignum vitae tree are supposed to restore energy. Marijuana is used for people with asthmatic conditions and is often taken as a tea against a cold. It has also been used successfully in the treatment of glaucoma, which is a common problem in Jamaica. The periwinkle, which has also recently been used by pharma-ceutical companies in the preparation of drugs to control cancer, is used by the Jamaicans as a tea for the treatment of diabetes. Pimento berries are steeped in alchohol to create a draught against stomach ache. Rum itself is a popular rub and is used with lime-juice and honey as a medicine for coughs and colds.

Anatomy of a Forest

Forest covers about a quarter of Jamaica. Much of it is on precipitous and difficult terrain but until earlier this century there was barely a section of the island that couldn't be reached by the many paths and mule trails. Nowadays, since everyone travels by motor vehicle, these paths have become neglected and overgrown, but are still clear enough for walkers. Because of massive pressure on such a small area of accessible land, illegal cultivation and charcoal burning for fuel, Jamaica has a major problem with deforestation: over 7 per cent per annum is lost.

The forests change character as you climb further above sea level. On the coast are trees that are able to cope with high salinity: mangroves dominate on the low-lying areas around mudflats, lagoons and swamps, called morasses in Jamaica. They trap mud and debris with their riotous assembly of flying buttresses, and hang ghostly tendrils as they spread themselves wider and wider. Along the beaches the most common tree is the tall and shady sea almond, which produces hard, inedible fruits (nothing like an almond) and the sea grape, taller and bushier, which does fruit with a bunch of grapes, though these are an acquired taste—they start off green and bitter and by the time they turn purple they are just about edible. Another tree you will see fringing the beaches is the manchineel, which has a full crown of slightly crinkly leaves and produces small apples. These are dangerous; if you eat one the juice will quickly cause your throat to swell up so that you cannot breathe. They were called the 'apples of death' by Columbus. Even to shelter from the rain under the manchineel is dangerous, because the dripping water will scald your skin. Coconut palms grow on many of the beaches. Be careful of these too. People have been killed by falling coconuts.

Despite the verdant lushness of most of Jamaica, in the southwest, around Treasure Beach, there is an area of savanna with desert-like plants, and scrubby forests where there are cacti and thorny bushes. This kind of scrub is also found in Hellshire, just to the west of Kingston and in several spots along the southern coast of the island. In places the cacti are cultivated so that they grow into hedges.

Much of Jamaica's forest is jungly and wet, and has a canopy of 50–100ft. Trees here include the blue mahoe, Jamaica's national tree. Shrubs, herbs and mosses grow on the dank forest floor and ferns sprout among the broken rock and earth. Vines and bromeliads clamber up the slender trunks of the tall trees and take the nutrients they need from the air and the rainwater that runs down the trunks. In the upper branches there are orchids, and lianas, which link all the trees to the ground in a mass of hanging lines. Rainforest is usually thought of as impenetrably thick and tangled and, if there is any available sunlight, for instance on river-banks or at roadsides, it generally is. Inside a mature forest, though, the forest floor is often clear because less than 10 per cent of the sunlight actually penetrates the upper canopy. There is constant, almost visible growth and regeneration: the leaves are dropped by the trees and decomposed by bacteria and fungi, releasing nutrients into the soil which are then drawn back up into the trees by the root system.

Among the peaks of the Blue Mountains, at around 7000ft, there is a small stretch of dwarf or elfin forest of stunted trees, about 7 or 8 feet tall, their gnarled trunks covered in lichens and mosses.

Ornamental and Garden Plants

The colours and profusion of tropical flora are one of the most delightful surprises for a newcomer to the Caribbean; a large number of species bloom all year round. The Jamaicans all keep flowering gardens and most hotels are also set in magnificent grounds, with buildings festooned with flowering vines, and lawns exploding with curious and colourful exotic bushes. Flowering trees stand over it all with spectacular crowns of bright yellow or red blooms. They say the Jamaican gardener's most useful tool is the machete.

Perhaps the most typical Caribbean flower is the hibiscus, which comes in a million different colours and varieties, and is often used for decoration—you may find one on your pillow when you go to bed. They last for no more than a day. You will also see ixora, whose white, pink, yellow or red star-shaped flowerlets develop into the shape of a sphere, and allamanda, with its large, yellow, bell-like flowers. The periwinkle is a low bush with delicate purplish flowers; and plumbago flowers lie blue and white amid profuse greenery. Shrimp plants are odd—the small white and yellow flowers stand erect like tiny pagodas. Poinsettia is known as the 'Christmas tree' all over the Caribbean because its leaves turn from green to a vivid bright red in the winter months. Bougainvillea, whose light amd flimsy petals grow in a range of colours on long bramble-like fingers reaching out from the main plant, is very often trained into huge bushes and even hedges.

Some more exotic 'flowers' (often they look more like toys or ornaments than conventional flowers) include chenille, also called red-hot cat-tail (it dangles red and furry, about 8 or 10 inches long). You are very likely to see anthuria in Jamaica, shiny, rubbery-looking leaves of any colour from pink to deep red with erect serrated stamens. The heliconia family, related to the banana, has a number of flowering species, named after the shapes of their solid, waxy-looking blooms: lobster-claw, bird of paradise and beeswax. Similar-looking, with tall, slender stems and banana-like leaves, is the ginger family, which has flowers like waxy red flaming torches.

There are a number of plants and outsize grasses that do not actually flower but have colourful leaves, often cultivated in hedges or as ground-cover: crotons grow higgledy-piggledy in variegated red, yellow and green; purple heart sprouts in a tangle of purple leaves. Pandanus is also called screw pine because of its curly pine-cones, and walking palm, named for its curious, mangrove-like root system, is a riot of yellow-green hook-edged leaves, which soar and bend over like a messy head of hair. Ferns and large, jungle-like leaves such as monstera are also popular in hedges and borders. There are many decorative palms, including the golden palm, whose leaves are a waterfall of slender, curling fronds, and the sago palm, with its spiky trunk and tight, comb-like fronds. Japanese fan palms have saucer-shaped fronds on stalks, and another exotic version is the fishtail palm, whose fronds are seemingly ragged and torn in the shape of fish tails. Royal palms are the tallest and most elegant of them all, sometimes planted in alleys.

Jamaica has an amazing array of flowering trees; the flamboyant, which comes out in a riot of red blooms in July and August, appears in many public places around the island. Other flowering trees include frangipani, with its pink and white five-pointed stars for flowers, and the African tulip tree, also called flame of the forest, which blooms in large scarlet, tulip-like cups. The wood of the lignum vitae tree is some of the hardest produced by nature, and it was even used as a substitute for metal by shipwrights, but the tree produces a delicate blue flower, which has been selected as the national flower of Jamaica. Perhaps the most attractive of them all is the traveller's tree (more of a banana than a tree actually), whose leaves fold out in the shape of a fan, always pointing east and west. It takes its name from the fact that water collects in the spaces between the fronds, so travellers were able to drink from it.

Fauna

Birdlife

Over 250 species of birds appear in Jamaica during the year. A proportion are migrants; there are around 75 species of winter visitors and birds that pass through on their migratory routes north and south but Jamaica also has a large number of endemic species. Twenty-five species are found nowhere else in the world. Jamaica's national bird is the doctor bird, officially known as the streamer-tailed hummingbird. It is black and green, with a red beak and tiny iridescent chest feathers, with twin tail feathers more than twice the length of its body, which flash back and forth as it hops from flower to flower gathering its supply of nectar.

If you spend some time on the beach or near the coast you are quite likely to see a brown pelican, standing on a rock out to sea, flying in formation with others, or diving into the sea and scooping up fish in its pouch. High above the coastline you will see the familiar black streak, broad-winged and scissor-tailed, of the magnificent frigate bird. These birds steal food from other birds on the wing, swooping in from behind, grabbing a leg and shaking until the other bird regurgitates its meal, which the frigate then catches before it hits the water. Other smaller birds such as sandpipers run twittering along the sand together and, just behind the beach itself, making forays from the shoreside foliage, you will see different species of plovers. Many other gulls, boobies and terns inhabit the coast and also the cays to the south of the island, where there are few people and good feeding grounds.

A little further inland, the coastal morasses (at Negril, Black River and the eastern tip of the island) and the mangrove swamps and mudflats in shallow estuaries are difficult to get to, but they have some of the most exotic and abundant birdlife. Rails, bitterns and ducks stalk among the lilies and aerial roots of the mangroves and you might see gallinules and green-backed herons.

In the gardens and woods of low-lying areas, you will find myriad species—doves, thrushes and finches, mockingbirds and woodpeckers and a couple of hawks and owls. One of the most noticeable is the bananaquit, which has a black head and back and a yellow underside and is often seen hopping around in the search for food. You are bound to come across the smooth-billed ani (recognized by a rather uncomfortable and distinctly un-smooth protruberance on its bill)—it looks awkward on the ground as it swaggers around in search of insects, but it flies quickly and gracefully, often in flocks. The Jamaican oriole often searches for insects and fruits in gardens. It is known as Auntie Katie and is coloured black and yellow. Mockingbirds are found in the town as well as the countryside; they imitate other birds in their calls, and are quite loud and boisterous. The Zenaida dove, pinky brown in colour, the island's most common dove, can be spotted feeding on the ground in pairs.

Besides the streamertail there are two other hummingbirds that can be glimpsed flitting through the abundant gardens, or conducting extremely aggressive dog-fights over their territory. The mango hummingbird is 6 inches from tip to tail, with a shiny brown and purple back and black head and belly. The vervain humming-bird is tiny, so small that it is called the bee hummingbird. It is coloured grey-green with a grey-white underside and white flashes on its tail feathers.

Plenty of birds are brave enough to appear near human settlements. The Greater Antillean grackle, a black bird about 6 inches high, is called a 'cling-cling' in Jamaica because of its bell-like call; you are likely to notice it because of its habit of hopping up onto the table and eating out of the sugar-bowl or off an unattended plate. A very familiar sight, circling around the skies of both built-up and rural areas, is the John Crow, a large black scavenger with a bald head and neck. And almost everywhere you go in Jamaica you will see the mournful cattle egret, white birds with hunched shoulders which attend cattle, either on the ground picking at the insects disturbed by grazing, or perched on their backs.

In the deeper and higher forest, there are species that are shy and keep away from human habitation. The Jamaican woodpecker is unique to the island. It feeds on insects from the trunks of trees and nests in a hole that it chips out with its beak. It stands 8 inches high, with black back, wings and tail and a ruddy underside, its head and neck bright red. There is a parakeet, with a green body, black wings and a brown underbelly, which flies around screeching in flocks. And there are two rare parrots, both unique to the island and severely endangered: one black-billed and one yellow-billed, both green with flashes of yellow or pink. They also screech and, like the parakeet, nest in holes in trees and feed on berries and fruits. The Greater Antillean bullfinch has the run of the lower woodlands and mountain forests; it is small and black and makes a rasping buzzing noise.

As you climb higher into the mountains you may come across the Jamaican tody, called robin redbreast and the rasta bird, named for its red and yellow colouring, which lays its eggs at the end of a 2ft underground tunnel. There are a number of small flycatchers and you might also see the Jamaican eleania or the Blue Mountain vireo or one of the handful of migrant warblers. In the heights, listen out for the whistle of the solitaire, a single, mournful tone at intervals; it is un-birdlike but very beautiful and rather eerie.

The best times to go birding are in the early morning and around dusk. There are not many arranged bird-watching tours of Jamaica, but contact one of the specialist outdoor and adventure operators listed in **Practical A–Z** and they will organize something; phone a couple of days in advance. Marshall's Pen near Mandeville often allows tours of the property. Again, phone in advance. Ornithologists and bird clubs can arrange trips through the Gosse Bird Club, ✆/📠 978 5121.

Animals

The animal life of Jamaica is not nearly as varied as the birdlife. However, there are many reptiles, ranging from the crocodiles of the Black River swamp and the Jamaican boa (rarely seen), which grows up to 15ft in length, to the tiny lizards that find their way all over the walls and the ceiling. A sound you will definitely become accustomed to is the call of the tree frog. It peeps rhythmically with a 'twee... twee... twee...', particularly after rain, when a whole chorus pings and peeps in unison. They are small, greeny, transparent and very difficult to see. The Jamaican bullfrog, actually a large toad, makes a noise so loud that it sounds like a generator. The snoring frog found on the island is the second-largest tree frog in the world and its call is like a wheezy snore. Jamaica's iguanas, overgrown lizards with armour plating like mini-dinosaurs, were thought to be near extinction, but they are occasionally seen in dry scrubland and recently some specimens over 5 feet long have been sighted in the Hellshire Hills. Some freshwater crayfish and terrapins live in the rivers.

The few rodents include the coney, a Jamaican native relative of the guinea pig. It is extremely shy and rarely spotted, surviving only in very remote areas. You are more likely to see a mongoose, as it crosses the road in the day. This animal was imported from the Far East in the 1870s in order to control the cane-field rats that were causing so much damage in the fields. Unfortunately for the farmers, once it had exterminated the rats it found other easy prey in the local birds and the farmers' chickens, as well as the lizards and snakes that controlled pests and insects.

There are innumerable insects in Jamaica. Remember to take insect repellant. You are most likely to come across the mosquito and the sandfly, both of which bite— sandflies are barely visible, but will cause a very irritating if harmless itch. As the name suggests, they live in sand and they come out particularly in the late afternoon. The most spectacular insects are the fireflies, which you will occasionally glimpse after dark, glowing as they search for a mate. There are more than 100 species of butterflies in Jamaica, a fifth of which are found nowhere else in the world. The yellow and black giant swallowtail butterfly is one of the largest in the Americas. There are about 20 species of bats in Jamaica; they are nocturnal, living on insects and fruit and occasionally sipping nectar from flowers.

Corals and Marine Life

Jamaica is almost as fertile beneath the surface of the sea as it is above; the fish life has been depleted in places by over-fishing but the reefs are dramatic displays of colour. Some corals are so pretty that it is quite hard to remember that they are animals rather than flowers.

Perhaps the most distinctive are brain corals, like boulders with a similar patterning to the surface of the human brain. Pillar coral stands like a forest of furry, upward-pointing fingers and other encrusting corals smother a rockface like a rust, sending out small erect protrusions.

Staghorn coral grows in a complicated tangle of little antlers which divide and subdivide, and elkhorn forms large branches like vast upturned palms. Near the surface of the water, corals are tightly bunched as they compete for space and sunlight. They feed by trapping nutrients that hang in the water in the flower-like tentacles of their polyps. As you descend, and leave the sunlight behind, the colours deepen and the corals themselves become larger.

Other corals are shaped more like fans and feathers; they wave with the passing current, sifting the nutrients from the water as it passes through them. They are two-dimensional and have a lung-like patterning. Sea fans are so hard that the Arawaks and Caribs used them as graters.

There are also any number of sponges, most of which are in the shape of a tube or barrel, and they come in endless colours. Sea anemones attach themselves to rock, as do feather-duster and plume worms—as soon as there is any disturbance in the water around them they whip back into their sheaths for protection.

Hiding in the cracks of the rocks are an array of crustaceans including crabs and lobsters. If you see a collection of black spikes protruding from a hole in a rock, leave it well alone because it is a sea urchin—at a touch, spines will break off, lodge in your skin and cause a very painful swelling and infection. Then there are all the minuscule shrimps and starfish, quite difficult even for a patient diver to see, and other even more exotic creatures such as sea cucumbers and octopi. Eels also live in crevices.

There are hundreds of species of fish, of which the most common are angelfish, parrotfish, wrasses and chromis, snappers and groupers. Parrotfish nibble at the reef, crunching up the polyps and spitting out granules of sand. Damselfish include the sergeant major, which is recognized by its three yellow and black stripes and extremely aggressive behaviour when it comes to defending its eggs. Trumpetfish are long and thin and curious in that they hang vertically from the surface of the water. Larger reef fish include the massive barracuda and grouper. Occasionally you may see rays.

Some shrimps and small fish work as 'cleaners'; they have a symbiotic arrangement with larger fish in which they clean their mouths and gills of edible debris. The larger fish loiters at an unaccustomed angle and the cleaner sets about it, picking around inside its mouth, getting a meal in the process, safe in the understanding that the larger fish will not eat it.

Farther off the coasts there are schools of blackfin and allison tuna, which once in a while will come to the surface to play and eat, jumping and hopping over the waves. They do not grow particularly large, but a bluefin can grow huge. Other large fish include wahoo, white marlin, and sailfish, which have a vertical wing on their back. The largest of all is the blue marlin, which can weigh up to 1000lbs.

Three species of turtles visit the coastline to lay their eggs. The females crawl up onto the beach during the night and bury their eggs in the sand, digging a hole with their flippers and then covering it again before swimming off (*see* p.240). Unfortunately, the turtle eggs are often dug up to be eaten and the turtles themselves have been hunted to near extinction. Another animal that used to be seen in great numbers and which is now very rare is the manatee, a lumbering great walrus-like creature without tusks. They are occasionally seen on the south coast around Milk River.

Jamaica Life

Religions

Jamaica has a mind-boggling proliferation of religions—and more church buildings per head of the population than anywhere else in the world. The Jamaicans seem happy to embrace new churches, particularly those of the Evangelist groups based in the States, and a number of religions have been developed here; the best known is Rastafari (see below).

All the established churches of the world are represented: the Anglican Church, the official church of the island during British rule, is the largest of the Protestant churches, but you also will find the Presbyterians (now merged with the Congregationalists into the United Church of Jamaica) and Protestant offshoots such as the Baptists, the Methodists and Moravians, the dissenter churches that established missions in Jamaica at the beginning of the 19th century. There are plenty of Roman Catholics and there is also an Islamic and a Jewish presence in the island, as well as a number of lesser-known faiths such as Bah'ai. There are also Seventh Day Adventists, and many of the various Churches of God.

Many of the churches, with their history of missionary work and involvement in education, still run schools around the island. And while you are in Jamaica you may well come across some of today's missionaries, including the Mormons (dressed in pressed white shirts and black trousers). Others have come on aid and assistance programmes.

Church services tend to be livelier in Jamaica than in Europe, particularly the Evangelist ceremonies, where you will see (and hear as you pass them on Sunday afternoons) singing and clapping, and the impassioned speaking of the preacher, a central figure in the Jamaican church and often an important figure in the community. There are many messianic churches in Jamaica, where a charismatic leader gathers a following around him and a church is born.

The influence of African beliefs is also evident in some Jamaican practices, some of which are similar to the voodoo of Haiti. Practices include drumming and dancing and often possession. The Jamaicans call these beliefs Revival and Kumina; people who usually attend the more mainstream churches sometimes turn to them as an alternative, but would rarely admit to having participated in ceremonies that are disapproved of in the community at large.

Revival is a mix of African and European beliefs. There are two main branches, Pukumina (which is also spelt Pocomania) and Revival Zion. Both feature use of the Bible and belief in the Trinity, but also invocation of spirits in the worlds beyond direct human experience. Zion is closer to the established churches; the spirits it deals with are heavenly spirits such as the saints and angels, whereas Pukumina deals with spirits such as dead ancestors. Led by a Captain or a Mother, the ceremonies include drumming, dancing and singing. The spirits are attracted by the dancing and special rhythms on the drums and take over the body of a person at the ceremony. The leader then interprets what the problem is or what is to be done from the actions of the person possessed. You will occasionally see Revival 'bands' at special events around Jamaica. Wearing distinctive turbans and simple, coloured shirts, they will perform their dances and singing (though you would not expect to see a possession).

Kumina is regarded as more purely African. It is thought to have been brought to Jamaica by indentured African labourers after the abolition of slavery, and features the invocation of spirits, specifically those of dead relatives. It enables humankind to communicate with and exercise a measure of control over their world, for instance over duppies, spirits of 'deads' (dead people) who wander the earth because they have not been laid to rest properly and who sometimes interfere in the human dimension. Their realm is the dark, and until quite recently many Jamaicans would be scared to go out at night for this reason. (As the country develops, these beliefs are steadily being rationalized as backward and superstitious, particularly by the youth, and the advent of electric street light in towns has denied the duppies such freedom of movement at night.) Kumina ceremonies, or 'duties', are held as rites of passage, especially at death and burial, but also at births and weddings. In their duties, followers attract spirits with items of a special colour, foods and by their drum rhythms. When a participant in the ceremony has become possessed, the leader then controls the spirit and interprets its needs.

Some of the adherents of these cults, often the leaders themselves, are practitioners of herb medicine and the closely associated practice of obeah, the Jamaican equivalent of witchcraft (*see* p.54).

Rastas

Jamaica is a country where spiritual attitudes and beliefs seem to crystallize readily into new religions; the one that has become best known abroad is Rastafari (not rastafarianism, which is seen as yet another example of white intellectual imperialism). Rastafarians are known for their dreadlocks and reggae music and also for their connection with ganja, but the quiet and peaceful ideals that true adherents follow, in fear of Jah (God), are often overlooked.

Rasta beliefs were born in the thirties after the Ethiopian war and the crowning of Haile Selassie as King of Ethiopia, and matured with the influence of Marcus Garvey, and his ideas on black self-respect and nationalism. Rastafari has a strong African heritage and is politically charged—with an emphasis on Garvey's rejection of the white-dominated world and its value system of materialism and imperialism.

Rastas regard Africa as the spiritual home of all Africans if not actual heaven on earth. They think of themselves as one of the lost tribes of Israel and consider that they were brought to 'Babylon' (the white-dominated world and consequently hell on earth) by the white man; their aim is eventual return to Africa, spiritually if not physically. Rastas think of the black race as superior to whites, but they are not necessarily hostile to individual whites, as long they approach with 'rispeck'.

Their spiritual leader was the Emperor of Ethiopia, Haile Selassie, or Ras (prince) Tafari (to be feared), King of Kings, Lord of Lords, the Conquering Lion of Judah. He was the Black Messiah and his Kingdom was the Promised Land. Haile Selassie died in 1975, but is still revered by the rastas, who do not believe that he is dead. The rastas reinterpreted the Bible with the precept that God was a black man (after Marcus Garvey). Of course this involved a rejection of the established churches and institutions on the island and so for many years the rastas were unpopular within mainstream Jamaica and suffered considerable harassment by the police. They are more or less tolerated now and have gained some acceptance through their association with reggae, but they still seem to have a lot less sympathy within Jamaica than outside.

There are different rasta sects, but as a rule genuine rastas are gentle people who follow their avowed beliefs of 'peace and love', often living in remote places in the mountains. They eat I-tal (natural) food, which is mostly vegetarian—sometimes meat, but no pork—and many are herbalists. They are teetotal and do not smoke tobacco. They do regard ganja as sacred and the 'chalice' (pipe), as it is known, is supposed to bring purification and inner wisdom. The most distinctive feature of the rastas is of course their dreadlocks, which gives them, some say, the bearing of a proud African lion. Rastas believe that they should not cut their hair, and they grow it in dreads that become matted like felt. They often wear the colours of the Ethiopian flag, red, gold and green, usually with black. The main rasta ceremony is the Nyabingi, in which there is drumming and dancing, much like the other Jamaican folk religions.

There are some opportunist pseudo-rastas, known as 'rent-a-dreads', around the tourist areas in Jamaica (where a proper, Jah-fearing rasta would never be seen dead). In almost all cases they are regular hustlers.

Obeah

Old habits die hard. Even though Jamaica is developing and modernizing, it still holds on to its superstitions—dreams, duppies (*see* p.53) and obeah—particularly in the country. Dreams are interpreted for prophecy and insight: typical interpretations are that green in a dream (perhaps clothes or a field) heralds disappointment, and that a dream of eating or picking ripe fruit will bring money.

And obeah is still practised. An expatriate man described how his house was blessed by the local obeahwoman when he moved in, at the insistence of the Jamaicans who lived with him: blood was sprinkled at the corners of the house and a chicken was placed in a box and buried. The obeahwoman then stood on the box and the chicken expired with a series of clucks and squawks.

The Jamaican version of black magic, obeah is a tool that its devotees can use to affect their lives through spells and specially prepared potions. It is a link between the world of conscious human experience and the superior world of the spirits and the dead.

Obeah originated in Africa (where in some places it is still called obi) and was brought to Jamaica by the slaves. It was officially banned as early as 1720, regarded as subversive because of its links with many of the slave rebellions. The word 'science' is another word for obeah and takes in the strongest form, called De Lawrence, followers of which claim their spirits fly around the world in their dreams. Many Jamaicans are reluctant even to admit that it exists, but obeah is still a real influence in Jamaican life, mostly in the country, although its hold even there is diminishing with industrial development and with the more modern preoccupations (American satellite tv) of the the younger generation.

Obeah is important at certain rites of passage. At birth blessings are performed to protect the newborn child from the spirits; and when a house is being built a goat is killed, its blood mixed with white rum and then sprinkled on the ground before the first ground-breaking. People will also use obeah to affect the outcome of a court case or an exam, or to have their way in a matter of love or, if a person gets ill, to see if a bad spirit is responsible and could be driven out. For illness, curative spells are prepared, using herbs, roots and oils (many experts in obeah are also bush doctors) and other naturally occurring things such as blood and bones, and instructions given for how they are to be used.

On a more sinister note, obeah can be used to exact revenge by putting a hex on somebody—this is where voodoo dolls are used. The hex will often need something personal, for instance a garment soaked with the potential victim's sweat, or some of their hair or nails (some people in the Caribbean make a point of burning their cut hair and nails). The only way for the victim to break the spell is to consult another, stronger obeahman.

Obeah also touches modern, urban life and it is known to reach high places: occasionally a bank manager or a government official is exposed in the papers for his involvement in obeah. If you do become interested you will hear some fantastic stories, but you should be very careful, because mere interest will be seen as an intrusion.

Music

Visitors joke that the Jamaicans switch the roll of their gait as they walk down the street, in response to each different rhythm played in the successive shops. Music is an essential part of Jamaican life; it's played everywhere, constantly, and almost always at high volume. On Friday and Saturday nights, stacks of speakers 15 feet high appear by the side of the road, higher than the bar that has the sound system.

Music is one of Jamaica's most successful exports—ska became well known in the sixties, and in the seventies reggae exploded to fame and found willing listeners around the world. If you go to Jamaica you will discover just how vibrant and active the scene is. It has moved on, hardening up into rap-style dancehall in the eighties and softening again in the nineties with gentler rhythms and more 'cultural' lyrics. If you are a music fan, Jamaica is particularly accessible at the moment. In Jamaica music is all about dancing, and the rhythms you hear there are well geared for that but, like so much Caribbean music, reggae and other Jamaican sounds have a strong element of comment, sometimes rebellious, sometimes visionary, at other times satirical or just plain slack (vulgar). Though it is difficult for a newcomer to understand the patois, lyrics are a constant source of Jamaican gossip and hilarity as singers address topical and universal issues in their songs.

Mento was the most popular Jamaican dance music from the first part of the century until the early fifties. Its heritage is complicated, with Latin American, European and African Jamaican influences; it is also similar to many Caribbean string band sounds. Mento is often compared to Trinidadian calypso and mento songs do often broach the subjects of love and life in the same way as calypso. However, mento has the typical off-beat rhythm which has come to be associated with reggae. You still see the occasional mento band at local Jamaican celebrations, though most of the players are quite old now. Bands used to consist of accoustic guitars, a fiddle, a ukelele and a boomer box (a sit-on sound-box with metal teeth that are plucked), which provided the bass. The instruments are now electrified, but the bands still play all the old Jamaican classics such as *Jamaica Farewell* and the *Banana Boat Song*.

With the arrival of electric sound systems in the late fifties, things began to change quickly. DJs would import rhythm and blues records from the States and play them to audiences in the original wriggly-tin-walled 'dance-halls'; when the supply of new records from America began to run dry, the DJs mixed their own sounds. The rhythm that crystallized was **ska**, a riotous, very quick and compulsive dance beat, influenced by rhythm and blues and jazz, which the local musicians had been playing until then, and elements of Jamaican folk and religious music. The best-known band was the Skatalites.

The ska dance style also had folk roots. The flex-kneed shuffle in which dancers hold their body forward came directly out of Pukumina ceremonies. Ska was fundamentally dance music, but it had a strong edge of protest in a time of considerable tension in Jamaica. It was frowned on initially by the establishment but then at the time of Independence it came to be seen as an elemental expression of Jamaican creativity and originality.

After a few years the rhythm was slowed down, literally reduced in speed by half, and the result was **rocksteady**, with its heavier drumbeat, more melodic bass and increased lyrical content, packed with social comment. The sound of rocksteady is much more mellow than ska, with the rocking, easy-dancing rhythm of reggae, pinned to a rumbling bassline.The best known singers of the era were Alton Ellis and Jackie Edwards; others such as Desmond Dekker, Jimmy Cliff and Ken Boothe started with rocksteady and then continued into the reggae era. Many of the singers of the rocksteady rhythm portrayed themselves as 'rude boys', rebellious Jamaican youth who vaunted a tough, gangster lifestyle.

Reggae appeared 1968–9, with a faster tempo than rocksteady and an extra lilt to the rhythm itself. It adopted some of the traditions of ska and rocksteady, with similar dance styles and a strong element of protest. Reggae is often gentle-sounding melodic music, but this belies the lyrics, which are often quite angry. It was also heavily influenced by rasta ideas, which gave it a fringe image within Jamaica itself. Reggae was soon an international phenomenon and its exponents became famous around the world. The biggest name is of course Bob Marley (*see* below), but other reggae stars include Jimmy Cliff, Peter Tosh, Gregory Isaacs and groups such as Toots and the Maytals, Burning Spear, Black Uhuru and Third World. Reggae has also flourished abroad, among the large expatriate Jamaican community in Britain for example, where groups like Steel Pulse and Aswad have grown up.

In Jamaica reggae was eclipsed in the mid-eighties and for the last 10 years the big music has been **dancehall**, a compulsive and monotonous rap grafted onto a hard reggae beat. There is little melody—delivery is all—and the DJs sing their lyrics over a number of established rhythms (many of them taken from other songs). Some examples of rhythms are cherry-o, punani, taxi; most recently pepper-seed, bulldog and ketté drum have been popular. Singers, as opposed to DJs, tend to sing more melodically and slowly. Like all the Jamaican rhythms, dancehall has a strong lyric content, sung in a very raw patois that is often difficult for a visitor to understand. The songs address topical and universal issues, often with a fair dose of violence and sex—and, for this reason are known as slack songs. Popular DJs include Shabba Ranks and Buju Banton, who caused great controversy in the States recently because of their views on homosexuality, Ninjaman, Yellowman, Beenieman and a singer-DJ duo called Chakademus and Pliers.

Recently though, dancehall seems to have faded a little in popularity and many of the heavyweight DJs have adopted a culture style closer to that of the singers. Led by the radio station Irie FM, many of them have renounced their vulgar and violent lyrics, slowing down their delivery and cutting out the rat-a-tat rap in favour of more melodic sound. It has more of a feel of the older reggae of the seventies and early eighties. Suddenly Jamaican music is more accessible to outsiders again. Popular singers include Tony Rebel, Beresford Hammond, who is big on love ballads, Garnett Silk (now dead), Everton Blender, Tony Curtis, Luciano and Spanner Banner (brother of Pliers).

Bob Marley

The world's most famous reggae artist and Jamaica's first international music star, Robert Nesta Marley, was born in the Parish of St Ann on the north coast, in the village of Nine Mile. He was the son of a black Jamaican woman, Cedella Booker, and an older white Jamaican, Norval Marley, who had little to do with her after the birth of her son. When Marley was about 10, his mother moved to the Trenchtown district of Kingston. Much of his protest music comes out of his experiences there, expressed in such songs as *Trenchtown Rock*. He was apprenticed to be a welder but like so many young Jamaicans he wanted to make it big on the music scene.

His first group, the Wailin' Wailers, formed in 1963 with Bunny Wailer and Peter Tosh, released a string of ska songs, very popular on the Jamaican scene. But success in Jamaica alone did not bring in much money and the band split for a while. Marley married Rita Anderson (a vocalist in her own right and a member of the I-threes) in February 1966. By 1968 the vocal trio, who presented themselves as 'rude boys' (Bunny Wailer served a term in jail), started to produce music under their own label, Tuff Gong; they now became involved with the rasta faith for which they, and reggae generally, would become so well known.

Marley's ability as a songwriter caught the eye of American singer Johnny Nash, who covered his *Stir it Up* and made a hit of it in the USA and UK. Soon after, Marley was able to sign with Island Records, owned by Jamaican producer, Chris Blackwell. In 1973 they released *Catch A Fire*, which was designed to appeal to an international rather than simply a Jamaican market. Peter Tosh and Bunny Wailer left the group soon after and it was re-formed as Bob Marley and the Wailers, backed by the I-Threes (Marcia Griffiths, Rita Marley and Judy Mowatt). International popularity finally came with huge critical acclaim and massive sales; it continued to grow as they released an album a year and toured around the world. In December 1976, Marley survived an assassination attempt at his home on Hope Road in Kingston. As arranged, he played at the Peace Treaty Festival (against gang warfare in Jamaica) the next day, but after that he went into exile in Miami for 18 months. He returned only to sing at the famous One Love Peace Concert in the spring of 1978 in which the two Jamaican political leaders, Prime Minister Michael Manley and opposition leader Edward Seaga, joined hands on stage. He continued to tour to huge acclaim and and to have massive success with albums such as *Survival* and *Uprising*.

Marley was first diagnosed with cancer in 1977, and by 1980 it had spread throughout his body, causing him to collapse while on stage in the USA. He died in Miami on 11 May 1981. In recognition of his success as a songwriter and singer, and as Jamaica's first international music superstar, he was awarded the Order of Merit, the highest Jamaican award. He was buried at Nine Mile in St Ann, where you can visit his mausoleum and his house (site of the old Tuff Gong Studio) on Hope Road in New Kingston.

The Music Scene

To be a successful reggae singer is the dream of many a Jamaican yout'; it's a way to escape from impoverished circumstances to fame and fortune. Jamaica has quite a problem with unemployed youth, and many, known as idlers or loafers (*iglers* or *loafters*), hang around the tourist areas in particular. And these *iglers*, like the rude boys of the sixties, are now often celebrated in song: in 1996 a famous song about a woman who wouldn't have truck with an '*igle jubie'* (juvenile). The *igle jubie's* female counterpart is a *sketelle*—a word that takes in the idea of easy sexual morals.

Many would-be stars start out in a local club or 'on a corner', where they sing their own lyrics to the established rhythms played in intervals during the regular parties. If they are lucky they will get to travel with a 'set'; these are sound systems which work the concert party circuit—you see their names all around the island on advertising placards nailed to the telegraph poles—Stone Love, Gemini, Travellers City Rock and Metromedia. If a budding singer is popular enough on the performing circuit, the next step is to cut a record in one of the many studios, for example Sonic Sound, Dynamic, Studio 1 or Bob Marley's old studio, Tuff Gong.

At the large concerts the backing music is usually provided by an established band: Sly and Robbie, The 809 Band, Sagittarius, Lloyd Parkes and We the People. Since Reggae Sunsplash left Montego Bay for Kingston and then the north coast at Ocho Rios, it has lost popularity. Instead you can hear Sumfest in the summer (usually in August). The format is similar to the old Sunsplash, a five-day bonanza of reggae (beach party, vintage night, dancehall night and two international nights), featuring individual singers, DJs and some big bands. In the winter months you can go to evening concerts such as Reggae Kwanzah (after the African word for celebration) and Sting, both of which are held in Montego Bay.

These are usually fun events, more like a day at the races than a concert in the European style, with games being played at the rumshops and stalls that line the back of the concert area. Reggae artists come from all over the world, and they each play a set of a couple of songs: you see about 20 performers in a night. It usually gets started at about 10pm and goes on until dawn, often beyond.

You get a good idea of Jamaican music from just wandering around the streets of Kingston, but to see it Jamaican-style, you have to get out into the concerts and clubs; ask around in Kingston or Negril. You may find a world-famous band playing to a crowd of just a few hundred.

Just as the rhythms constantly develop, going in and out of favour and then picked up 20 years after they were first made hits, so do the dances. Popular styles in recent times are the Bogle, in which dancers brandish imaginary guns (and occasionally real ones too); the Erckle, a general comic display in imitation of the squeaky little no-hoper with the amazing dance-style in the American comedy *Family Matters*; the Tattie, a study in self-admiration and narcissistic body-language, and the Butterfly in which dancers flap their legs like wings.

Though the Jamaicans are sold on their own rhythm, reggae, you may well hear some calypso while in the island, particularly in the tourist hotels. Calypso originated in Trinidad in the eastern Caribbean and the favourite sounds of Trinidad carnival (held at Mardi Gras) filter their way through each year in preparation for the Jamaican carnival, held in Kingston in April. The best-known Jamaican calypso band is Byron Lee and the Dragonnaires.

Listen in to some of the excellent music played by the Jamaican radio stations (*see* p.23). Try RJR or best of all Irie FM, which plays non-stop culture reggae. Most clubs and record shops will sell you a cassette of the latest tunes.

Jerk

The jerk centres all over the island are among the best local Jamaican restaurants. Despite their name, they are not for the socially ungainly (there are even executive jerk centres), but a place where you order a meal of seasoned meat, which you eat with a festival (a sweet and heavy roll) and baked breadfruit or sweet potato.

Jerk is a special Jamaican way of barbecuing meats slowly over a wood fire set in the ground. The technique was supposedly developed by the Maroons who lived in the mountains in the 18th century and who would cure pig-meat for sale. Traditionally they would kill early in the week and cook it in an underground oven for a couple of days before taking it to market on Friday or Saturday. Nowadays the process is rather quicker. The fresh meat is seasoned with a marinade (with as many as 20 spices including peppers, scallions, pimento and ginger—each chef has his own special recipe) and then it is cooked over a pit on slats of wood. Chickens are chopped down the middle and splayed flat on the grill, along with whole backs of pork, complete with curly tail. Almost anything can be jerked including pork, chicken, 'spear ribs', sausage, fish and even lobster.

The home of jerk is Boston Bay, beneath the John Crow Mountains in Portland Parish in the east, where the Maroons lived. There are a number of shacks at the roadside, where they start to cook early in the morning—don't arrive after 4pm or it will all be gone. When you get your order, the cook will suddenly whip out a machete and proceed to chop the meat into bite-size pieces before throwing it onto a piece of paper. You will then be asked if you want hot pepper sauce. Jerk seasoning is pretty spicy already, so you might try one tiny dash on a corner of the meal. If you are not one for hot sauces, beware: Jamaican hot pepper sauce is vicious and searing and affects everything edible for miles around.

Country Life

Dawn is a serene time in rural Jamaica. Sounds carry well on the still, cool air of the receding night and you will hear the beginning of the day's activity; the wheezy beating of wings as a flock of cattle egrets fly off to their daily duties in the pastures and the sharp smack of metal on wood as someone prepares the firewood. Palls of woodsmoke rise in the valleys and, just before sun-up, as the moisture starts to condense, mist begins to pool in the hollows. Later, in the gathering heat of the day, this steel grey curtain is burned off to reveal the million greens of the forested hillsides.

The day begins early in rural Jamaica, at around 4am, with a 'tea' (a catch-all Jamaican word for tea, coffee and also locally made cocoa). By dawn the country workers will all be at their plots, reached by the lacework of trails that cover the whole of the island, often as much as an hour's walk away. They tend the neat rows of sweet potatoes and small forests of spiky-leafed cassava, yams with their vines trained over small climbing frames and cho-cho hanging from trellises. They stop mid-morning for a meal, perhaps brought from home by one of their children and then continue to work past midday. Harvested produce is packed into bags and set aside to be taken off to market.

Work is usually finished by early afternoon when the sun is at its hottest; the workers make their way home, riding donkeys or walking slowly in their rubber boots, machetes at their side. Agriculture is by far Jamaica's largest employer and it is a way of life that has changed little since Emancipation in the 1830s, when the slaves left the plantations and set up their own villages. Houses are more usually built of concrete now, but there are still many traditional wooden homes around the country, set in a 'yard' of beaten earth, in the shadow of a tree.

Every village, however small, has its rum shop, a small shack where villagers stop to pass the time of day, and most will also have a 'tuck shop' which sells dry goods such as biscuits, soap powder and sweets. There are also 'mobile haberdasheries', vans which go to remote areas to sell goods that the small shop would not stock, particularly material and ribbons, as the name implies.

The laboured crawl of an old truck winding around the country roads is a regular sight in Jamaica. Inside it will be loaded to the gunwales with produce from outlying settlements—bags of yam still covered in earth and huge bunches of plantain or green banana—all headed down to market in the main towns. The market ladies are there too, sometimes just chatting, or singing late at night.

Generally the men remain behind to tend the fields while the women and sometimes the older children go to town. A truck does the rounds through the country, often at 2 or 3 in the morning, and the market ladies load up with their sacks of produce and head for the main towns. They arrive and set up on the streets and in the red-tin-roofed market buildings by about 5 or 6—they have to arrive that early to get the best spots for selling. In Kingston the market ladies arrive by about 2 or 3 in the morning (they set off early the evening before because they come from as far away as Manchester and the eastern tip of St Thomas) and they grab what sleep they can at the stall before it all gets going at around dawn. Often they will stay for two days before returning home.

Sports and Games

Dominoes is the essential Jamaican, and Caribbean-wide, pastime. If you travel around the island you will soon recognize the slap of the chips hitting the table. The game is usually set out under a tree outside a rum shop at the side of the road and it is played almost exclusively by men. The slapping and the mock aggression are all about intimidation and show that you're on top of the game.

The format is the same as dominoes all over the world, but in Jamaica they often play in pairs. The partners use codes to send information to one another—these have to be changed often so that the opposition does not catch on. If you do get into a game, you'd be well advised not to play for high stakes.

Another popular pastime is **bingo**, often played in the local communities, mainly by women, but sometimes played for large stakes in venues such as the National Arena, where the main prizes would be cars and white goods for the kitchen. There is a whole etiquette and special language (much of it very rude or 'slack') which goes with the calling of the numbers, also referred to as seeds. These are a few examples: 5 is a thief, 8 a belly-(pregnant)woman, 13 the police or the beast (and bad luck), 16 a girl (sweet 16), 22 a nurse, 27 a fire-chief, 29 a preacher and 30 a rummer or drunkard. 38 and 45 are both guns, 10 an outdoor loo, 11 two legs in bed, 25 Christmas morning, 37 crab-lice and 69 is dirty people (Jamaicans do not have a high opinion of oral sex). 31 and 35 are unpublishable.

Cricket is a national preoccupation. Just about the only time that the dancehall music is silenced on the radio is when there is a test commentary. You will see the game played all over the island, occasionally on regular cricket pitches, but more usually in the streets (join in if they toss you the ball), in yards, on country roads and even on the beaches (a bit of a sloping pitch and fielders at square leg might have to swim for it). Even the hustlers are soft on you if there is a match being played and the West Indies or Jamaica are winning.

Sabina Park in Kingston is one of the five host venues for the test matches (the others are on the islands of Antigua, Barbados and Trinidad, and in Guyana in South America). It is well worth attending a match, not least for the high-grade heckling from the colourful crowd.

The most famous early cricketer from Jamaica was George Headley. In the eighties the big names were the bowler Michael Holding and keeper-batsman Geoffrey Dujon. Current players include the fast bowler Courtney Walsh (recently vice-captain of the West Indies team) and the batsman Jimmy Adams. The Red Stripe Cup is the annual Caribbean inter-island cricket competition and this fiercely contested event is held each January.

The Entrepreneurial Jamaicans

It must have looked like a piece of absurdist drama. An almost empty, tropical airport terminal, a fan whirring lazily overhead and a single, frail woman at the (only) check-in desk surrounded by a vast pile of suitcases and cardboard boxes all done up with string. Panicked passenger (guide book writer) races in stage left, with ten minutes to go before take off, and stands around behind it all, waving frantically and stretching tall over the luggage to get the attention of the check-in lady.

Eventually my gesticulations caught her attention. She laughed and told me not to worry; the flight would not be leaving for a while and there was plenty of room on the plane. Looking at the woman's mountain of luggage I seriously doubted it. How on earth could one person have so much? There were suitcases enough for 20 people. And she was chatting away animatedly, probably negotiating to be allowed to take most of it on board as hand-luggage.

She was what is known as a higgler or in sexy modern jargon, an ICI (Informal Commercial Importer). They travel abroad around the Caribbean to ports known for their bulk sales and duty-free zones (Curaçao, Haiti, Central America) and cities in the States such as Miami and even New York. There they buy goods in bulk and bring them back to the island to sell. The most popular imports are clothes and shoes, but they also bring in some small manufactured goods as well such as toys and tools, anything to order, anything that might make a little money. You will spot them in the customs halls at the airports, haranguing the customs officers to let them bring it all in without tax.

The goods are sold to market dealers and from here they flood into the daily markets around the island. Or they can be taken to the weekly 'flea markets' (such as the one in Falmouth, see p.112, which serves the whole of the west of the island) where they are sold to shopkeepers and local dealers.

The Jamaicans are great small-business people and entrepreneurs and the best places to see them in action are the many markets. These range in size from a roadside fruit stall to the buzzing press of the Parade in downtown Kingston. It is well worth visiting a Jamaican market just to see the bustle and activity. Vendors line the roadside so that pedestrians are slowed down and detained near their stalls. Most do not use tables. Instead the produce is laid out on a blanket on the ground. This is 'ben dung' plaza, where, to make your selection, you literally do have to ben dung. You will notice how carefully everything is displayed with an eye to design and decoration. There is often a musical stall around, with a handsome stack of speakers to keep the decibel count up, and cassettes neatly arranged.

There are fruit stalls at the roadside literally everywhere in Jamaica and these too are always decorated with care. People even sell in the traffic—on the main thoroughfares into Kingston they sell yellow dusters (called shamoys) in the traffic jams. Vendors walk among the cars or stand like trees between the lanes of traffic, their arms like branches with handfuls of yellow dusters hung by their corners for maximum visual effect. If you are driving around the country you may well come across a 'mobile haberdashery' (see pp.61–2).

The Jamaican entrepreneurial spirit stretches to other areas too, not all strictly on the right side of the law. Hustlers apply their characteristic Jamaican energy and ingenuity when they are 'doing a lickle business'. This business may be as innocent as getting a box of fruits for you from the market, or making up a cassette of current music, but if they can bamboozle you into paying too much then they will. The Jamaicans have a sneaking admiration for tricksters and enjoy hearing stories about how a clever operator beats a stronger opponent. This character is even written into island folklore, as Anancy.

Anancy comes from Africa and he is known all over the Caribbean. He is a spider, low down in the hierarchy of the African jungle, sometimes lame and often the butt of jokes. But he can turn himself into other animals, and he is quick-witted and full of tricks. Anancy is the lovable layabout, and he would always rather win a meal by cleverness and sleight of hand than by graft.

Jamaican hustling has a distinct edge of Anancy. A quick-witted trick to con a tip (or something far larger) out of a tourist is regarded as fair play—the cleverer the con the more fun. It is all done with brisk good humour, though it can be a little uncomfortable when you are asked for an outrageous sum of money for a service that you only agreed to under duress.

One visitor went out jogging, and after a few hundred yards found himself shadowed by another runner, who kept pace with him for about 5 miles. He presumed that his companion was simply out for some exercise as well. At the end of the run he fell into conversation with the man, only to discover that he had run all the way alongside providing security and wanted to be paid for it.

Style

Where else but Jamica would a hustler, dressed in a charcoal grey suit, briefcase in hand, arrive by canoe? As he hopped out into the smallest waves and onto the sand he rolled down his trouser legs (his feet were bare), struck a commuterish pose and marched off to the office... along the 5 miles of sand on Negril Beach. He was off to sell some gold chains and coral knick-knacks to the tourists.

The Jamaicans have a highly defined sense of style, evident as much in their manner as in their appearance. They are demonstrative, often noisy and boisterous and they love a verbal spat, talking as loudly as football fans whose team has just won an important match. It is quite normal to find people loudly lambasting each other in public (mostly in jest). It can be a group at the market, or just three people at a bus stop, but all the shouting and quipping and carrying on, and the timing of course, make it seem like a theatre of the street (often as playful as pantomime, sometimes as silly as farce).

A drive through the country is a feast for the eyes. Posses of schoolchildren race by and goats meander in and out of the chaos. Passers-by cut a theatrical dash along the pavement, dancing as they make their way through the crowd—there is a special hop and skip step to pushing a hand-cart through the streets. A greeting will often be a shout from one side of the road to the other, followed by an elaborate series of handshakes (if one of the greeters happens to be driving at the time, the car stops in the middle of the road, with the traffic queueing up behind). Even the traffic police in Jamaica, dressed in the peaked caps and white gloves of officialdom, do their job with great flourish and aplomb; you'll see them break into robotics from time to time as they direct the lines of cars.

At the simplest level, the Jamaicans are extremely careful with the presentation of the goods for sale at markets and in the street. Manufactured goods (anything from clothes to cassettes, shoes to cigarettes, or chewing gum) are invariably laid out in colourful patterns, red after green after white in sequence. At the roadside, fruit stalls look wonderful, colour-coordinated, as oranges (coloured green or orange) hang side by side in plastic bags of three, interspersed with the red of ackee fruit; limes are piled in pyramids of four and water-melons cut and stacked carefully so that the green of the skin is offset against the bright red pulp. One vendor selling umbrellas on the Parade in downtown Kingston displays them in threes, standing against one another in pyramids. Goodness knows what he does when he only has two umbrellas left to sell. And the sales patter is all part of the fun of it. All sellers have to come up with something original as they weave through the crowds shouting. It's not enough just to cry: Nuts! Wrigleys! or Bag-Juice! Box-Drink! And so, to beat the competition, they throw in an extra hiss: Nutssss! Wrigleysss!

And the appearance of every islander displays distinctive Jamaican style. Where clothes need not be warm they are likely to be decorative. Women dress in the brightest fabrics, with vivid colours in violent juxtaposition; men's T-shirts are slit into a hundred slivers of cotton between nipple and waist and the tails of their belts are left to hang extra long. Many Jamaicans wear hats, whether it be the head-tie of the market ladies, the mock-piratical red handkerchief around the head, or the huge woollen tam o'shanter in which rastas gather their locks. Rastas wear red, gold and green and are known for the swagger in their walk; for this and for their manes of dreadlocks, they compare themselves to lions, the kings of the jungle.

Hair is an important decorative feature for Jamaican men and women. Most Jamaican hair grows in tight curls called 'kinky', and there seems to be a general concern with straightening it. The most popular method of styling hair at the moment is 'creaming': the hair is straightened with a chemical solution. The scalp is oiled, then the cream is combed in and left, then it's neutralized with another solution, then washed out and the hair set in curlers. The result is straight and rigid and will last for weeks. Dreadlocks, twined and matted hair that is neither washed nor cut, with a texture almost like felt, are not that popular at the moment except with the rastas themselves. Perhaps the most distinctive and best-known style (mainly because so many tourists have it done) is braiding: the hair is plaited into many braids, and often hair extensions made of human hair are attached to the natural growth. This takes a good three hours every month as each braid has to be removed and replaited into the natural hair. Children's hair is often twisted into mini-hydras clipped with colourful plastic baubles, in a style called 'cane-row' because the series of squares it creates is like a sugarcane field that has recently been planted. Men tend to wear their hair short nowadays (hardly anyone has the huge afro that was so popular in the seventies), but they cut an amazing amount of decoration into it. The rabbit tail, a tiny tuft of often bleached white hair at the top of the neck, on an otherwise completely shaven head, was quite popular at the time of writing. Nike ticks on the back of the neck are popular—it looks as though half the population of the island is earning advertising money—and eyebrows can be shaved in a series of long and short flashes, sending some obscure message in Morse code. One man had his hair styled in the shape of a spider's web; his skull was completely shaved except for the gossamer-thin curved strands of the web spun from the crown to the sideboards and behind the ears.

The Jamaicans love gold; you will see people with a ring on each finger and so much of the stuff around their neck that you might confuse them for a mayor. You begin to worry that the life-guards will sink from the weight. Gold teeth are very popular, sometimes with a stone inset, and occasionally you will see a gold tooth with the inevitable Nike tick engraved on it.

And the current fashions in the black communities in the States have been adopted here: youths wander around with uncomfortably thick and heavy baggy jeans, often worn back to front, the crotch swinging somewhere between their knees, and a forest of shoelaces undone on their baseball boots. American baseball caps and all the sports gear are *de rigueur* in some circles.

There are the dedicated followers of fashion, but most Jamaicans are creative and slightly rebellious in their attitude to clothes. Sometimes mere decoration tips into eccentricity. Why do Jamaicans wear their sunglasses on the back of their heads rather than on their eyes, and why would a man wear a pair of welding goggles on the back of his head when he is quite obviously dressed to go out for the evening? It is not so much that everyone seems to ride children's bicycles around the island (they are obviously cheaper). It is more that they seem to enjoy the absurdity of riding such tiny and inappropriate machines. And they ride them with great style, pedalling around imaginary cones or rocking back and forth to some private rhythm. I saw one boy riding down a hill at an impossibly uncomfortable angle, body leaning out one side and a tangle of legs around the seat and pedals. It looked as though he was about to perform some fearsome and complicated BMX trick; but no, it was just for fun. After a hundred yards he merely switched position to the other side in some weird expression of symmetry.

A visitor's part in all of this can be fun, even just as an observer; but if you venture out into the markets you will find yourself quickly drawn into the scene, although it is unlikely you'll understand all the quickfire backchat, delivered in raw patois.

Bus stations, often next to the market, are something of an experience: conductors almost kidnap potential passengers as they walk by, their intended destination only a secondary consideration. Picking my way through a series of stalls in 'ben dung' plaza in downtown Kingston, I was beckoned by a woman stallholder, sitting on a low stool with her skirts rolled up over her knees, baskets of fruit laid out neatly before her. She looked up in feigned surprise to see a white face and, once she had my attention (and that of the crowd), said: 'Ooh daalin', come daalin', come squeeze me mangoes'. The whole crowd erupted into a screech of sharp laughter, which gradually subsided through repetitions into 'Heh, heh, heh', as it rippled around the street. You will begin to recognise this laugh around the island. It accompanies any sharp comment or wisecrack. Once, in the tourist centre of Montego Bay, where every white visitor seems to travel by taxi (or at least is encouraged to do so by taxi drivers), I went for a jog. Few Jamaicans do this— 'Well, man, you know, it a long way... an' it HOT!'—so it caused just a little stir among some children; they ran alongside for a while, with exaggerated and uncomfortable-looking runners' movements. But a hundred yards down the road the issue was settled by a fellow who was sitting in the shade by the roadside. His eye followed me as I struggled past in the heat, with a look somewhere between bemusement, pity and disgust, and then he turned away, dismissing me with a wave and three simple words: 'Get a taxi'.

All around there was a chorus of wheezy laughter: 'Heh, heh, heh... '

Encounter with a Hustler

Step outside your hotel in the main tourist resorts, and you are likely to be approached by a hustler. Often it will be within the first 48 hours of your arrival, or, if you are white-skinned, before you have a little colour; people who do not tan can expect it to go on for the full length of their visit. You will be barraged with questions and demands but just stand your ground, don't be browbeaten, and make sure you demand as much 'rispeck' as they no doubt expect from you. Periodically the hustlers are thrown out of town but they always come back. There are tourist police in some of the towns, dressed in blue, who may able to help if the going gets a little tough.

Hustlers can make a good living in Jamaica and some are very good at their job, knowing when to lay off because someone is a little angry, or when to put the pressure on someone who is about to break and hand over some money. They will run through an arsenal of techniques, varying from sympathy to occasional threats of violence. They even have different techniques for different nationalities (cheery and up-front with Americans, a little cooler and more conspiratorial with Europeans). They will often tell slightly fanciful but credible stories to persuade you that you must lend them a little money or hand some over as an advance for a favour.

It is not all bad, though. Jamaicans love to talk to people in the street, even tourists, and it is quite possible to have a chat with a hustler which is not entirely geared towards his gain. It is part of their nature to be all things to everybody and so if you say the right thing you often find that they suddenly change attitude and treat you with genuine interest. Most Jamaicans will be flattered if you take an interest in their country (enough of the tourists who come to the island barely know where they are, and only care about the quality of the beach). The funny thing is that once you have had a good chat, you feel a little more disposed to hand over some small change when the question eventually comes:

So you can do a lickle sometin' fer me?

You should not part with any money if you want to see it again—you probably would not do so with a person who approached you in the street at home. A typical encounter with a hustler will probably run something like this.

So, white man, wha' 'appenin?

There is no real answer to this question—of course it is simply designed to detain you and draw you in to conversation. They can usually tell a Briton from an American or another European, and so they might say: *Hey, Englan!* or *Yo Deutch!* Another favourite is:

Hey, white man, I saw you yesterday...

It is probably not true. If you stop, you will probably be asked:

So, wha' canna do fer yer?

Another open-ended question, with the offer of a service implied. If you say that you don't need anything, they will begin to run through their list of options. You have joined conversation and that was half the point of the question. One smart aleck tourist, annoyed at being asked the same question over and over again, decided to ask the same question in return. He got the lightning reply that a thousand dollars would do nicely.

The inventory of services and products on offer ranges from a box of fruits from the market, a cassette of recent reggae, or some aloe vera for your sunburn, to seedier offers of a prostitute or a visit to a go-go club. Once again, it is not all bad. Many hustlers would be happy to do a little honest business. For instance they will accompany you to a concert where you would not go on your own. Just be wary about giving any money up front.

There are numerous illegal drugs on offer in Jamaica. Ganja is what the island is best known for, and it is easily available and widely used, though officially illegal, but there is also cocaine and crack, which has become a problem over the last few years.

A lickle smoke (ganja)? *Blow* (cocaine)?

Or the seller might simply communicate with a tap on the nose or a puff on an imaginary cigarette. The product is obvious, though not necessarily of reliable quality. If he is having no joy with you, your hustler may switch tack and ask:

> *A girl? A boy?* And then in desperation: *Mebbe a aloe rub* (a massage with oil of aloe)?

If you do not want to be detained, the best thing is to walk on and say: 'Is cool, is cool, man', or 'Is arright', and denote 'no' with a slight wave of the hand. It shows a certain acquaintance with the country and that you are not just an ordinary tourist ready to be fleeced. You can become selectively deaf, but the most insistent will make sure to pin you down. If you simply walk by, ignoring them, then the tricks start:

> *So, why you doan' wanna talk to me, man. I is a Jamaican, an' dis my country. One love, man.*

It stirs a certain feeling of guilt in the person being hustled, and will catch a lot of people who would otherwise not stop. You can no doubt learn the five-stage hand-shake that goes with 'peace and love'. Then there's a cheaper line that some of them use when you try to walk past:

> *So why you doan' wanna stop and talk to me, man? You doan like black people, man? You prejudiced?*

And so it goes on. Being hustled can be uncomfortable, but it can also be fun. Just be careful; do not be led off the main streets and do not hand over large amounts of money for anything because you will probably not see it again.

There is a wonderful hustler in Kingston, who dresses like a professional person and claims to be a civil servant. His story is that his car has broken down and that he needs money to free it from the garage but that he can't get any money in town because the banks are closed... thing is, his daughter is ill out of town and he has to go out to see her... it's actually fun being hustled by him.

History

Jamaica's history is a story of conquering and colonization, piracy and planting, turmoil and terror in the constant wars, great riches and miserable subjection in slavery on the plantations.

Ten centuries before package tourists dreamt of their Caribbean island idyll, the Arawak Indians were already living it. They led a simple and gentle existence, peaceful and perfectly in tune with their benevolent island environment. The Arawaks called their island Xamayca, which has variously been translated as the 'land of springs' and as the 'land of wood and water'—both of these sound quite likely but are, in fact, without foundation.

There were around 100,000 Arawaks living in Jamaica when Europeans first arrived in the New World in 1492. Originally they came from South America and in the centuries following the birth of Christ they island-hopped up the chain of the Lesser Antilles, settling Puerto Rico, Hispaniola, Jamaica, Cuba and the Bahamas.

The Arawaks were quite short in stature, had light brown skin and straight black hair. They wore few clothes—married women wore a square of cotton around their middle, men and children went uncovered—but they decorated their bodies with paint of all colours, particularly black, yellow and red. They also wore colourful feathers or garlands of flowers around their necks, calves and upper arms. Like the Caribs, they would deform their skulls, binding them with slats of wood so that their foreheads sloped back to a high point. This hardened the bone so much that it could withstand club blows; it was even known to break the Spaniards' metal swords.

They lived like a Stone Age people, gathering food from the wild, including Jamaica's many tropical fruits, and cultivating some crops. Cassava, grated and then strained to get rid of its poisonous juice, was their staple, but they also planted maize and sweet potatoes. Seafood, fish, turtle and manatee (a large aquatic herbivore, like a walrus without tusks) were also an important part of their diet. The Arawaks lived in round houses called *caneyes*, with walls made from cane and a conical palm-thatch roof. They made simple earthenware pots and ate from gourds (the dried shells of the inedible calabash fruit). Their beds were hammocks woven from cotton, which they cultivated. As pets they kept birds in cages and a breed of small dog called an *alcos*, which never barked. They were fond of dancing and a game called *bato*, in which a ball was hit back and forth between teams using their heads and feet but not their hands. They drank a good deal at their ceremonies, of alchohol made from maize and from cassava, and they smoked themselves into a stupor using the *tabaco*. The Arawak word for tobacco was actually *cohiba*, now remembered in a brand of Cuban cigars; a *tabaco* was the hollow, double-pronged tube which they used to blast smoke up each other's noses.

Most Arawak settlements in Jamaica were along the coast because they depended so heavily on the sea and the coastline must have been fairly developed when the Spaniards first saw it. The Arawaks were excellent swimmers and fishermen. They built canoes that could hold as many as 50 people, from silk cotton trees, which they felled and stretched using fire and stone tools. Arawak weapons were clubs and spears sometimes tipped by flint or bone. They fished with harpoons, cotton nets and lines with bone hooks and they also had a clever trick using a remora: these sucker fish, with a line and a buoy attached, would swim off and stick to a larger fish or a turtle. The fisherman would simply follow the buoy until the catch was exhausted and then pull it in. There was also an ingenious method for catching ducks. Calabashes were floated downriver among the flock, then the hunter would swim by with a calabash on his head and grab the ducks by the feet, drowning them and stuffing them into a bag.

Arawak communities were governed by *caciques*, who were religious as well as civil leaders. The *caciques* had larger houses, with ceremonial furniture including chairs shaped as animals, and they were the keepers of the tribe's religious idols, called *zemis*. The main Arawak deity was Jocahuna, but others, gods of the elements, were represented in the *zemis*, which were made from clay, wood or even cotton. Heaven was Coyaba (a name given to more than one hotel around the Caribbean), where life was spent dancing and feasting on an endless supply of the finest fruit, particularly guava and mammee apple, safe from illness, hurricanes and attacks by the Caribs.

It did not take long for their way of life to be destroyed by the Spaniards. The very presence of the Europeans was deadly because the Arawaks had no immunity to new European diseases. Thousands died in epidemics of smallpox; in return the Arawaks passed on syphilis. The Spaniards justified colonization in terms of bringing Christianity to the Indians. In return for their gift, they forced the Indians to work on their plantations and to feed the colonists. Unofficially the Indians were cruelly over-worked and abused in Jamaica, particularly in the hunt for gold. In some cases they were killed for sport, after which the Spaniards simply went to nearby islands to find more. For their part the Arawaks quickly became depressed and melancholy; mothers aborted or killed their babies and many committed suicide by eating earth or the poisonous juice of cassava. One leader (from Hispaniola) was due to be executed for not becoming a Christian. Why did he not convert, the Spaniards asked, when he would go to heaven? He replied that he didn't want to go to the European heaven because it was probably full of Spaniards.

The Arrival of the Europeans

The Arawaks' idyllic lifestyle was already doomed, though, even before the Europeans arrived at the end of the 15th century. Another tribe of South American Indians, the Caribs, had followed them along the island chain. The Caribs are portrayed as warmongering and territorial. At the time of Columbus's arrival they were raiding Arawak settlements (mainly on Puerto Rico and Hispaniola, but occasionally on Jamaica), stealing women and killing the menfolk. They would probably have wiped the Arawaks out without Spanish help. As it was, within a hundred years of discovery by the Europeans the Arawaks were nearly all dead. Just a few communities survived hidden in the mountains in the larger islands. You can still see Arawak Indian features in faces in the Dominican Republic and parts of Cuba, where there was some intermarriage with the early European settlers, but there is no trace of them now in the Jamaicans.

Christopher Columbus

The first European caller was Columbus, who visited Jamaica on two of his four voyages to the New World. Though he was appointed the Viceroy of the Indies and the Admiral of the Ocean Sea, he had a special connection with Jamaica: the island was granted to him as a personal possession by Queen Isabella of Spain in recognition of his services to the Crown, and it was also to be the scene of one of the saddest episodes of his life.

He first visited Jamaica during his second voyage, in 1494. After sailing up the island chain and through the Virgin Islands he dropped his 1500 colonists off in Hispaniola and set off to the west, touching the south coast of Cuba. He was told that he might find here the gold he so desperately needed to restore credibility to his teetering enterprise, on an island called Yameye.

The crossing was difficult because of freak winds, but on 5 May he arrived on the north coast of Jamaica and his confidence and his usual effusive, optimistic tone returned. Jamaica was 'the fairest island that eyes have beheld; the land seems to touch the sky...' He reached land at what is now St Ann's Bay. The reception was initially unwelcoming as 70 canoes came out with what appeared to be hostile intent, but Columbus scattered them with blank cannon shot, and after that the Indians were happy to exchange food for Spanish trinkets. He moved along the coast for the next week, mending his boat and taking on supplies but, to his distress, not discovering gold. When he reached what is now Montego Bay (which he named the Golfo de Buen Tiempo or Fairweather Gulf), Columbus turned his two ships northwards back to Cuba. A month later, he returned. Starting again at Montego Bay, he rounded the western tip of the island at Negril and followed the wooded southern coast, greeted everywhere by Arawak *caciques,* who brought him gifts of food—one *cacique* even wanted to return to Castile with him. From here he sailed back to Hispaniola and then home.

His next visit, nearly 10 years later in 1503, was during his fourth journey to the New World. He had been expressly forbidden to return to Hispaniola (during his previous sojourn there, he had found the colony in disarray and been forced to make a treaty with the rebels; the episode had ended in the revoking of his viceregal authority and his return to Spain in chains), but he had been permitted to explore the area. By this stage he was embittered and arthritic and he had lost his fascination for the islands and his benevolence towards the Arawaks, whom earlier he had regarded as the gentlest people he had ever come across. His two small ships, the *Capitana* and *Santiago* were worm-eaten and unseaworthy after exploration of the South American coast and he had to beach them in St Ann's Bay. The ships sank and the crews set up camp on the beach; two of Columbus's crew, Diego Mendez and Bartolome Fieschi, offered to paddle to the colony in Hispaniola by canoe to get help. They made it, but Columbus's unpopularity in the colony meant that the governor, Ovando, would not allow him to be rescued. To make matters worse Ovando actually sent a ship to report on Columbus. They made contact, gave Columbus some salt pork and some wine, took a letter and left without him. On Jamaica some of his crew mutinied and made a break for safety themselves; worse still, the supplies of food arranged with the Indians dried up. So Columbus, who had read that there was to be a lunar eclipse, warned them that if they did not resume the supplies then God would show his anger by hiding the moon. The moon duly disappeared. The Indians were awestruck and begged him to arrange for its return, which of course he did after an hour or so. The supplies of food did not run short again.

Eventually, Mendez was able to charter a small ship at his own expense and rescue the admiral. Columbus left the island in June 1504 and they sailed for Hispaniola. Soon after, he returned to Spain for the last time where in 1506 he died, a sad and ridiculed man, having lost his earlier power and influence.

Jamaica was left untouched for a few years after Columbus's visit but, in 1510, the colonists set up their first town, Sevilla la Nueva (of which only a few foundations remain), on the north coast near St Ann's Bay. It proved to be an unhealthy spot, and so eventually the settlers moved off to the south coast, to the place where Spanish Town is now. St Jago de la Vega, as the town was known, became their principal settlement and remained the island capital into British times.

Jamaica remained a backwater during the century and a half of the Spanish occupation, undeveloped and neglected by officials preoccupied with the gold-rich areas in Mexico and Central America. The colony was used mainly as a supply station for the other islands and so it became a ranch as the colonists farmed pigs for their fat (the word *manteca*, from which Montego Bay derives, means pig-fat) and cattle for hides. The islanders also sold provisions to passing ships en route from the mainland colonies to Havana (where ships gathered before making the Atlantic crossing together). Little evidence remains of Spain's influence in Jamaica. Under the Spanish, there were a small number of colonial towns scattered across the island with hardly any roads, and the north coast was almost entirely unpopulated. Only a few Spanish names live on, mostly in geographical features such as rivers and mountains.

Buccaneers and Pirates

It was during the Spanish time that freebooters and pirates began to appear around the coasts of Jamaica, heralding a huge Caribbean problem to come. French and Dutch interlopers appeared in the Caribbean in the early 1500s and by the end of the century pirates were infesting Jamaica's tortuous coastline. Initially they came to trade, which was illegal under Spanish laws, but they were also quite happy to make a quick raid on the settlements and ranches, ransoming them for all their worth, torturing the inhabitants to find out where they had hidden their money and then leaving with anything they could carry.

The official neglect of Jamaica made it an easy target for the English in 1655. In fact, Jamaica was captured as an afterthought. According to Cromwell's Western Design (to take over as much Spanish territory in the New World as possible), the English should have taken Hispaniola rather than Jamaica but, due to military incompetence and rivalry between the expedition leaders Penn and Venables, the raid on Santo Domingo was a failure. To make amends they descended on Jamaica, which was almost undefended, with 38 ships and 8000 men. They landed in Kingston harbour and marched on Spanish Town, capturing it without loss of life.

For their part, the Spanish settlers presumed that the 1655 attack would be much the same as the previous ones and that when the invasion force had left they would be able to move back into their houses, dig up their money and carry on with their lives. But of course the British never left. They took over the town (what was left of it after their destruction) and deported the surprised Spaniards, who, as they left, armed their slaves and let them free so that they should harry the English troops. Later known as the Maroons (from *cimarron,* the Spanish word for wild), the descendants of these slaves were influential in Jamaican life until the 19th century.

Under Cromwell's instructions the occupying army was not permitted to leave the island (though Penn and Venables themselves headed for England and were both promptly locked up for their incompetence) and the young colony floundered, diseased, without food and regularly attacked by the Maroons. However settlers began to arrive, 1600 from Nevis and 300 from New England, as well as 'a thousand Irish boys and girls' who were simply rounded up and transported to swell the numbers, and the planting began. In addition, indentured labourers came out, exchanging their passage for five or seven years of work on a plantation and the promise of land to settle after their term was up.

In 1658 the former Spanish governor of the island, Ysasi, raided the north coast and set up a fort there, but he was defeated by a force sent around from Spanish Town. Ysasi retreated into the hills with the Maroons and held out there for two more years but he was never able to take the island back. Eventually he and his followers left for Cuba in canoes in 1660. There were fears among the colonists after the restoration of Charles II that he might hand the island back to Spain, but Jamaica was ceded permanently to England in the Treaty of Madrid in 1670.

Though Cromwell's Western Design may have failed, Jamaica turned out to be a very convenient base for attacking the Spaniards 'in their Indies'. There was a definite policy in Jamaica, perhaps with the nodded assent of King Charles II, to take any advantage against the Spaniards in order to decrease their hold on the Americas.

The buccaneers, a bunch of misfits and scallywags, were an invaluable fighting force for the governors of the island in their struggle against the Spaniards, and they were welcome on Jamaica for the wealth they brought from their raids on shipping and settlements, but when the region was at peace these 'brethren of the coast' could not be sanctioned officially. The base for their expeditions was Port Royal, which quickly mushroomed into the richest town in the New World.

The Buccaneers of Port Royal

The place was a gilded Hades, and Mammon held sovereign sway over its people. Bearded seamen, bronzed and weather-stained, bedecked with priceless jewellery and the finest silks of the Orient, swaggered along its quays and gambled with the heavy gold coins whose value no one cared to estimate. The drinking shops were filled with cups of gold and silver, embellished with flashing gems torn from half a hundred cathedrals. Each house was a treasure store. Common seamen hung their ears with heavy gold rings studded with the costliest gems. Dagger thrusts were common as brawls,

and the body of a murdered man would remiain in the
dancing room until the dancing was over. Gold and precious
stones were cheap, but life was cheaper. And every man in
that crowd of pirates lived beneath the shadow of the gallows.

A planter called Henderson describes life in Port Royal

The buccaneers came to Port Royal soon after the British took over Jamaica, but their original home was in the remote northwestern areas of Hispaniola. They were a rag-tag bunch of sharpshooters, adventurers and runaways of all nationalities: sailors who had jumped ship, indentured labourers who had deserted their plantations, even some second sons of well-to-do families who were looking for a life of adventure. In Hispaniola they would shoot the cattle that had escaped from the Spanish ranches and cure the meat for sale to passing ships. They lived in pairs and, according to their own moral code, shared all their possessions, even wives if they had them. The word bucca-neer comes from the *boucan*, the frame on which they they smoked their meat, and the word bacon also derives from the same name.

The buccaneers were rabid in their hatred of the Spaniards, who hunted them ruthlessly and eventually forced them off the Hispaniolan mainland onto the island of Tortuga. By the middle of the 17th century the buccaneers were beginning to take to the sea, capturing Spanish ships and sailing farther and farther from Tortuga itself. Gradually they turned into pirates.

They were ferocious and tenaciously brave, often taking large vessels against the odds. They were also notoriously brutal and would enjoy torturing people before they killed them. L'Ollonois, a Frenchman, once executed a whole ship's crew, licking the blood off his sword as he ran them through. He tore the heart out of another man and ate it.

Their apparently lawless life was in fact governed by an idiosyncratic moral code. The fundamental rule was 'No prey, no pay'. Spoils were divided equally among the crew, with a slightly higher share allotted the captain, quartermaster, surgeon and pilot and a bonus for the man who first spotted the prize. First, though, crew-members who had been injured were compen-sated: a limb was worth 600 pieces of eight and a finger or an eye 100.

The capture of Jamaica by the English gave the buccaneers a perfect base from which to work, where they could repair their ships, offload their loot and make merry until it was time to go to sea again in search of more. In times of war the governor of Jamaica had good reason to be grateful to them because they could be employed to attack enemy ships (they were given 'let-ters of marque' which legitimized their activities), but they were problematic allies; their loyalties were to themselves alone and, when peace resumed, they were reluctant to give up their 'sweet trade'—so called because of the rich pickings it offered.

On return from their expeditions, the buccaneers would spend wildly until the money ran out. Some were known to spend two or three thousand pieces of eight in a night and wake up broke. Roche Brasiliano was notorious for forcing passers-by to stop to have a drink with him at gunpoint. At other times he would just run up and down, throwing beer on pedestrians or attacking them. Prostitutes and strumpets were handsomely paid to entertain them, one of whom is described as 'common as a barber's chair: no sooner was one out, but another was in'. One fellow was heard to offer 500 pieces of eight just to see a particular woman naked.

The most famous of the buccaneers, and their leader for a time, was Henry Morgan. Morgan was born in Wales and travelled to Barbados, probably as an indentured labourer. From there, he is supposed to have made his way to Tortuga, joining Mansvelt's crew and eventually becoming its leader when the captain died. Morgan was bold, amazingly successful in his raids, some of which netted up to half a million pieces of eight, and a very successful leader of the unruly buccaneers. His prizes included Puerto Principe in Cuba and Puerto Bello in Panama, one of the strongest cities in the Spanish New World. Like all the buccaneers, Morgan was ruthless and cunning. On one attack he actually used a human shield of monks and nuns to storm some battlements. But by sacking Panama City (in which he netted 750,000 pieces of eight) he went too far. Under a cloud of disgrace, Morgan and the Jamaican governor Modyford were taken to London in chains. He fared well, however, was feted around the town, and was soon freed and back in Jamaica.

He returned with a knighthood and the lieutenant governorship of the island and, now a gamekeeper rather than a poacher, he was charged with stamping out the trade of which he had been the finest practitioner. He promptly hanged a few of his former partners. Now that the threat from the Spanish islands had been annulled by the buccaneers, the English started to trade with them. Henry Morgan died in 1688, largely as a result of his excessive appetites for drink and high living. According to the doctor, Sir Hans Sloane, he was: 'Lean, fallow coloured, his Eyes a little Yellowish, and Belly a little jetting out or prominent... much given to drinking and sitting up late'.

When the official word came to stamp the buccaneers out, some gave up the sweet trade in the many amnesties, but others became fully fledged pirates who scourged the area for the next 30 or 40 years; those who were caught were tried and hanged (often on the cays just near to Port Royal). A huge number of merchant ships plied the Caribbean waters, carrying every conceivable product, from Caribbean goods such as sugar, rum, indigo and cochineal to slaves arriving from Africa and cargoes of silk, foodstuffs and manfactured goods. Once they had left Port Royal, the buccaneers turned pirates were beholden to no nation and so they would plunder any ship at will. Steadily they became more and more unpopular and they were hunted by the authorities. Rewards were put out on their heads of course (there are stories of someone actually pickling a pirate's severed head in order to claim a prize). The town of Port Royal itself received its comeuppance in 1692 in the form of a massive earthquake which destroyed it in seconds (*see* p.213).

Calico Jack

The most notorious pirates in Jamaican annals were 'Calico' Jack Rackham (so called because of a supposed penchant for calico underclothes) and his henchwomen Anne Bonney and Mary Read. They were captured together off the coast of the island in 1720. Having been sighted off Ocho Rios they were followed by a naval vessel and run to ground off Negril where they had put in for a party. They came across nine turtlers and Rackham forced them at gun-point to join them for a bowl of punch. When the naval ship swooped in Rackham tried to get away but he was cornered and surrendered. His ship was taken under escort to Port Royal, where he was tried and hanged on what is now Rackham's Cay.

It was discovered to general amazement that two of his crew were women. They too were tried and would have been hanged, but they 'pleaded their bellies', meaning that they were pregnant. Mary Read died in jail of a fever and Anne Bonney gave birth and was eventually freed. She saw Rackham on the day of his execution and is supposed to have said to him that she was sorry to see him there, but if he had fought like a man, he need not have been hanged like a dog. The nine turtlers were also tried and despite their entreaties that they had been drinking only under threat of death by Rackham, they were executed as well.

The Maroon Wars

The 18th century in Jamaica was a time of massive development and prosperity. The increasing value of the colonies inevitably triggered a succession of wars— some were started in Europe and spilled over into the Caribbean, others developed in the Caribbean itself when a string of irritant raids flared into outright aggression. Jamaica was never actually captured but the threat of invasion hung over the island, particularly during the American War of Independence when the British were sorely stretched throughout their American colonies; they lost the States but held onto most of their Caribbean islands. Jamaica itself was plagued by the Maroons until the treaty of 1739.

The Maroons had waged a successful guerrilla campaign against the British settlers and authorities for eighty years. Even in the 1660s the English had tried to treat with them, because it was obvious that they would develop into a problem, but the peace did not last.

They hid out in the remotest mountain ranges, in two communities at either end of the island. The Windward Maroons lived in the Blue and John Crow Mountains to the east and the Leeward Maroons were based around the barely accessible fringes of the Cockpit Country. They hunted pigs and tended a few crops, settling small townships in the security of the mountains. Roused by drums and the 'abeng' (a cow-horn), they would raid the plantations at night, descending from the hills to attack, torching the fields and stealing cattle. And then when the soldiers were sent after them they defended themselves expertly, ambushing the troops along the narrow mountain paths and then filtering away into the forest.

Their numbers swelled steadily as slaves ran away from the plantations and joined them. Led by men such as Cudjoe, Accompong and Cuffee, they forced the island government to sue for peace, and eventually, under a treaty signed in 1739, the Leeward Maroons were granted two areas of land to themselves, around the villages of Accompong and Maroon Town. Here they would be left undisturbed. A year later the Windward Maroons, led by Quao (the brother of Nanny, who is a Jamaican national hero) treated with the English as well. According to the treaty, the Maroons were given considerable autonomy and self-government. The Maroon leader was made a colonel and the community permitted to handle its own judicial affairs (with the exception of the death penalty, which had to be referred to a magistrate).

For their part, the Maroons promised to cease their attacks on the plantations and the military. They also agreed to return runaway slaves and, if called upon, to hunt them down, a fact which makes many Jamaicans a little ambivalent about them still. They were required to do so a number of times, notably during Tacky's Rebellion in 1760, when a band of Coromantee slaves broke into a fort and stole arms and ammunition, and then took to the hills. Tacky was killed by one of the Maroon hunters.

In 1795 when the French colony of Saint Domingue was thrown into revolt and the whole Caribbean was in a high state of tension, a small incident blew up into a Second Maroon War. This time 300 Maroons from Maroon Town held out against 4500 trained troops and militia, once again waging a guerrilla war against the government, and torching estates. Eventually, after an exhausting fight that lasted for months, the governor brought in some tracker dogs from Cuba and the Maroons knew their time was up. They treated. Under the terms of the treaty they should have been allowed to settle elsewhere on the island, but the majority were deported to Nova Scotia and then eventually shipped to Sierra Leone.

Maroon autonomy still exists to this day, and they are still responsible for their own legal affairs and elect their own colonel. Their culture has always been distinct from that of mainstream Jamaica: though it is gradually dying out now, the Maroons had their own language, with a stronger thread of African words, which are still recognized by Africans today. The drums (the long drum and the cutter drum, made from mahoe covered with goat-skin) beat out African rhythms that have been passed down the generations.

Central to Maroon life was the 'play' or 'duty', in which the community contacted its ancestors' spirits at crucial moments, for instance when an important decision had to be made or when a person was ill. It still continues today. Started by a call on the abeng, the play involves singing, drumming and dancing—eventually the spirits appear, taking over a dancer; depending on which spirit arrives the people decide what should be done. In the case of an ill person, an evil spirit is cast out with the right singing. Maroon culture is kept alive only by the older members of the village; the language is no longer used much and the youth really prefer regular Jamaican dances to the plays of their elders.

It is possible to visit the Maroon villages on the fringe of the Cockpit Country and high up above Port Antonio, though it must be mentioned that nowadays they are not that different from most remote Jamaican villages. The Windward Maroons in Moore Town now have a simple museum. The attraction is really in their extraordinary story, though you might enjoy attending the celebrations held in honour of the treaties.

The Plantations and the Slave Trade

During the 18th century Jamaica became Britain's wealthiest and most valuable colony in the West Indies. The basis of the wealth was sugar and Jamaica was turned into a massive sugar factory, for a while the largest producer in the world.

The appetite for sugar in Europe was voracious. It was an alternative to honey, readily available in almost limitless quantity, which was suitable for use as a sweetener in the newly fashionable hot drinks such as tea and coffee. The planters and merchants enjoyed immense wealth; they built their great houses on the estates and their town houses in the capital. Their wealth, however, was created by exploiting a massive workforce of slave labour: Africans were shipped across the Atlantic in hundreds of thousands. At the beginning of the century the British won the Asiento, the contract to supply the Spanish islands and mainland with slaves, and Kingston in Jamaica became one of the centres of the trade.

The slave trade to the Caribbean began as early as 1517, when a friar in Hispaniola, Bartolome de las Casas, suggested bringing Africans to the Caribbean to replace the Arawak Indians, who were dying out alarmingly quickly. At that time slavery was fairly established throughout Europe and the Arab World. Prisoners of war could usually expect to be sold into slavery and some people actually sold themselves into slavery in order to pay off their debts.

But plantation slavery of the sort that grew up in the Caribbean islands was something new. It involved vast numbers and it was more systematized and far more brutal. It also entrenched racist views that had not existed before that time, but which still linger today. It grew into a huge transatlantic business called the triangular trade: ships would leave their home ports in the metropolitan countries with manufactured goods, arms and liquor for the African slave traders, slaves would be shipped from Africa to the colonies and sugar and rum would be transported from the Caribbean back to the metropolitan countries. The notorious 'Middle Passage', in which the slaves were often packed into holds so tightly that they could not sit up, lasted anything from three weeks to three months.

The slaves were collected on the Guinea coast, in the bight of West Africa. Some were criminals or prisoners of war, but the majority were simple villagers who had been captured by slave raiding parties sponsored by the local African leaders, and who were sold to the 'factors' of the slave trading companies, bartered in return for drink, weapons and other goods. The captives were tied together by the neck and driven to the coast where they were branded and then held in corrals or in the cells inside the huge coastal fortresses, to await transportation by ship.

Most of the captives had never even seen the sea before, so the ocean journey was terrifying as well as appallingly uncomfortable. At the moment of departure the crew stood by with torches until they were out of sight of land, threatening to set the ship alight if the slaves rebelled. They were packed into the holds, chained by the feet, sometimes so tightly that there was only enough room for them to lie on their sides. They could not sit up (there were usually two platforms to an average 5-foot deck) and the air was so foul that people actually died of suffocation. They were fed a meagre amount each day and there were no sanitary arrangements. Once underway, if the weather was fine the slaves were permitted to go up on deck, chained together in pairs, where the traders watched over them with guns to prevent rebellion. Some committed suicide by jumping overboard in their pairs. Though the traders kept as many people alive as possible (there would be no profit on a dead slave), an average of 12 per cent of the slaves died on these transatlantic trips. The traders themselves lived in fear of the privateers and pirates and sometimes foreign navies who cruised the Caribbean waters.

When they neared land the slaves would be fed and 'oiled' so that they looked healthier (open wounds were sometimes disguised with an application of rust) and then as the ship came into harbour its arrival would be announced with a gunshot. The exhausted and famished slaves (who often thought they were being sold to cannibals to be eaten) would be transferred onto land and then paraded through the streets before being sold at public auction. One type of auction was called the 'scramble', in which purchasers would pay an agreed price in advance for the slaves they wanted: on the shot of a gun they would race aboard or into the quayside corral to make their selection—first come, first served. Dealers would often buy a whole ship-load in order to sell them on to the other islands.

Slaves in the British colonies had no legal rights, and they were believed not to have souls. They could not own property, they were barred from giving evidence in court against a free man and they could not be christened or marry in church (unlike in the Catholic islands, where slave owners were obliged to baptise their slaves and give them religious instruction). In Jamaica religious education was left to the dissenter churches such as the Moravians and Methodists who arrived in the Caribbean towards the end of the 18th century. Some slaves, however, particularly craftsmen and artisans, were permitted by their owners to hire themselves out for work and were able eventually to buy their freedom. These former slaves would often keep slaves of their own.

The first year on a plantation, called the 'seasoning', was known to be the hardest for a newly arrived slave. Cut off from family and their homeland, they had to learn a new language and accustom themselves to the harsh regime of plantation life. There was a deliberate effort to sever their connections with their former life. Slaves of the same tribe and language would be separated because it was thought that singly they would be more compliant. Life expectancy was only seven years for imported slaves anyway, but many died within the first twelve months.

Work was a six-day week, which started at dawn to the call of a conch horn and lasted until dusk, or longer during the harvest. Cane-cutting was exhausting work, particularly so in the tropical sun, and so there was always a slave-driver, often a slave himself, who used a whip to make sure that nobody slackened the pace. Not all slaves were set to work in the field. Some worked in the factory, handling the cane-crushing and clarification of the juice into sugar. Others worked as household servants, cooking and caring for the planter's or overseer's family and children.

Punishment was brutal in an already brutal age—like soldiers and sailors, slaves could expect to be flogged within an inch of their life for misdemeanours. On the plantation, where it was in the planters' interests to keep the slaves alive, punishment was decided on by the overseer and it was entirely unregulated. Those laws that existed were stacked up in the planters' favour. Whippings were commonplace, as were mutilations. Repeat offenders would have their tongues and noses slit, even limbs amputated to stop them running away. There was no law against killing a black man in the British colonies until the early 1800s.

Sunday offered a respite from the back-breaking routine of work in the fields and a chance to tell stories and to dance and sing, the three main sources of entertainment. Later on slaves were given some education and religious instruction by the churches, who offered a faith (Christianity) in a world that was purposely kept spiritually arid by many planters. Slaves would also tend their plots and take the excess produce to the Sunday market, which enabled them to make a little extra money. There were just a few holidays each year, and these were celebrated with extravagant parties where Junkanoo characters (carnival figures) and 'set girls' or dancers would entertain the crowds to the music of roving bands and singers.

The nucleus of a sugar estate was like a small town. It was built around the factory itself: the mill, the boiling house, the still-house for making rum and warehouses for storing the sugar loaves and rum barrels. Close by were the outhouses, stables and workshops (for carpenters, coopers and blacksmiths) and a short distance off were the slave quarters; sometimes there was a dormitory, but more usually separate small houses of mud and palm thatch and their 'provision grounds', where the slaves were encouraged to grow their own food. The plantation estate house, where the owner or overseer lived, was further off, usually set on top of a hill; great houses such as Rose Hall and Greenwood were built to show off their owner's prosperity, but most Jamaican planters aspired to return to live in comfort to England. The wealth of the planters, often expressed in ostentatious luxury and lavish entertainment, was the stuff of legend; there was actually an 18th-century expression 'as rich as a West Indian planter'.

Many slave revolts were rumbled before they started and their ring-leaders executed but, if they got going, they could hold the island to ransom for months. The most successful revolt came to be known as Tacky's Rebellion, after the plantation slave who led it. Tacky and a band of rebels in the Parish of St Mary stole weapons and powder from Port Maria and took to the hills, causing havoc on the plantations as they went. The militia and then the Maroons were sent out against them. Tacky was hunted down and shot, and his followers committed suicide rather than surrender. Revolts broke out all over the island and it was months before the old order was reimposed. The effects of the French Revolution caused a major rebellion in the nearby French colony of St Domingue (now Haiti) and refugees fled into Jamaica from there but, despite the tense situation, it did not break into open revolt.

The endless wars and treaties continued into the first part of the 19th century, but by 1816 the borders of empire were fixed; Jamaica remained in British hands until Independence in 1962. In 1831, with unsatisfied hopes of emancipation in the air, Jamaica's slaves erupted again in massive revolt. It was led by Sam 'Daddy' Sharpe, a slave who was also a Baptist preacher. He had intended the revolt to be a simple sit-down strike during Christmas week, but soon the whole island was in turmoil as sugar estates were burned. Many of the leaders were executed and Sharpe himself was hanged. However, the rebellion was enough for Parliament in London to force through the Emancipation Act for all the West Indian islands in 1834.

Abolition of the Slave Trade and Emancipation

During the early 18th century there was little moral debate about slavery. It was an accepted institution pretty well all over the world and only a few groups, such as the Quakers, stood out against it. In the second part of the century, particularly from the 1770s, however, there was a rising tide of feeling against slavery, spreading outwards from the metropolitan countries. Even so, it wasn't until the early 1800s that they managed to bring the end of the slave trade while slavery itself was finally banned only after another 30 years had passed.

Led by men such as Thomas Clarkson and William Wilberforce, the Society for the Abolition of the Slave Trade was established in 1787. They raised public awareness of the maltreatment of slaves through a campaign of pamphlets and lecturing throughout the country. But for abolition to be made law it had to be passed in Parliament, where the West Indian planters were well represented. The abolitionists won support among the dissenting churches and then lost it because of their association with the liberal revolutionary movement in France (the revolutionaries abolished slavery, but it was re-established when Napoleon took over again), but eventually the pressure was strong enough and in 1807 laws were enacted outlawing the trade in slaves in British ships.

A number of other European countries followed suit soon afterwards (Denmark had banned the trade six years before) and Britain sent her ships out against the remaining traders. The demand for slaves was still there of course and the price went up; despite its illegality (and not all countries had banned it) the slave trade flourished. There was a good deal of smuggling, and blind eyes were turned because the profits were so large. Eventually it became clear that the trade would not be prevented until slavery itself was abolished.

Attempts were made to improve the situation of the slaves on the plantations, with laws for the banning of the whip in the field and permission for religious observance, but the planters were against any changes on the grounds that they would threaten their livelihood. The pressure to abolish slavery increased, however. Petitions were signed in Britain itself and eventually a bill to free all slaves was passed in Parliament.

For four years there was a system of 'apprenticeship', under which the former slaves were still attached to the plantations, but in 1838 the slaves were freed completely and the Proclamation of Emancipation was read from the steps of the King's House in Spanish Town. The slaves voted with their feet and most of them left the plantations. The situation in Jamaica was by no means universal. The French islands did not liberate their slaves until 1848 and, just 90 miles away, Cuba continued with slavery. They were still importing slaves even up to 1865 and slavery itself was not abolished there until 1888.

Once freed some of the slaves took plots of land and turned to subsistence agriculture. With the help of Baptists, Methodists and other missionaries they formed free villages. Others stayed on the estates, where they had to pay for rent, food and clothing out of their meagre earnings. For their part, the planters fared badly and went steadily into debt. Some attempts were made to revive their fortunes by importing modern machinery and immigrant workers (East Indians mainly, but also some voluntary Africans), but the industry continued to decline. In 1846 protective tariffs on the importation of foreign goods into the UK were lifted and suddenly the colonies had to compete with countries where slavery was still legal. Soon after, sugar from beet from Europe became a viable and cheaper alternative to cane sugar and the Caribbean sugar industry was left high and dry.

The island descended into appalling poverty, and the misery of the peasant farmers (the former slaves and their descendants) was worsened by droughts and epidemics in the 1850s, low wages (when they could get work at all), and then the price of imported food which increased vastly during the American Civil War. Their cause was adopted by men like the self-educated mulatto lawyer George William Gordon and the preacher Paul Bogle.

Matters came to a head under Governor Eyre in 1865, when Gordon and Bogle took a petition to him in Spanish Town. He refused to see them. Back in Morant Bay Bogle led a march on the Court House and a warrant was put out for his arrest. Later there was a riot at the Court House, which was put down brutally. Gordon was blamed for the rebellion and hanged. Bogle was hunted down by the Maroons and tried in Morant Bay, where he was sentenced and hanged in the arch of the Court House where his rebellion had taken place. Statues of him stand at the Court House today and in National Heroes Park. Governor Eyre was recalled and dismissed from the colonial service, but his last act was to get the Jamaican Assembly to vote its own demise, giving up the power it had held since the 1660s and handing it over to the Colonial Office in London. In 1872 the capital was removed to Kingston.

Political Change and the Spirit of Nationhood

With the decline of the 'plantocracy', the pattern of life and politics in Jamaica for the 20th century was set. Black and mulatto Jamaicans began to enter the civil service and be elected to the local assemblies. In the second half of the 1800s the government funded public services, including medical and education services, and public works such as roads, railways and irrigation works. Investment was allowed in from outside. There was a growth in the export of tropical products, with the banana trade flourishing in the 1880s and even a small revival in the fortunes of sugar.

Pressure for political change grew ever stronger at the beginning of the 20th century, particularly in the wake of the Depression in the 1930s. One Jamaican figure who founded and commanded international influence with his Universal Negro Improvement Association, was Marcus Mosiah Garvey.

In the early years of this century, with the slogan 'Up you mighty race, you can accomplish what you will', he brought black men and women around the world pride and self-respect in a way that had never been possible before under colonial rule.

Garvey was born in 1887 in St Ann's Bay (where there is a statue to him out-side the parish library), the youngest of eleven children, and he was apprenticed to be a printer in Kingston. As a young man he travelled around the Caribbean and South America: he was appalled by the widespread poverty and general subjection of the blacks and devoted himself to improving their lot. In 1914 he founded the Universal Negro Improvement Association, which aimed to unite 'all the negro peoples of the world into one great body to establish a country and a government exclusively their own'. It proved hugely popular and by the 1920s it had become an interna-tional movement, with 1200 offices around the world—700 in the States and others in Latin America, the Caribbean, in African countries, and even as far off as Australia. They were all linked by the newspaper, the *Negro World* and later *The Blackman*. The UNIA encouraged the establishment of businesses by blacks, such as groceries, tailoring businesses and a shipping line, the Black Star Line (which took its name from the White Star Line). There was even an aim to go 'Back to Africa', to create a model state.

Garvey became a champion of blacks everywhere, but he was generally dis-liked by the white establishment (in the States he was seen as a 'dangerous agitator') and in 1922 he was charged with using the US Mail to defraud. He served part of a jail-term in Atlanta and was deported to Jamaica. Here, despite more opposition from the colonial authorities, he continued his cam-paigns. He formed the People's Political Party which ran on demands for labour reforms and wider political representation. Although it did not have any success while he was in Jamaica, it set the pattern for later political development on the island. In 1935 Garvey moved his offices to London, where he died in 1940. History was quite unkind to the man and his move-ment was eclipsed and forgotten. He was ridiculed and criticized during his lifetime, but he was a visionary and he successfully caught the spirit of the age with his calls to self-reliance and nationhood. In 1964 his remains were flown back in triumph to Jamaica, where he was buried in National Heroes' Park.

There were labour riots all over the Caribbean in 1938. Soon after this the Jamaican trade unions were born, and then out of them came political parties. Steadily the pressure for political reform changed into a demand for political power and an eventual demand for Independence. In 1944 adult suffrage for all Jamaicans was introduced, the first in the Caribbean, and in 1957 the last of the colonial sec-retaries on the Legislative Council were replaced by elected Jamaican officials; cabinet government and full internal autonomy were also granted. The two leaders who emerged were the flamboyant Alexander Bustamante, later leader of the

Jamaica Labour Party (JLP) and his cousin Norman Manley of the People's National Party (PNP).

In the run-up to Independence there was a move to unite all the British Caribbean islands into a federation. The idea had been suggested before and had not proved successful, but in 1958 the West Indies Federation was formed, encompassing Jamaica, Trinidad, Barbados and the Windward and Leeward Islands (but not the mainland countries of Guyana and Belize), with its parliament based in Chaguaramas in Trinidad. But the federation ran into problems and, in a referendum put to them by Bustamante in 1961, the Jamaicans decided to withdraw.

Within the year, on 6 August 1962, Jamaica became the first British Caribbean island to take independence. Alexander Bustamante, at the head of the Jamaica Labour Party, was elected the first Prime Minister of the independent island.

Politics after Independence

Today Jamaica is an independent parliamentary democracy and a member of the British Commonwealth. The British queen is head of state and she is represented on the island by the Governor General, an honorary appointment, usually made to a former politician, at present Sir Howard Cooke. The Jamaican Parliament, set up following the Westminster model, is made up of a 60-member House of Representatives, elected every five years, and a smaller 21-member Senate, to which members are appointed on the advice of the Prime Minister (13) and leader of the opposition (8). Governmental policy is steered by the 12-member Cabinet which consists of the Prime Minister and other ministers and senators. The judicial system is based on British law and the highest court of appeal is the Privy Council in London. Recently there has been some discussion about Jamaica leaving the Commonwealth but it looks fairly unlikely at the moment. Privy Council rulings on certain Jamaican death-row prisoners have been viewed as unwelcome interference; there has been talk of setting up a Caribbean Court of Appeal as the final judicial arbiter.

Politics in Jamaica tends to be partisan and territorial (some say tribal) in that each party has its areas of committed supporters, particularly in Kingston (where Rema and Tivoli Gardens are JLP strongholds and Arnett Gardens and Jones Town are the heartlands of the PNP). At the grass roots level, these areas are given assistance when their party is in power; correspondingly they receive no support when the opposition is in power (justifiably in some respects, because of course the opposition's areas have been neglected in the meanwhile). Support in more influential circles finds subsequent patronage with government contracts and appointments. For all its rough edges, and the political parties have resorted to armed gangs in the past, Jamaican democracy is honourably respected in most quarters and plenty of people work hard to maintain it. The civil service does not change wholesale when a new party is elected and the judiciary is not under too much pressure to conform to the government wishes. Elections in Jamaica do tend to be somewhat traumatic, however, despite efforts to calm them in recent years and they are always hard, if not entirely honourably, fought.

After Independence, politics continued to be dominated by the same two political parties. In 1972 the PNP was returned with Michael Manley (Norman Manley's son) at the helm. He pursued a policy of democratic socialism based on principles of government control and social reform, introduced a statutory minimum wage and improved working conditions. Free education was provided up to secondary level and social welfare programmes and land reforms were put in place, redistributing farmland. Companies were nationalized, foreign capital restricted and levies made payable on imports. He became a major voice on the international stage within the Third World Movement. Manley also courted Cuba, which angered the United States and frightened off all capital, both Jamaican and foreign; the public sector debt grew. Basic foods were not available in the shops, unemployment rose to intolerable levels and there was considerable unrest around the island.

At the height of the political troubles in 1978, the shortages had reached a critical point, teams of gunmen were roaming the streets and making politically motivated killings and violence and gang activity flourished. Bob Marley, who had survived an attempt on his life in 1976 (*see* p.58), returned to Jamaica from Miami as a national hero and was persuaded to play in a concert, the One Love Peace Concert on April 22nd. During the song *Jamming* he managed to get Prime Minister Michael Manley and leader of the Opposition Edward Seaga to stand together on the stage and to hold hands in a show of unity against violence. There is a classic photograph of the two leaders clasping hands over the head of Marley in the centre.

After two terms, Manley was voted out in Jamaica's most violent election in 1980, during which 750 people died. It returned the JLP, led by Edward Seaga, with a massive majority. Seaga severed links with Cuba and re-established them with the USA. He dismantled the protectionist policies, allowing foreign capital in. He renegotiated loans from the IMF who in turn demanded austerity measures and certain political policies. Unemployment rose and so, again, did the cost of living.

Seaga survived for two political terms. He was re-elected in December 1983, uncontested by the PNP because they felt the vote was declared at too short notice, but voted out in 1989. The incoming Prime Minister was again Michael Manley at the head of the PNP, who rode on a less radical ticket than before, but he had to retire through ill-health in 1992. He was succeeded by P. J. Patterson, who was re-elected in 1993. Elections are due some time before March 1998.

Much as elsewhere around the democratic world there seems to be an ingrained pessimism about politics in Jamaica at the moment. Turnout at elections used to be well over 90 per cent but has dropped dramatically, and many think that the people have been sold out by the politicians. Life seems to go on getting harder and harder, with just a few people at the top of the pile (among them politicians and their cronies) actually feeling the benefits. Many Jamaicans claim that their leaders have gone into politics in order to make money and for self-advancement rather than to serve their constituents.

This feeling of disillusionment is not helped by the fact that the two main parties have very much the same agenda at the moment. Twenty years ago the situation was polarized with the PNP on one side, with a broadly socialist programme, and the JLP in opposition, favouring monetarist policies. The main complaint now is that politics is muddling through with short-term measures to try to shore up the continuing downward spiral of the economy.

In late 1995 there were the rumblings of political change when some members of Seaga's Jamaica Labour Party (in opposition at the moment) broke away and formed a new political party, the NDM or the New Democratic Movement. They cited dissatisfaction with the iron-willed and unbending leadership style of Edward Seaga. One member of the PNP, formerly of the JLP, went over as well. The party has so far adopted a centrist stance.

The Economy

The three pillars of the Jamaican economy are agriculture, the mining of bauxite, which provides alumina for aluminium, and tourism. Agriculture employs a large number of people (about a quarter of the workforce) and contributes just less than 10 per cent of the GDP. There are still many small farms in Jamaica and, as the economy has become more difficult over the last few years, many more people have turned to growing provisions for sale. Sugar is grown for export, as are bananas, coffee and cocoa, which is made into chocolate.

Bauxite and its derivative alumina are Jamaica's largest export earners (providing about half the entire income from exports), but the industry employs very small numbers of people. You are quite likely to see a couple of the transhipment points if you travel along the north coast, outside Ocho Rios and in Discovery Bay. Production began in 1953 and by 1957 Jamaica had become the largest producer in the world. Other industries include manufacture of garments for export and food, beverages and tobacco, of which a small amount is exported.

Tourism is the largest earner of foreign exchange and in 1993 Jamaica had over a million and a half visitors, earning around US$1000 million. Tourism employs a huge number of people, both directly in the hotels, but also invisibly in the services that support the industry: taxi-drivers, food suppliers, etc.

The most notorious unofficial earner in Jamaica is the illegal drugs industry and, at one stage, this was thought to outearn all others. There are two main sources: the export of marijuana cultivated in Jamaica, mainly to the US; and the transhipment of cocaine en route from South America to the States. Both of these have been reduced, with considerable financial and logistical support from the DEA. Ganja can no longer be grown in large open plots because of helicopter cover, and there are observer stations all around the Caribbean tracking the movement of ships. However the trade certainly continues and weed is widely available in Jamaica. Cultivation is carried out under a screen of other plants and in hedgerows where it is not so visible. Experts say the best ganja comes from Westmorland at the moment.

Transhipment has become ever more sophisticated as well. Cargoes are often flown in by plane and dropped into the sea just offshore so that they can be retrieved by 'fishermen' (there are stories that canisters are fitted with delayed fuses so that they will surface on a particular date and time). Then they are re-exported, by individual carriers by plane, or welded onto a ship's hull and taken off at its destination, unknown to the crew.

The state of the economy has a much more immediate effect on the standard of living in Jamaica than it would in a larger country and the decline in recent years has touched every aspect of Jamaican life. An island suffers all the familiar problems, but in addition it has the problem that it must import goods that it cannot produce, for example (in Jamaica) cars, medicines and white goods. Inflation has been severe and there has been a depreciation of the Jamaican dollar on the world currency market. This means that the price of essentials, particularly anything that has to be imported, has gone up immeasurably.

The cost of borrowing is extremely high because interest rates are huge, and so businessmen are controlled by the banks. This is not good for the confidence of the young executives who should be the driving force behind the economy. Many who can, leave for a better life elsewhere. For those who cannot, it seems like a desperate situation from which there is no escape.

Falmouth Church

Montego Bay and the Northwest

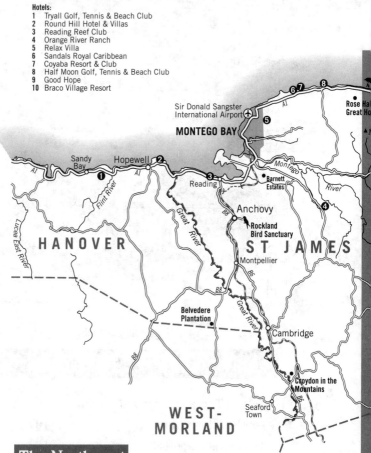

Hotels:
1 Tryall Golf, Tennis & Beach Club
2 Round Hill Hotel & Villas
3 Reading Reef Club
4 Orange River Ranch
5 Relax Villa
6 Sandals Royal Caribbean
7 Coyaba Resort & Club
8 Half Moon Golf, Tennis & Beach Club
9 Good Hope
10 Braco Village Resort

The Northwest

Like migratory birds on their annual journey south, tourists and travellers flock to warmer regions during the winter months. Montego Bay and the northwest are the heartland of Jamaican tourism, and this is where they come. Wheeling on outstretched wings, they fly in to land by the jumbo-load, filling the hotels that have encrusted the town and the beaches along the north coast, to luxuriate in the warmth of the sun and the sea.

Montego Bay is the biggest and busiest of Jamaica's resort towns. Here you will find some of the island's most expensive and opulent

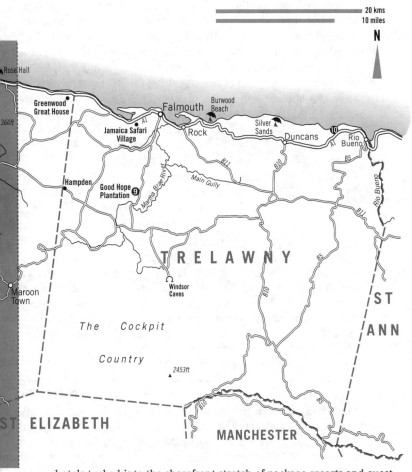

hotels tucked into the shorefront stretch of package resorts and guest houses; there is also a string of lively restaurants and bars, and the beaches where you can enjoy various watersports. The town itself is really only the gravitational centre of the hotels scattered along the coast for several miles. For all that it offers, Montego Bay also has some of the less pleasant features of tourism too—the hustling on the streets of the town is probably worse than anywhere on the island.

It is quite possible to spend a week in Mo Bay without venturing beyond the confines of your hotel complex or out of the immediate area of the town, existing on a diet of sunning, swimming and water-sports but, for those whose tastes are more varied, there is plenty to discover beyond the coastal strip. There are the most famous of the Jamaican great houses (the northwest was immensely rich from sugar in centuries past) and a number of working plantations, fruit farms and even a couple of sugar factories. Also there is the historic town of Falmouth, with the finest examples of Georgian architecture in the Caribbean (in distress at the moment, but under restoration).

Getting to Montego Bay

Montego Bay is well served by **air**. Besides being the international airport for the north of the island, it has a charter-plane terminal. Try Air Jamaica Express, ✆ 957 4051, for scheduled international flights. If you wish to charter a plane, contact Tim Air, ✆ 952 2516, 957 3374, ✆ 979 1113, or Airways International, ✆ 952 5299, 957 4051, ✆ 940 0005.

The new Montego Bay **bus** terminal is at the harbour end of Barnett St, next to Courts Store (the yellow building) and the fire station. Plenty of buses come from Negril and Ocho Rios, starting early in the morning, around 6am, and continuing to leave until 7pm. The Kingston buses start even earlier and there are plenty of them. If you want to get to Montego Bay from Port Antonio, there is a direct service, usually twice a day, which makes a single stop in Ocho Rios. The journey takes about six hours. If you miss the direct bus, you can always go via Ocho Rios anyway. To reach the south coast you must go via Savanna-la-Mar.

Getting Around the Area

Minibuses and **Ladas** (private taxis) ply all the local roads until after dusk; catch them from just below Sam Sharpe Square, on the junction of Market Street and Strand Street. **Share taxis** headed west towards Hopewell leave from St James Street. Generally local travel is cheap, but you should be careful to agree the price before getting in, particularly if you get in on the open road, because at the sight of a tourist some of these vehicles meta-morphose mysteriously into private taxis (sometimes even throwing the other passengers out), and charge accordingly.

There are limitless **private taxis** available around Montego Bay. They will offer themselves to you more often than not, but if you need to order one, you can go to any hotel front desk and contact any of the tour companies listed below, or phone the **Doctor's Cave Taxi Stand**, ✆ 952 0521, or the **Wexford Taxi Stand**, ✆ 952 3820. If you are standing looking vacant

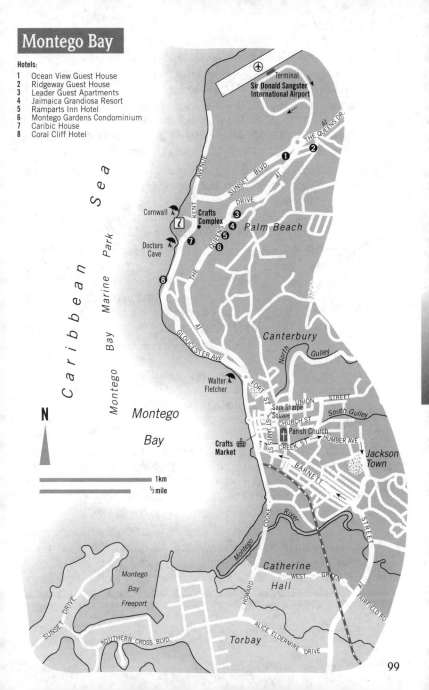

Montego Bay

Hotels:

1 Ocean View Guest House
2 Ridgeway Guest House
3 Leader Guest Apartments
4 Jaimaica Grandiosa Resort
5 Ramparts Inn Hotel
6 Montego Gardens Condominium
7 Caribic House
8 Coral Cliff Hotel

Terminal
Sir Donald Sangster
International Airport

THE QUEENS DR.

A1

SUNSET BLVD.

KENT AVENUE

DRIVE

Cornwall

Crafts Complex

Palm Beach

Doctors Cave

QUEENS

THE

A1

GLOUCESTER AVE

Caribbean Sea

Montego Bay Marine Park

Montego Bay

Canterbury

North Gulley

Walter Fletcher

FORT ST

UNION STREET

Sam Sharpe Square

CHURCH ST

South Gulley

ST JAMES ST

Parish Church

CREEK ST

HUMBER AVE

Crafts Market

BARNETT

Jackson Town

Montego River

Cooke River

Catherine Hall

WEST GREEN

STREET

Montego Bay Freeport

SUNSET DRIVE

HOWARD

ALICE ELDERMIRE DRIVE

FAIRFIELD RD

A1

SOUTHERN CROSS BLVD.

Torbay

N

1km
½ mile

you might even find yourself accosted by the driver of a horse and cart, particularly outside Jack Tar on Gloucester Avenue.

Plenty of **car hire** companies have offices at the airport. Some of the companies are: **Avis**, ✆ 952 4543, ✉ 979 1067; US toll free 1 800 331 1212; **Budget**, ✆/✉ 952 3838; US toll free ✆ 1 800 527 0700; **Hertz**, ✆ 979 0438, ✉ 979 0439; US toll free ✆ 1 800 654 3131; **Island Car Rentals**, ✆/✉ 952 5771; Jamaica toll free ✆ 800 843 4678; and **Jamaica Car Rentals**, ✆ 952 9496, ✉ 952 6951; US toll free ✆ 1 800 237 7533.

The companies with outlets at the airport tend to be a little more expensive. Companies based elsewhere, but still registered with the tourist board include **Caribbean Car Rentals**, ✆/✉ 952 0664, **Anna Car Rentals**, ✆ 953 2766, ✉ 953 2391, **Travel International**, ✆ 952 9362, ✉ 952 9358, and **Leo's Car Rentals**, ✆ 952 5662, ✉ 952 5662.

Motorbikes are available in the town. Contact **Montego Bike Rentals,** ✆ 952 4984, opposite Walter Fletcher Beach and **Tropic Ride Car, Jeep and Bike Rentals**, ✆ 952 7096, a little out of town to the east (they will pick up and deliver). **Scooters** are quite difficult to come by, contact the motorbike companies, but **bicycles** can be hired from Montego Bike Rentals above if they are not available through your hotel.

Tours

There are literally limitless organized tours taking in all of the 'sights' in the Montego Bay area, sometimes two or three in a day, in a bus-borne package that includes transfers and often lunch. If you are travelling independently but have no transport then this may be the easiest way to see the surrounding countryside (if you don't mind being part of a group). Tours are most easily booked through the tour desk of a hotel, but you can contact the tour companies directly on the numbers below. If you are travelling in a small group and wish to tailor-make your own tour, taxi drivers (many of whom drive for the tour companies anyway) are available at an hourly rate of about US$25–30, and about US$100 a day.

Some of the most popular tours are visits to the **Cockpit Country**, the **Appleton Rum Distillery**, the working plantations and the great houses in the area. There are also dinner outings, including a candle-lit dinner on the Great River. The **Hilton High Day Tour** offers a tour of a small plantation, with walking, riding and breakfast and lunch on the estate house veranda, ✆ 952 3343.

Some of the leading companies are: **Forsythe**, ✆ 952 0394, **Greenlight,** ✆ 952 2636 and **Caribbean Cruise and Tours**, ✆ 952 6260.

Sun Holiday, ✆ 979 0725, offers some of the usual tours but also has trips to Cuba (Santiago for the day and a weekend in Havana); and **Caribic Vacations**, ✆ 952 5013, has some more original tours which you may be able to join. They run two-, four- and seven-day trips around the island with all accommodation and stops arranged, specializing in Bob Marley and reggae tours. Most of these companies will tailor-make a tour for you.

There are surprisingly few companies who arrange anything more adventurous in the way of walking or hiking around Montego Bay. You can always contact one of the 'adventure tours' companies listed at the beginning of the book to see if they have anything scheduled in the area.

Tourist Information

The main **tourist office** is in the north of the town, next to Cornwall Beach on Gloucester Avenue, ✆ 952 4425, ✉ 952 3587. There is an information desk here but you will also find **information booths** dotted elsewhere around the town: at Sangster International Airport, upstairs before the immigration desk, ✆ 952 2462; opposite the St James Parish library just outside the downtown area; at the Crafts Market in town; at the cruise ship pier; and there is also a desk at Rose Hall.

In a medical **emergency**, there is an accident and emergency room at the Cornwall Regional Hospital on Mt Salem, ✆ 952 5100, and at Falmouth Hospital, ✆ 954 3250. If it is not an emergency you can also contact the Eldemire Hospital at 3 Orange St in the middle of town, ✆ 952 2620; if you prefer, there is a woman doctor, Dr Campbell Forrester, at 17 Kerr Crescent, ✆ 952 3898, and there is a paediatrician, Dr Byfield, at 13 Market Street, ✆ 952 5833.

Banks can be found both in the town centre around Sam Sharpe Square and along Gloucester Avenue, the main tourist area. The main **post office** is in the centre of town, but there is an office for stamps on the hotel strip on Gloucester Avenue (next to the entrance to Doctor's Cave Beach) and a desk at the airport. Diplomatic representation is all in Kingston, but there is a **US Consulate** at St James Place, Gloucester Avenue, ✆ 952 0160, and a **Canadian Consulate** on the same road, ✆ 952 6192. If there is no laundry facility in your guest house, there is a **launderette** in Love Lane in downtown Montego Bay.

There are any number of **shopping** strips, malls and markets around Montego Bay—and hotels often have a selection of shops too—most of which stock the usual wooden machetes and bags of Blue Mountain coffee for the cruise ship passengers. The best **bookshop** in town, with a special section of Jamaican books, is The Book Shop in the Life of Jamaica Mall, opposite the Montego Bay Crafts Market.

You will find numerous **art galleries** around Montego Bay, and paintings by local and expatriate artists are also on display in many restaurants and hotels, for example, the eccentric paintings by Jonathan Routh are exhibited at Tryall Hotel. Try the Gallery of West Indian Art, © 952 4547, at 1 Orange Lane in town, on the corner opposite the St James Parish church, which has work from Jamaica and around the Caribbean; also Heaven's Art Gallery, 1 Church Lane, © 952 2852, and in Reading to the west of town, Budhai's Gallery, which has an interesting collection of paintings in a house right on the road.

Beaches

The coastline that stretches east and west either side of Montego Bay has some excellent beaches; the mountainous backdrop of St James undulates in many bights and coves, and the coral reefs offshore provide lovely light sand.

Many of the beaches here are part of hotel developments and so there is often difficulty with access: every beach is public up to the high water mark, but you may not be permitted to cross private land to get to it. If you are staying in a hotel with a beach, facilities for some watersports will usually be available (check before you make a booking if this is important to you). Otherwise you can enjoy watersports on the public beaches in town.

In Montego Bay itself you will find three public beaches (where admission is charged) along Gloucester Avenue, within walking distance of many of the town hotels. The most popular, actually the original Jamaican bathing beach, **Doctor's Cave** beach, is very attractive and often quite lively. There is an enclosed swimming area with some watersports and changing facilities, and a bar and restaurant on a raised area with sea almond trees. Renovations were due in summer 1996. Not far off is **Cornwall** beach, where sports include jetskiing, snorkelling and beach volleyball; there are changing rooms with cold water, a restaurant and a bar, and some entertainment (evening DJ). Closer to the centre of town and slightly less popular is **Walter Fletcher** beach, a mounded curve of good white sand between man-made causeways, with a snack bar and changing facilities. If you would prefer not to pay an entry fee you can go up to the top of Kent Avenue to **Dead End** beach, also known as Buccaneer Beach, a small strip of passable sand with a bar nearby. There are no watersports or facilities and you are advised not to leave your belongings unattended in this area. **Tropical Beach** is another public beach where there's a small admission charge, on a quite remote part of Kent Avenue beyond the airport, cut in two by the extension of the runway; it offers a snack bar and picnic area under the trees, the constant pulse of reggae, and some watersports.

Beyond the town, hotels have been built on most of the good beaches, and this is where there are problems with public access.

Doctor's Cave Beach

Some hotels permit visitors and allow them to use their facilities, though many are all-inclusive and would demand a day's fee. As you head west of Montego Bay you will find a beach with a bar at **Old Steamer Beach** beyond Reading, though the old steamer of the name is now nearly completely disintegrated. Beyond here the best beaches are inaccessible, though you will find some good shorefront bars.

About 12 miles east of Montego Bay you come to a beach club at **Rose Hall** (*adm US$8*), where you will find superb sand and hammocks strung between the trees, plus non-motorized watersports, including sailing in kayaks and sunfish, and windsurfing and snorkelling. A little bit further on is **Bush Cay**, a pleasant beach with gently shelving sand at the end of the pine-covered causeway opposite Glistening Waters. It is quite remote—be careful about security. At **Burwood**, there is a small public beach with a little bar on a thin strip of sand protected by an offshore reef; it's popular with the Jamaicans at the weekends, but quiet otherwise. Still further east there is a nice strip of sand protected by a reef at **Silver Sands** in the villa complex (where you will have to pay admission), with changing facilities. There is a bar and restaurant where you can get lunch under the trees, with a view of the waves between the cannon and sea almond.

The Montego Bay Marine Park

Instituted in 1992, the Montego Bay Marine Park extends along the shore between the airport in the east and the Great River to the west of the town, about 9 miles altogether in length and about a mile broad. The words 'marine park' are a little misleading—local fishermen are permitted to fish here and there is a major port within its boundary—the area is more of a managed restoration project which aims to stem the extensive destruction to the offshore environment.

The coral life, which took a considerable beating during Hurricane Gilbert in 1988, seems to be in quite good condition now. Many of the corals lie within 30 feet of the surface, in spur and groove formations, with sand channels running between extended coral outcrops, and there are plenty of smaller fish: schools of exotic-looking blue chromis flit over the tangled spikes of staghorn and the sea fans and whips that quiver on the current. There are occasional rays and turtles.

In some areas of the park, the coral heads are close enough to the surface to see with a snorkel, and there are also plenty of operators in Montego Bay who will take you out on a dive (*see* below). Or you can view the corals in the dry from the glass-bottomed boat (*expensive*) run by Mobay Undersea Tours, which departs from Pier One. It is large and quite invasive, but the view is good and by feeding the fish they make sure that you see plenty—a hundred twittering sergeant majors (named for their yellow and black stripes), all clambering over one another to get hand-held fodder. If you prefer a smaller, less invasive boat, contact the operators on the main beaches.

Watersports

The best public beach for watersports in Montego Bay is Cornwall beach (jetskis, bouncy bananas, pedalos, snorkelling and glass-bottomed boat trips). Doctor's Cave Beach also has some sports. Watersports operators in Montego Bay are: **Seaworld**, ✆ 953 2180, ✉ 953 2550 and **Resort Divers and Watersports**, ✆ 952 4285.

Scuba diving on the reefs of the Montego Bay Marine Park can be arranged through **Poseidon Divers**, ✆ 952 3624, ✉ 952 3079, who are based at the Reading Reef Club and at Margueritaville in town, and can offer instruction in a number of languages, **Reef Keeper Divers** at Walter Fletcher Beach in town, ✆ 979 0102, ✉ 979 0101, and through **Tango Divers,** ✆ 952 3474. Other operators include **Scuba Connection**, ✆ 952 4780, at the Sea Gardens Hotel and **Seaworld Resorts**, ✆ 953 5018, which operates from a number of hotels.

There are numerous **sailing** trips and daytime, sunset and evening yacht tours on offer, many of which depart from Pier One in town; transportation from your hotel to the departure point and back is usually included in the price. For a day's **snorkelling** on a wooden ketch or schooner with lunch and a reggae picnic contact **Calico Sailing**, ✆ 952 5860, evenings ✆ 979 6863. *Rapsody* offers similar day and sunset sails on a catamaran, and the most rumbustious and rum-soaked of them all are the trips on the *Jamaica Queen IV*: day, dinner, sunset and disco cruises with a loud sound system, ✆ 953 3992.

Deep-sea fishing is also available through Calico Sailing and through **Rapsody Charters**, ✆ 979 0104, ✉ 979 0101.

Land Sports

There are **tennis** courts at most of the large hotels, many of them floodlit at night. If you are not staying in a hotel, you can contact the **Montego Bay Racquet Club**, ✆ 952 0020. And there are courts at Walter Fletcher beach, ✆ 952 0100.

A number of stables in the Montego Bay area offer **horse riding**. The **Half Moon** complex has some stables, ✆ 953 2286, where you can join a trail-ride in the hills and then a swim in the sea (there are even dressage and polo lessons if you feel you're missing out), and you can also contact **Oasis**, ✆ 953 3013, at Rose Hall. There are a couple of other stables set in the immensely fertile valleys inland from the coast, and a visit to one of these makes an excellent day out. South of Mo Bay is the **Orange River Ranch**, ✆ 979 3294, where there are endless stretches of country to explore, and further east there is a charming spot at **Good Hope**, ✆ 995 2825, south of Trelawny, where you can ride through working fruit plantations in the hills on the fringe of the cockpit country.

There are also a number of **golf courses** around the Montego Bay area, three of which you will pass stretched along the coastal road to the east of Montego Bay. The first is **Ironshore**, which is quite simple and good for beginners; then there is the **Half Moon** course, *green fees expensive*, which is always well maintained and an interesting course to play, with some good par 3s and 5s and luxuriant fairways. **Rose Hall** is yet farther east. If you are staying to the west of the town, there is another good course at **Tryall**, where the sea breezes are sometimes a challenge.

River rafting is an essential Jamaican activity and there are two places where this is possible around Montego Bay. To the west is the **Great River**, ✆ 952 5047, where the trip lasts about an hour and takes you through Mountain Valley. Alternatively you can ride the **Martha Brae River**, ✆ 952 0889, near Falmouth, which meanders through fantastic greenery; the trip takes about an hour and a half.

The City of Montego Bay

Montego Bay, or Mo Bay, as it is usually known, is Jamaica's second city. It has a dual identity: the busy Jamaican town and the major tourist resort. Downtown there is mayhem as the schoolchildren and handcart boys weave in and out of the traffic and the roadside stalls, where limers loiter chatting with the market ladies among the constant calls of 'Bag-juice!' and the pulse of dancehall music. Behind this, old-time Montego Bay looks on from its Georgian stone buildings and timber houses. And then, just a few hundred yards away, there is a completely different life: the Montego Bay shoreline is lined with humming factory-like hotels and the beaches are awash with lobster-red tourists sizzling in coconut oil. Rude-boys joust on their jetskis and higglers apply their high-pressure selling techniques.

Montego Bay is the capital of St James Parish and it has around 85,000 inhabitants. It became a city in 1981 and it is the only town on the island apart from Kingston that is a commercial, industrial and cultural centre. It is also a major port, which serves businesses in the area as well as the cruise ships.

The magnificent bay which gives the town its name was first named by Columbus for its favourable winds, the 'Golfo de Buen Tiempo', but when the Spaniards settled the area it came to be called '*manteca*' after the butter or pig fat that was its trade. When the British took over in the 1650s development was slow because of the constant threat from the Maroons in the mountains, but once that receded in the mid-1700s Montego Bay began to develop quickly, thriving as the shipment point for the sugar trade.

By about 1770 the town was enjoying its most prosperous years. There were 400 houses and most of the monumental buildings, the parish church and other stone buildings behind Sam Sharpe Square, date from this time. A few years later, at the beginning of the 19th century, the visitor Matthew 'Monk' Lewis (called so because of his scandalous and best-selling book *The Monk*) thought Montego Bay the prettiest town in Jamaica. Business took a dive in the mid-1800s when the sugar trade collapsed, but in the last years of the 19th century the trade in bananas brought some prosperity.

The latest boom, tourism, began in 1906 with the opening of Doctor's Cave beach and then of the first hotel in 1924. Mo Bay was not the first tourist resort on the island (Port Antonio makes that claim), but it is certainly the largest now. The trade has changed the town—a modern commercial city has taken over the downtown area, swamping the traditional wood and stone houses in a sea of concrete office blocks and, inland, suburbs have spread over the hills in all directions. Not far beyond these dormitory towns, however, you will find farmland where the hurry and hustle of city life seems a world away.

Around the Town

The centre of the town itself is **Sam Sharpe Square**, named after one of Jamaica's national heroes, though it is still occasionally called Charles Square as it was originally known before Independence. The square is laid with stone, shaded in places by bauhinia or bullfoot trees, with a fountain in a central roundabout. Normally you would expect to see the court house here, but the grand two-storey building with pillars and pediments was burned in 1968 and so only the shell of the lower storey remains in the southwestern corner of the square. Just across from here you will see the Cage, a brick and stone building with a small steeple which was used as a lock-up for 'vagrants, drunks, runaways and slaves' who were found still out after curfew at 3pm. Next to it is a statue of Sam Sharpe himself, preaching (he was a deacon at the Baptist church). His 1831 rebellion went far further than his intended sit-down strike—plantations were torched and riots continued for months. It speeded the eventual end of slavery, but Sam Sharpe himself was hanged in the square.

The St James Parish **Church** is an imposing stone structure straight out of 18th-century England that stands in a large, grassy graveyard behind the square. Built in 1778, it has tall arched windows, a square tower and a mahogany interior. It has been restored since it was nearly destroyed in a hurricane in 1951. Montego Bay's main **market** (as opposed to the craft market) is on Fustic Street, down at the end of Railway Lane; here you can see the traditional way of buying ground provisions (starchy vegetables, especially potato and plantain) West Indian style.

To the north of the downtown area, past the small Fort Montego, you come into Montego Bay's main tourist drag. **Gloucester Avenue** is a mile-long strip of all-day cafés, mid-range package hotels and dreary fluorescent-lit tourist shops muscling in for streetfront space. There is constant daytime and evening activity, with the traffic, taxi-drivers and hustlers who will accost you with a 'taxi-buddy?' or a 'hey, wha' canna do fer yer?'. Behind the hotels are two of Mo Bay's public beaches: Doctor's Cave and Cornwall beach.

The main road swings west to the airport along Sunset Boulevard, but Gloucester Avenue itself leads into Kent Avenue, which touches the shore and culminates in a dead end, and the Dead End Bar. It is a popular place to sit out or walk, in the early evenings, and watch the planes on their final approach to the airport.

Head south from the town centre and you will pass **Pier One** (a bar and marina) and the Montego Bay Crafts Market, a collection of stalls selling locally made arts and crafts. Further on, you come to the concert venue, Reggae Sumfest Entertainment Centre and then the Freeport area, a peninsula covered with wispy casuarina pine trees, where you will find the the cruise ship terminal and the Montego Bay Yacht Club.

South and West of Montego Bay

You will get a better feel for Jamaica if you travel beyond the main tourist towns, and there is plenty to visit within easy reach of Montego Bay. The **Barnett Estates**, *open daily, adm includes a drink and tour of the house and plantation*, a working sugar, mango and coconut plantation, are just out of town to the south. The great house, which dates from the 18th century, is in excellent condition and offers a revealing demonstration of a West Indian planter's life of two centuries ago. The ground floor is built of stone, with some defensive features (against the Maroons who would come this close to the town to make their attacks), and upstairs it has sand-dashed wooden walls, jalousie windows and large verandas all the way around.

The house is furnished with original antique chairs, some with the family's coat of arms, and silver platters and goblets on the dining room table. Upstairs there are pineapple headboards on the four-poster beds and in the office is an old rum chest (used to send sample rum back to the absentee landlord), with a lead bottom to stop it shifting in the hold on a rough crossing. The kitchen is in an outhouse (against the threat of fire), and there you will see old orange and lime squeezers and some of the herbs that were used before modern medicine. The visit to the plantation is by trolley bus and you will pass through the mango and coconut walks and taste the milk and flesh of a coconut cut down for you. You will also hear the story of sugar-cane, with descriptions of 'ratooning' and torching before harvest (it gets rid of the 'trash' and the rodents and 'brings up the sap' of the plant itself).

To the southeast, the land quickly gets rougher and more mountainous, with small villages dotted around the steep-sided valleys. Eventually you come to the **Cockpit Country**, a remote and weird landscape of shaggy limestone hillocks. It is an extra-ordinary sight, a series of regular, 300ft, cone-shaped bumps jostling one another like some diabolic eggbox. The cockpits, carved by water out of a limestone plateau, are steep-sided, circular bowls shaped like the cock-fighting pits that give them their name. If you fly between Montego Bay and Kingston, be sure to look out of the window because the aerial view shows the cockpits in all their extraordi-nary majesty. The water still flows, but below the surface of the land, and it emerges at the edge of the Cockpit Country in river heads. It has also dug out caves from the limestone, including Windsor Caves on the north side, Peace Cave near Accompong and Wondrous Caves near Elderslie. The Cockpit Country was also the Maroon heartland, and in the south is the infamous area once known to sol-diers as the 'land of the look-behind'–it was so treacherous that they had to ride back to back on their horses. The Maroons held out here, in settlements where the villages of Accompong, Maroon Town and Quick Step are today, descending to attack the plantations at night.

West of here, off the road to Cambridge, you will find **Croydon in the Mountains**, *open Mon–Fri, adm*, a working plantation ranged over the ridges of the high mountains. After a tour of the cocoa walks and coffee fields and plantain and banana plantations, you will be shown the process of coffee-making (pulping, fermenting, drying, hulling, selecting, roasting, and eventually grinding and brewing). The farm is also interesting for the many varieties of pineapple it grows: bullhead, natty, cowboy, Natal queen, honey and smooth Cayenne. Facilities include a restaurant. The Baptist and Jamaican national hero Sam Sharpe is sup-posed to have come from this area.

Close by is **Seaford Town**, the home of the descendants of a community of German settlers who arrived in 1835. The town is really quite similar to most Jamaican villages except that the 200 villagers are almost all white, with blond hair and blue eyes; it is still a fairly exclusive community, to the point of inbreeding. When they dance they surprise you by holding themselves exactly like any other Jamaican.

Further west is **Belvedere Plantation**, *adm*, another working plantation. The approach to the old estate buildings is through citrus, pineapple and banana plantations. You will see a riverside garden with plants such as puss-tail, anatto, which provides red food dye (and lipstick of a sort), and shame-a-lady. The great house is in ruins, but a post-emancipation village has been created with displays of traditional village skills (weaving, blacksmithing), a herbalist's garden and a small crusher where you can get a drink of cane-juice. There's also a pool and a river to swim in, and a snack bar for local fare.

Off the road back into town, in Anchovy, is the **Rockland Bird Sanctuary**, *open daily, 2.30–5, adm*, where every afternoon a stream of Jamaica's colourful birdlife heads in for feeding, wings thrumming as they flit through the greenery. You sit on a peaceful veranda surrounded by greenery and sugar-filled feeding bowls while warblers and finches eat out of your hand and hummingbirds, including the mango and the streamertail (Jamaica's national bird, usually known as the doctor bird), actually sit on your finger while they feed. There are also walks through the forest where you will see insect-feeders such as the Jamaican tody (with a green body and red flashes), a number of cuckoos and the yellow and black Jamaican oriole.

The border between the parishes of St James and Hanover is defined by the Great River, on which you can take a river rafting trip. From here the main road passes along the coast to Round Hill, which, apart from being one of the island's smartest hotels, is a landmark for planes on their approach to Montego Bay airport. The Hanover coastline is quite windswept, but inland it is extremely fertile. Pass through the town of Sandy Bay, which boasts the original Cool Runnings bar (from the 1993 film of the same name), and you come to the town of Lucea (*see* p.137). Tryall, another of the island's finest hotels, is marked by the open fairways of a golf course and a derelict water-wheel at the roadside. South of here, Mayfield Falls is quite difficult to find but repays the effort (*see* **Negril**, p.137).

East of Montego Bay into Trelawny Parish

The area to the east of Montego Bay, in the parishes of St James and Trelawny, was once almost entirely planted with sugar cane. There were literally hundreds of estates, each with their own sugar-works, rum distilleries and estate houses. It was the power-house of Jamaica's wealth 200 years ago (and at that time Jamaica was the wealthiest colony in the world).

Now that the sugar industry has declined, most of the estates have been abandoned or turned to other crops, their stone outhouses simply left to be reclaimed by the overgrowth. But a number of the old great houses survive: Greenwood and Rose Hall are the most famous in Jamaica. And there are areas of Trelawny that are still carpeted with sugar-cane. At Hampden you can see a working sugar estate and factory. Falmouth, set on a broad, protected harbour, was the main port for all this trade. The grandeur of its old central buildings stands out incongruously amid the run-down warehouses and the modern Jamaican town, a reminder of how prosperous the town once was.

As you leave Montego Bay to the east the road passes the airport and then follows the coastline, making its way between the golf courses and local villages on one side and the hotels ranged along the shoreline on the other. The ridge that runs all the way from Montego Bay to Ocho Rios rises to a height of several hundred feet a mile or so inland; it is steadily becoming more developed as the Jamaicans build their houses with a view.

After 10 miles or so you come to **Rose Hall** great house, ✆ 953 2323, *open daily 9.30–6, adm about US$10*, the most famous in Jamaica. It is a Georgian mansion with a stone base and a plastered upper storey, high on the hillside, with a fantastic panorama over the coast. Built in the 1770s, Rose Hall was restored in the 1960s to its former splendour, with mahogany floors, interior windows and doorways, panelling and wooden ceilings. It is decorated with silk wallpaper printed with palms and birds, ornamented with chandeliers and furnished with mostly European antiques. There's a bar downstairs and a restaurant.

Rose Hall is most famous for the story of its mistress Annie Palmer, who came here in 1820, and the fanciful legends of underground tunnels, bloodstains and hauntings. A renowned beauty, Annie Palmer was widely feared as a black magician, and she is also supposed to have dispatched three husbands (by poison, by stabbing and then pouring boiling oil into his ears, and by strangling) and innumerable lovers, including slaves, whom she simply killed when she was bored of them. She was 4ft 11ins high and was murdered in her bed. There is little evidence to support the legend, an amusing version of which was written up by H. G. de Lisser in his *White Witch of Rose Hall*, though maybe you'll be convinced by the ghostly faces that appear in photographs taken by tourists.

Set high on the ridge 4 miles farther on is **Greenwood Great House**, *open daily, 9–6, adm*, home of the Barrett family from which the poet Elizabeth Barrett Browning is descended. Built in the late 1700s, it is still lived in. On view are musical instruments, including wind-up organs and an excellent polyphon, the Barrett family library, and some old carriages and portraits. From the veranda, the view is so broad that you can see the curvature of the earth.

Inland and to the south is the sugar factory and estate house at **Hampden**. They stand in a huge broad valley of growing cane and are best visited during the harvest season, from January until July. Built in 1936–9, the factory is still in use and when it is working the air of the whole valley hangs heavy with the industrial-sweet smell of the crushed cane. Lorries bring cane from the surrounding area and dump it in the yard. Cranes on massive gantries bundle it into huge maws, where cross-carriers separate and wash it and get rid of the stones and the trash, and treadlers beat it and cut it to length. From here it passes through four mills that squeeze the last drop of juice out of it, leaving only bagasse (which is almost completely dry and is taken off to fire the steam turbine). The juice is sluiced off to the juice tank, mixed with lime and separated from any remaining dirt before being clarified in huge white plastered vats. It is then evaporated in vacuum pans and the sugar is crystallized in a centrifuge. The by-product, molasses, is used to make rum. First the skimmings are fermented in bubbling, oily black vats, with some cane juice, local spring water and dunder, for about six days. Then it is distilled (boiled through low wines and high wines, and condensed) to produce white rum at about 85–90 per cent volume by alchohol. Hampden factory processes about 160,000 tonnes of sugar a year, giving roughly a million litres of alchohol, much of which is used in manufacturing chocolates.

The great house at Hampden straddles the borders of St James Parish and Trelawny; its distinctive large roofs sweep down between dormers and overhang the balconies. On the ground floor (where the rum used to be stored) and first storey there are the original mahogany floors and furniture, including solid four-posters with palm motifs.

Among the small villages and agricultural grounds to the south of here you will find some interesting caves at **Windsor**, *adm*, on the edge of the Cockpit Country. You will be led through the cavern by torchlight to look over a 45-ft drop and shown rock formations in the shape of a hand and of Moses. If you're in luck, the guide will also play you a tune on the stalactites.

Back on the main coastal road to the north of here you might take a quick look at **Jamaica Safari Village**, *adm*, on the straight stretch of road leading down towards Falmouth, at the edge of the mangrove swamp. It is really a small zoo, where you will see snakes, a lioness and plenty of Jamaican crocodiles, which swim in the dis-coloured water with a lazy switch of the tail or sun themselves with a huge diabolic and toothy smile. The place is famous as the location in the James Bond film *Live and Let Die*, from which James Bond escapes a sticky marooning by using the backs of crocodiles as stepping stones. The island is overgrown now. You will also hear the story of Ross Kananga, the stuntman who owned the farm, and ended up with 193 stitches after an earlier take of the stunt. There's a bar, and a warning sign: 'Trespassers will be Eaten'.

Falmouth

A couple of miles farther on you come to Falmouth, the capital of Trelawny parish and site of some of the finest Georgian architecture on the island, set around a magnificent protected harbour. The town was founded in 1790 and for a time it was the busiest port on the north coast. Once the derelict warehouses that you see as you leave the town to the east buzzed with activity exporting all the sugar from the estates up in the fertile hills. Now Falmouth is a fairly ordinary Jamaican town.

Falmouth is still known for its land markets, though. Every Wednesday there is a 'flea market'; the streets are lined with vendors selling anything from kitchenware, clothes and shoes to human hair (for braiding). These 'informal commercial travellers' buy foreign goods abroad and sell wholesale to shopkeepers, who flock to the market from all over the western area of the island. Saturday is also popular as vegetable market day. The main road passes through the centre of the town, where you will find the red-tin-roofed market building and next to it a roundabout, a circular tank which once held the town's water supply. Just north of here, towards the sea, is the old heart of the town, where many of the Georgian buildings are still standing. Some are built of stone, others have timber-frame upper storeys on stonework bases, with balconies supported on stilts, reaching out over the pavement; some have been restored recently.

Look out for the court house on Water Square, a neo-classical building of stone with rounded arches, pillars and pediment and a double staircase. On Market Street you will find the post office and the Methodist manse. The Barrett Browning house was in the process of being restored at the time of writing. On the point itself, there is an old fortress, with one cannon on a roller, covering the whole of the bay; the barrack buildings have become a school.

The first monumental building you are likely to see on arriving in the town is St Peter's Parish Church, supposedly a copy of Falmouth Church in Cornwall in England. In yellow stone and pebble-dash plaster, with a square tower and balustrade, this Jamaican national monument has wooden floors and pews, with old marble tablets set into the walls commemorating the great and good of the town. The church is a little distressed now, the gravestones uncared for and the grass mown only by goats.

Falmouth harbour, almost closed off by a spit of land and reefs, is a shallow lagoon, part salt water and part fresh from the outlet of the Martha Brae River. The lagoon is known for its phosphorescence, caused by microscopic protozoa that undergo a chemical reaction which makes them glow when agitated. It is best seen on a moonless night—as you stir up the water you will see whorls of eerie green light. You can arrange a trip onto the lagoon through Glistening Waters restaurant.

Good Hope great house, *no adm, but you'll need to buy lunch or dinner, expensive,* is an old plantation estate house set on the top of a hill, quite a long way inland and only reached along rickety country roads, but with a magnificent view across a stretch of fantastic Jamaican landscape that takes in spectacular Cockpit Country. It has been restored as a small and extremely attractive hotel. You can visit for the day, or for lunch or dinner, and then relax in one of the drawing rooms which overlook the neatly ordered rows of papaya and orange orchards in the plantation grounds.

From here, the road winds its way east, touching the coast, where there are stalls selling wood carvings, and then heading inland; it passes through the small town of **Duncans**, where just a few pretty old wooden buildings are left among the more modern development. Soon after this you pass the plane by the side of the road that has been turned into a bar (it was an old ganja runner that crashed) and then you come to a couple of travel halts and then to the small town of Rio Bueno. At the head of the deep bay you cross the Rio Bueno river, which marks the border with the Parish of St Ann.

© (809–)

Where to Stay

Montego Bay has the widest selection of hotels on the island, with a string of the island's famous and luxurious retreats as well as a number of the chain all-inclusives. There are also plenty of very pleasant places to stop over in all categories if you are travelling around the island.

luxury

Round Hill Hotel and Villas, PO Box 64, Montego Bay, © 952 5150–5, ✆ 952 2505, UK reservations © 0171 730 7144, US © 1 800 424 5500, is the smartest and most sophisticated resort on the island. The pineapple of traditional West Indian welcome is the leitmotif of the hotel's décor. Round Hill lies 8 miles to the west of Montego Bay and has 27 villas set in hillside gardens; the pool, the blocks, each containing the 36 private rooms, the central foyer and the dining room are ranged around an amphitheatrical slope, with the private bay below them, where there is a private beach protected by an offshore reef. Recently redesigned by Ralph Lauren, the décor uses traditional Jamaican styles, with white louvred screens and latticework offsetting the dark blue and dark green colours of the awnings. Round Hill is elegant but also relaxing, managed by staff who have been here for years and has seen generations of returning guests. Watersports and a number of other activities are available if the library palls.

Another enclave of low-key, high luxury lies a few miles further west at the **Tryall Golf, Tennis and Beach Club**, PO Box 1206, Montego Bay, ✆ 956 5660–3, ✆ 956 5673, US and Canada reservations ✆ 1 800 336 4571. The great house, an elegant conglomeration of buildings with overhanging eaves, terraces and balustrades, set around the stone shell of an old plantation house, stands on the crest of a hill amid palm trees, with the golf course and the sea stretching before it. There are 47 very comfortable rooms and 55 villas ranged on the hills behind (these are self-contained, with pools, gardeners and maid service, but you can use the facilities of the hotel). Scuba and other watersports are available if you are feeling active, including tennis and golf; otherwise laze around over lunch and afternoon tea on the veranda.

The **Half Moon Golf, Tennis and Beach Club**, PO Box 80, Montego Bay, ✆ 953 2211, ✆ 953 1731, US reservations ✆ 1 800 237 3237, European representative Windotel ✆ 0171 730 7144, lies 8 miles east of Montego Bay. It is a sumptuous resort, set in manicured gardens and buildings of old colonial grandeur, giving onto a lovely half-moon curve of beach. A motif of neo-classical black and white runs through the resort, from the atrium of the great house to the chequerboard floors and classical columns of many of the rooms. Half Moon is a large hotel (as it does get quite full): there are 340 rooms in all, with 39 swimming-pools, 13 tennis courts and four squash courts, a childrens' entertainment centre, and plenty of watersports (jetskis excluded) with stables and, across the road, a golf course. The rooms are set in low blocks attached to the main house; there are also huge suites on the seafront, and villas around the grounds.

very expensive

A smaller beach resort in a more contemporary Caribbean style, with tall blocks standing over a pool above the beach and the broad expanse of sea, is **Coyaba Resort and Club**, Little River PO, ✆ 953 9150, ✆ 953 2244. There are 50 very comfortable rooms, with terracotta tiles and mock antique furniture; each has a balcony. There is a personable and intimate air about the interior of the hotel. Life centres on the beach, however, where there is a bar and a deck stretching out into the shallow water towards a reef. Dining takes place in the pretty, vine-covered restaurant or above the beach itself. There's a fitness centre and watersports; all-inclusive packages are available.

Braco Village Resort, Rio Bueno PO, Trelawny, ✆ 954 0000–19, ✉ 954 0020, US reservations ✆ 1 800 654 1337, is an all-inclusive hotel with a difference, a good way east of Montego Bay. The hotel is set in a purpose-built 'village', which replicates most attractive features of a traditional Jamaican town, styled 'Georgian to Gingerbread'. There is a village square with a Georgian court house at the centre; around it are shops, pizza parlours and ice cream stalls set in brick-buildings and sand-dashed wooden houses, a jerk centre, a tin-roofed market building (the main dining room) and an original tin-walled dancehall (the discotheque and club, indoor and air-conditioned). The rooms are in blocks that reflect an eclectic variety of Jamaican architectural styles—there is an acreage of latticework and gingerbread decorations on the balconies and verandas, under the shingle and tin roofs and gazebo turrets. Braco Reef is 'theme Jamaica' there's no doubt, with coconut, sugar-cane and peanut vendors on the 'street' who are mere shadows of their counterparts outside the hotel compound, but you do get a good beach holiday plus a taste of Jamaican life here without ever taking out your wallet. There are the regular amenities such as the vast meandering swimming pool and the beachfront watersports (there is also a clothes-optional beach), a sports room with clinician, 4 restaurants, and all the conveniences of modern life in the rooms—13 satellite channels, air-conditioning and fans.

expensive

Good Hope, PO Box 50, Falmouth, ✆/✉ 954 3289, UK reservations ✆ 0800 614 790, US ✆ 1 800 *OUT POST*, is set in a restored 18th-century estate house overlooking a fantastic stretch of Trelawny countryside, a patchwork of rich red-brown earth and orchards, against a backdrop of the Cockpit Country. Built of stone and wood, with huge windows and breezy louvres, the house has original antique furniture, planters' chairs, vast glass hurricane lamps, four-poster beds and commodes, all on the original floor of wild orange wood. There are only 10 bedrooms, scattered around the main house, the garden buildings and stables, and so Good Hope never seems full. There is a pool and tennis court, and you can take a ride on horseback through the valley beneath the house—or you can simply watch from the drawing room or the veranda as the view alters constantly with the changing light of the day. Ideal for the lazy life among old Jamaican plantation elegance.

The **Reading Reef Club**, PO Box 225, Reading Post Office, ✆ 952 5909, 🖷 952 7217, US reservations ✆ 1 800 223 6510, sits on the waterfront across the bay a little out of the town, and is quiet and well off the beaten tourist trail. There are just 28 rooms in three villa-style blocks set in an attractive garden of traveller's palms and heliconia, and the resort stands around a pool on a pleasant if slightly pebbly beach. The rooms are brightly decorated and furnished with wicker; each has ceiling fans as well as air-conditioning and some have balconies looking out onto the sea. There are some suites. The friendly bar has a wonderful view and, above it, the restaurant serves fine international and Caribbean food, including curried lobster and catch of the day as well as pastas. There is a dive shop on the premises and snorkelling right offshore.

For a more usual all-inclusive holiday in a busy beach hotel, offering a diet of constant activity and entertainment, and mostly buffet food, you can try either of the two Sandals resorts in Montego Bay, of which the better is probably **Sandals Royal Caribbean**.

moderate

Montego Bay and its surrounding area has a number of smaller hotels which still have a certain style. They are ideal for more independent travellers who want a stopover on arrival in Jamaica or are passing through while touring the island.

The **Relax Villa** Resort, 26 Hobbs Ave, White Sands Beach PO, ✆/🖷 952 7218, US and Canada reservations ✆ 1 800 742 4276, is close to the airport, in a couple of modern blocks set in the tropical gardens of a hillside estate. It's friendly and well run, with large rooms and (one-, two- and three-bedroom) apartments, all of them comfortably decorated in bright white and pastel colours, with balconies, air-conditioning and fans, TVs, etc. The beaches are not within walking distance, but easy to get to by car or taxi. Pick-up from the airport is offered and car-hire is available at a reasonable price here. It's a good place to start your holiday.

Orange River Ranch, PO Box 822, Montego Bay, ✆ 979 3294, is set in 989 acres of fertile Jamaican countryside just south of Montego Bay. The hotel is on a remote and quiet hillside (though tours visit occasionally); its central house has a wraparound veranda hung with flowering vines, and a white picket fence. Set in a modern block behind, the 24 rooms are slightly small but pretty and comfortable and many have an excellent view of the Orange River valley; fans, phones and a small veranda. Facilities include a pool, riding stables, and a shuttle service to the beach. Very peaceful, a good escape.

A comfortable town-based hotel (among the hundreds) is the **Jamaican Grandiosa Resort**, PO Box 139, Montego Bay, ✆ 979 3205, 📠 979 3203, on the Close behind Queen's Drive, high above Gloucester Avenue. It is very much a modern Jamaican hotel; a large block on the hillside with a terrace pool and an excellent view of the town and bay. Dressed up in pink, the 40 rooms, each with a balcony, are quite basic but comfortable. A beach shuttle is provided.

inexpensive

The **Ramparts Inn Hotel** at 5 Ramparts Close, ✆ 979 5258, also has a homely feel, set in an attractive hilltop house and garden with a view over the town and the expanse of Montego Bay. There are just 10 rooms, all air-conditioned, some with a view. The central areas include a pool on a deck, a bar and a TV room; there is a complementary beach shuttle. The restaurant serves breakfast and lunch.

There are also plenty of guest houses in Montego Bay, quite a few of them in the area close to the airport (some will pick you up when you arrive). In the tourist heartland of Gloucester Avenue you will find the ever busy **Caribic House**, ✆ 952 5013, 📠 952 0981, surrounded by bars and restaurants and in easy walking distance of all the beaches. Its 15 simple rooms have air-conditioning and some fans.

Perhaps the friendliest stopover in the area is the **Ocean View Guest House**, ✆ 952 2147, which is on Sunset Boulevard, just above the airport. There are 12 rooms, some air-conditioned and some with fan ventilation. Inexpensive meals are cooked to order and served in the busy central area (where there's a TV and some books), or under parasols on the veranda at the front. There is no pool, but a washroom you can use if you've been to the beach before flying out late in the day.

Alternatively you might try the **Ridgeway Guest House** just up the hill from the airport roundabout, ✆ 952 2709, 📠 940 0636, where there are rooms and self-contained apartments with fans and air-conditioning, and they offer meals cooked to order.

Further up the hill, on Leader Avenue off Queen's Drive, you will get a good rate at **Leader Guest Apartments**, ✆ 952 0361, where there are 21 rooms in a no-nonsense block at very good prices. The rooms have baths, hot and cold water, some balconies but there are no meals (nor kitchenettes, though it's OK to bring food into the rooms).

About 200yds south is the **Montego Gardens Condominium**, also off Queen's Drive, ☎ 952 1854, which offers studio apartments at an excellent price. They include kitchenettes, hot and cold water, some fans, some air-conditioning and TVs in the rooms; the pool and the bar are down below. The rates in some of these guest houses are negotiable, particularly if you are staying for more than a few days. You may also find that people will offer you a room if you are looking a bit lost at the airport. Be careful, but there are good deals available.

The **Coral Cliff Hotel**, PO Box 253, ☎ 952 4130, ✆ 952 6532, on Gloucester Avenue, has a traditional Jamaican charm and enjoys a lively crowd of repeat visitors. It has the air of a grand old villa from colonial times, with a large breezy balcony above the street and tropical gardens punctuated by vast royal palms. The interior is charming and homely, with wooden floors and airy corridors. There are 21 rooms in older Caribbean style (with stained wooden walls and dark-stained furniture) and above them a pool and 10 rooms in the newer block; the library area has chess and backgammon.

Eating Out

Montego Bay has a reasonable selection of restaurants, in and outside the hotels, some of them in very elegant surroundings. Most offer international fare using local ingredients; some present meals with a little more imagination than others. Very few places take Jamaican cuisine into elegant surroundings; for the best of Jamaican fare you have to go local.

Eating out is quite expensive in Mo Bay, but a number of restaurants sweeten the deal by offering complementary transport before and after the meal.

expensive

The finest restaurant around, for the cuisine and for the setting is **Norma's**, ☎ 979 2745, a few miles east of Montego Bay in Reading (signed from the road). You dine in the open air on a wooden deck beneath a huge sea almond tree, with the water washing quietly over the rocks beneath you, and the lights of Montego Bay sparkling on the hillside opposite. Norma uses the best of freshly bought local ingredients in some unlikely but satisfying combinations—the crisp flesh of an otaheite apple sits well in the rich body of a pumpkin soup; as main courses snapper is marinaded in lemon, lime and ugli fruit, capers and herbs and then grilled, chicken breast layered with cream cheese; desserts include a white chocolate and pear cheesecake with a lacing of rum. The menu changes nightly; it's open at lunchtime, but ideal for a lingering dinner for two. *Closed Mon.*

The **Town House**, Church Street, ✆ 952 2660, is set in an elegant Georgian mansion (variously a manse, masonic lodge, warehouse, hotel, synagogue and residence of the governor's mistress), overlooking the parish church. The dining rooms are in the brick-laid cellar (where the walls are covered with paintings, which you can buy if the desire should strike) and upstairs, with some tables looking over the street. The menu is international with some Jamaican flavours: red snapper is served as a papillotte, cooked in a cheese, wine and lobster sauce, and Jamaican chicken curry is served with breadfruit, ackee and plantain; puddings are English sherry trifle and fresh fruit sorbets.

On the hillside above Gloucester Avenue (approached by the road next to the Coral Cliff Hotel), you will find a very pleasant spot for lunch or dinner: **Tapas**, ✆ 952 2988. The name suggests Latin American food and the fare does include some Latin dishes—*pollo chimichanga* (with mustard tomato sauce, served with rice and red cabbage) and *carne asada*, a fillet steak marinaded in coffee, sugar and cayenne pepper—among mostly Mediterranean food (Greek, Italian and Spanish). Quiet and friendly in the setting of a Spanish colonial villa, Tapas is open for lunch and dinner.

moderate

On Orange Street is the **Georgian House**, ✆ 952 0632, set in a fine old West Indian town house. The dining room is oval, and decorated with an acreage of flounce, brass chandeliers and repro furniture, the cuisine is international with variations on a seafood theme—shrimp creole or sautéed in a white wine sauce, red snapper in a 'dip and fallback' rundown sauce— and steak, grilled with mushrooms, and exotic fruit salads and ice creams to follow. There is a pleasant courtyard and a bar downstairs in the cellars, where you can take a rum punch or a Red Stripe before dining.

Julia's, ✆ 952 1772, signed from the bottom of Bogue Hill, is an Italian restaurant with a dining area on a candle-lit terrace that overlooks the whole of Montego Bay. The set menu includes: soup, salad, a choice of pasta, for example *lasagna all' Julia*, with meat, mozzarella and parmesan, and an entrée (chicken parmesan or snapper in lemon and white wine). All the restaurants above offer complementary pick-up.

The **Houseboat**, ✆ 952 5817, is a fondue restaurant, an unlikely concept for the Caribbean, but an original one and actually quite fun. The houseboat itself sits on the lagoon in the Freeport area and you ride across to it on a small hand-drawn ferry floating on oil barrels. There are three courses, all of them fondues: cheese sauce and wine to begin with, into which you dip Jamaican hard-dough bread; then the meats and vegetables—steak, chicken, shrimp and plantain—with Béarnaise, spicy tomato and teriyaki sauces and mango chutney; and finally a chocolate fondue, made of local Jamaican chocolate, into which you dip fresh Caribbean fruits. Take a constitutional on the upper deck and admire the lights of the Bogue Hills.

Marguerite's has a superb setting on the waterfront at the heart of the Gloucester Avenue strip. It is both a smart restaurant on a seafront deck, which serves international fare with a Caribbean twist, and a bar-grill, with a waterslide off the roof to cool you down when the drinking in the sun becomes too much. A lively spot for a daytime or early evening drink.

Now in the centre of town on Gloucester Avenue, the **Native Restaurant**, ✆ 979 2769, specializes in Jamaican food on a breezy veranda. A long menu includes steamed or escoveitched fish and a volley of local vegetables like cho-cho and yam. A brisk and busy venue with some entertainment.

Just down the road you will find an ever popular spot for a trusty Jamaican meal (and some more regular international fare): **The Pelican**. It is set in a modern and aggressively air-conditioned room, with quick service, 'Please Wait to be Seated', but it pulls a lively crowd of Jamaicans and tourists and you can get a curry goat or a brown stew with rice cooked in coconut milk. The Sunday buffet at the **Wexford Hotel** just next door is also very popular. The well-to-do of Montego Bay congregate there for brunch or a Jamaican breakfast of saltfish and ackee with johnny cakes and a leisurely chat about business in town.

cheap

If you want to go a little more local try lunch at **Smokey Joe's** downtown, in a dingy dining room in a little alley off St James's Street. Delicious pumpkin soup is followed by curry goat and rice 'n' peas or a fish platter and a Red Stripe.

There are plenty of stalls around the downtown area for a lunchtime pattie and an ice cream. Finally, the **Pork Pit**, back on Gloucester Avenue, opposite Walter Fletcher beach, is a classic among jerk centres and something of an institution around Montego Bay. It serves excellent jerk—chicken and pork, some 'spear ribs' and sausage—which is hacked to pieces before you, tossed into a basket and thrust through the small window. You eat at picnic tables, mitigating the effect of their electrifying jerk sauce with a festival roll, yam or sweet potato. Also on offer are some Jamaican standards: steam fish and rice 'n' peas. There are endless bars which double as simple eateries along Gloucester Road, offering burgers, salads and sandwiches, usually with music, sometimes a live band. Many of these restaurants stay open all day.

Beyond Montego Bay

Beyond Montego Bay you will find plenty of places to stop and eat. There are many snack stalls and waterfront bars, and if you want something a little less authentic you can always go into one of the hotels. Many of the 'sights' have cafés and nearly all of the innumerable Jamaican bars serve a simple meal.

Beyond Falmouth, over the bridge in Rock, you will find an excellent stopover at **Glistening Waters**, ✆ 954 3229 (*moderate*), where you sit on a breezy wooden deck at the waterfront surrounded by deep-sea fishing boats. It serves a good conch as a starter and then wholesome Jamaican food: chicken or fish with a heap of coleslaw and coconut-flavoured rice. There is a lively crowd of Jamaicans at the weekend, and you can see the phosphorescence in the bay from here. The restaurant has a boat in which you can take a tour of the lagoon (*see* p.112).

There is a charming bar and restaurant for burgers, seafood and fries, **The Time and Place** (*moderate–cheap*), just down from the Trelawny Beach Hotel. Its thatch-covered bamboo shacks have a sandy floor, irresistible hammocks, upturned cable-barrels as tables and a rickety jetty that reaches out to infinity, with the shallow water lapping beneath it. Not far off is **Mama's Place**, which is known for its steam fish. As you go farther east, look out for the crashed plane that has been turned into a bar (*see* p.113).

As you come to Rio Bueno you pass a couple of travel halts where you can get a drink and a snack, even a game of dominoes over a white rum with some Jamaicans. In Rio Bueno itself there is a good restaurant right on the road, the **Lobster Bowl** (*moderate*), where you sit on the waterfront looking out onto the bay. While you wait for your meal you can take a look at the showrooms full of paintings and carvings; the restaurant doubles as a gallery. Lots of fish and lobster to easy reggae and jazz.

Entertainment and Nightlife

There is a string of bars along Gloucester Avenue. **Walter's** is probably the liveliest, a garden bar with television (you can keep up with the NFL at most bars in the area), popular with locals and tourists; you can sit inside or in the open air under parasols. **Hemingway's Pub**, just above it, is another busy watering hole; the air-conditioned lounge-bar has leather benches, stained wood and brass. **Marguerite's** is a much frequented bar right on the waterfront in town (*see* p.120). Nearby, **Tino's Reggae Café** is an easy outdoor haunt on the street, recognizable by the ever-present throb of heavy reggae bass-lines. **Pier One**, near the centre of the downtown area, is a very lively bar, particularly on Fridays, when it will often double as a dance venue.

There was a shortage of public discos at the time of writing (except in the all-inclusives, where you have to pay a heavy evening fee). **Hurricanes**, attached to Breezes hotel on the Gloucester Avenue strip, is very popular. **Sir Winston's**, a dungeon-like dance floor with mirrors, car-numberplates and loud dancehall music, is a much more Jamaican affair. Beyond the town nightlife is sparse, although the town of Sandy Bay, to the east of Montego Bay, is ever alive, with activity all night every night.

If you want to go to a Jamaican concert, look in the papers and on telegraph poles or ask around. There is a large venue at Catherine Hall Performing Centre on the southern outskirts of the town, where they stage Reggae Sumfest (the successor of Reggae Sunsplash, which moved elsewhere). A band sometimes plays during the evenings on Cornwall beach.

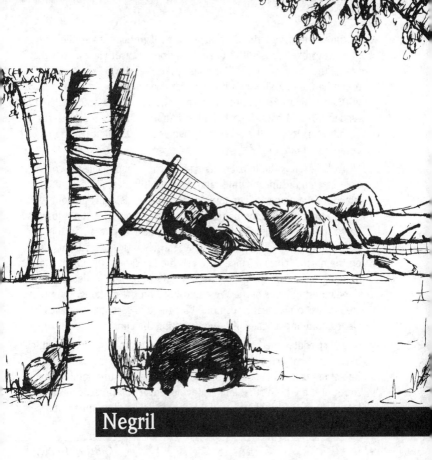

Negril

At the westernmost tip of Jamaica, on a magnificent five-mile stretch of powder-like sand, with the island's finest sunset view across the sea, is the town of Negril. For many years Negril was something of a hippy haunt and, although it has become one of the big players now, with a number of large hotels and a seemingly never-ending string of restaurants and bars, Negril still has a more laid-back feel than the other resort towns. It has recently been dubbed Jamaica's 'capital of casual'; naff but apt.

Negril's beach is the finest of its type on the island: a classic, continuous stretch of superb white sand. It is also the best place on the island for watersports. The town of Negril itself is really just one single stretch of development along the shorefront, divided into two halves by the roundabout, which lies at the town's heart. To the north, hotels, bars and restaurants all muscle in for beachfront space on the narrow coastal fringe between the beach and the Great Morass (a mangrove swamp). And to the south development jostles along the 4 meandering miles of the West End Road on the clifftops. Here there are endless cafés ideally positioned for the two essential pastimes in Negril, jumping off the cliffs and watching the sunset.

Negril straddles the borders of the two westernmost parishes, which between them make up the head and neck of the Jamaican turtle. The small parish of Hanover in the north and Westmorland to the south of it are both rural and undeveloped. If you investigate further inland from the beach you will find sugar flats and mountainous reaches of fertile land.

Getting to Negril

The closest international **airport** to Negril is at Montego Bay. Most resorts will include or arrange bus transfers; if you are travelling independently you will need to get to the main bus terminal in Mo Bay town (near the fire station in the centre of town) and take a bus from there. Buses run until late afternoon.

There are just a few direct **bus** services between Negril and Montego Bay (about 1½hrs). You usually have to change in Lucea or Savanna-la-Mar. The terminus in Negril is at the bus and taxi park over the bridge just north of the roundabout. Buses to Savanna-la-Mar leave from the cash-and-carry supermarket square on the road inland from the roundabout. The journey to Kingston takes about 5 hours and is best made via Savanna-la-Mar (*no direct services*).

Alternatively you may prefer to fly down to Negril. There is a small airstrip, at the top end of the town, served twice daily by hopper schedules from Mo Bay and Kingston: Air Jamaica Express, Negril ✆ 957 4051. Small charter planes are also available through Tim Air, ✆ 957 3374, in Negril, and Airways International, ✆ 957 4051. These charter companies fly each day; try to book ahead.

Getting Around the Area

Share taxis run up and down the beach road (officially called Norman Manley Boulevard) and in the other directions (for example, down West End Road, along the cliffs, and the Sav Road). They will stop anywhere along the route and they run constantly until mid-evening, and then become less frequent. There are limitless **private taxis** around Negril. These can be found at the bus stations or booked through hotel front desks, but if you're out and about they'll accost you all day long anyway (even if you're on a bicycle, in which case they offer to put it in the boot for you). If you need to phone for a taxi, you can contact Easy Going Cabs, ✆ 957 3227, or Gold Spoon Taxis, ✆ 957 4692. Some restaurants offer free transport from your hotel.

You will find **car hire** companies all along the beach road in Negril. Some recommended by the Tourist Board include: Rite Rate Car Rentals, ✆ 957 4267, on the beach road; Vernon's Car Rentals, ✆ 957 4698, in Fisherman's and near the roundabout; Elite Car Rentals, ✆ 957 4657, half-way down the beach road; Tanka's Car Rental, ✆ 957 4488, right on the roundabout and Action Tours, ✆ 957 3255, at the top of the beach road. Jeeps are available from some of these operators and also from Jus Jeep, ✆ 957 4835, on the cliffs.

Similarly, there are endless scooter- and bike-hire places. Contact Dependable Bike Rental, ✆ 957 4764 on the beach road, Tyke's Bike Rental, ✆ 957 4863 and CJ's Bike Rental, ✆ 957 4207. For a **scooter** you can contact Salmon's on the beach road, ✆ 957 4671 or Elvis Bikes and Scooters, ✆ 957 4732. If you want a **tractor bike**, contact Tanka or White Lion, ✆ 957 0227, midway down the beach road. Most car and bike hire companies offer a free pick-up service.

The land is good for cycling because it is so flat. **Bicycles** are available in quite a few of the hotels, but they are also for hire at Ragga Bikes (no telephone), about half a mile up from the roundabout.

Tours

You can visit Negril on a day trip from the other resort areas; trippers are drawn to the magnificent beach and other famous institutions such as sunset at **Rick's Café**. Contact a local tour operator or book through your hotel. If you are staying in Negril, you can book excursions to **Dunn's River Falls** at Ocho Rios, the **great houses** around Montego Bay and to the south coast area around **Black River**, or visit **YS Falls**, which is a little touristy but wonderful. Arrange these through hotel front desks or local tour operators such as JUTA, ✆ 957 9197 and also Caribic Vacations, ✆ 957 3309, who offer trips to Cuba.

The main **Jamaica Tourist Board** can be found in Jackson (formerly Adrija) Plaza, the shopping mall just south of the roundabout, ✆ 957 4243, ✉ 957 4489. However, there are three information **booths** (pink and white gazebos) in the town: one near the craft market (just north of the roundabout); one at the top of the main beach and a third quite a way down on the cliffs, near the Mariner's Inn.

In case of a **medical emergency** there is an emergency room at the Seven Mile Medical Clinic, ✆ 957 4888, about a mile up the beach road from the roundabout, but for more serious problems you will have to go to the main hospitals in Savanna-la-Mar or Montego Bay. For non-urgent problems, many of the hotels have nurse's stations; otherwise try the Seven Mile clinic.

The banks are in the middle of town, around the town square, as are most of the plazas, where there is some duty-free **shopping**. There are a couple of craft markets (just above the roundabout and at the top end of the beach) and there are galleries and craft shops dotted around the town.

The Beach

Negril Beach, or Seven Mile Beach, is a magnificent 5-mile-long stretch of palm-backed sand, 30 yards wide in places, which shelves gently into a reef-protected reach of bright turquoise water. It is a sun-trap, ideal for sunbathing but also for watersports and, as a continuous stretch, it can be walked along its entire length.

The beach has become steadily built up over the years, particularly around the southern end, and you will come across bars, watersports outfits, some of them attached to the hotels, and volleyball courts, where you can join an active crowd. If you want a patch of sand to yourself, with only walkers to disturb you, it is still just about possible to find one—try near the northern end.

You can expect to be hustled on Negril beach. You will be offered a whole inventory of drugs and services; it is all done with a certain amount of good humour and eccentric Jamaican style—there are masseuses who will start rubbing your legs from behind and I actually saw one hustler arrive by canoe, dressed in a suit with briefcase in hand, from which he proceeded to show his wares. The usual advice applies if you want to be left alone: a polite but persistent no.

Beach Bars

Negril has a string of excellent beach bars, where you can spend the day, taking a dip when the urge strikes and then retreating to the bar for a drink or a bite to eat. All of these bars operate during the evening as well.

Cosmo's is near the top end of the beach, set on its own strip of sand away from other development. You eat in an open-sided, thatched hut with a fantastic view of the sea, among a good mix of tourists and Jamaicans. It is known for its conch platters, served with bammy, but also does a range of grilled fish and other simpler dishes.

Headed south towards town, **Runaways**, ✆ 957 9180, doesn't have quite the same style—it is larger and a little brisker—but there is an excellent strip of sand on which to spend the day, dotted with beach chairs and palm-thatch umbrellas, with watersports and changing rooms nearby. Some Italian fare is served, also grilled fish and burgers.

Risky Business is a sports bar and grill nearer the main action at the bottom end of the beach; alternatively try **Chance's**, where you will find plenty to drink and a bobsleigh from the film *Cool Runnings* to admire.

Alfred's Ocean Palace, at the bottom end of the beach among all the hotels and guest houses, is ever popular, with a huge drinking and volley-ball-playing daytime crowd. Drinks, meals and lots of watersports.

Watersports

Negril is the best place in Jamaica for watersports: you can take a trip on a glass-bottomed boat, or try out a pedalo, a bouncy banana, a kayak or a jet-ski, a small sailing dingy, a parasailer or a windsurfer. Some of the island's best diving is around Negril and there are a number of snorkelling, picnic and sunset yacht cruises and deep-sea fishing.

Near the roundabout you will find **Blue Whale**, ✆ 957 4438, just close to the JTB information booth and the craft market and not far off there is **Aqua Nova Watersports** at the Negril Beach Club Hotel, ✆ 957 4323. Further up the beach try **Ogli's** at Foote Prints and at the top end of the beach near the Poinciana Hotel is **Ray's Watersports**, ✆ 957 4349.

Many of these outlets will offer **scuba diving**. Or you can try the **Negril Scuba Centre**, ✆ 957 4425, at the Negril Beach Club, **Sundivers**, ✆ 957 4069 or

Dolphin Divers, ✆ 957 4944, who will take you out to the reef. Most of the scuba companies and even the watersports shops offer free pick-up from your hotel. For those who are content with **snorkelling**, this is best off the cliffs and up in Bloody Bay. You can also take a boat out to Booby Cay, off Rutland Point.

For a boat-borne picnic (usually with sunbathing and snorkelling thrown in), there are a number of yachts based at the different hotels. Contact *Wild Ting* at Mahogany Inn, ✆ 957 4401 or the *Catamaran Cruise*, ✆ 957 9228.

Land Sports

As for sports on land, it is easy enough to arrange to play **tennis** (check with the hotel front desks; even some of the all-inclusives will be happy to let you in) and there is a **golf course**, the **Negril Hills** 18-hole course, ✆ 957 4638, not far from the town on the road to Sav-la-Mar. If you wish to go **horse-riding**, then contact **Rhodes Hall Plantation**, ✆ 957 4258 during the daytime, where you will ride through a coconut plantation and then take a canter along the beach, or try **Country and Western**, ✆ 957 3250, in Red Ground, who take trips into the hills behind Negril.

Around the Town

The town of Negril cannot claim much beauty or style. Thirty years ago it was a tiny fishing village: now it is really just a stretch of modern, fairly ugly, concrete buildings dotted along 10 or 12 miles of beach and cliffs; hotels, bars and restaurants shoulder to shoulder the whole way. Certainly there are enough watering holes and eateries to keep you busy during an average holiday. One couple decided to set off from the Lighthouse and to have a drink in every bar along the cliffs. It took them four evenings of hard work just to get as far as the roundabout.

There is not much recorded history of Negril—there is not even a consensus about how it got its name. Before the last 20 years of hotel construction, most of the activity here was illegal: initially there were pirates, who would lie in wait for ships en route from the Spanish Main to Havana. Calico Jack Rackham and his disguised women companions Anne Bonney and Mary Read were captured here in 1720, while on a rum blow-out. And later Negril was a transit point for smugglers.

The town remained a sleepy fishing village (only occasionally used as an assembly point for British naval sorties) until a road was built in 1959 and hippies began to wash up here. They rented floor space in the local houses and enjoyed the magic mushroom omelettes, the weed, the palm-backed beach and the sunsets. The smuggling continued, and Negril became a transhipment point for ganja.

The hippies may have gone (some no doubt return to their old haunt as company executives) and the town has gone above board—the big players of Jamaican tourism have built on the best beachfront space and Negril has been gentrified to the point of having a golf course. Even so, hanging out is still the main pastime here, and there is still a laid-back and easy-going air.

The town itself is in two halves—referred to as 'the beach' and 'the cliffs'—either side of the central roundabout. North along Norman Manley Boulevard the 5 miles of spectacular beach is steadily filling up with hotels (they are mostly resort-style hotels, some of them belonging to the big Jamaican chains); and south of the roundabout the 4 miles or so of ironshore cliffs offer some charming places to stay, set in fantastic gardens.

There are not really many sights in Negril, though you can always watch the evening antics at **Rick's Café**; the tradition is to jump 40 feet into the sea below at sunset. The Negril **Lighthouse** 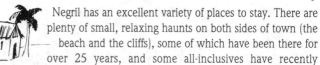 stands 100 feet tall and overlooks the most westerly point of the island (at the bottom of the West End Road). Oddly enough it doesn't have much of a view inland (just the undeveloped scrubland that is the backdrop to Negril) and so it is interesting mainly for the highly polished brass fittings of the old lighthouse lamp (1894–1956 kerosene; 1956–85 acetylene gas; solar since then), the logbooks and the huge glass lens. A sign informs you 'Permission to enter the premises must have the prior written approval of the Harbour Master'—but don't worry about it too much, you can usually get a look around, if you're prepared to climb the 103 steps.

You can take a boat trip into the **Great Morass**, a vast swamp behind Norman Manley Boulevard, where there are herons and other waders among the mangroves. **Bloody Bay**, the next bay north of the main beach, off the road to Montego Bay, is supposed to take its name from the whales that were beached and sectioned here, or alternatively from pirate battles of centuries past.

© (809–)   *Where to Stay*

Negril has an excellent variety of places to stay. There are plenty of small, relaxing haunts on both sides of town (the beach and the cliffs), some of which have been there for over 25 years, and some all-inclusives have recently appeared. Quite a few of the smaller hotels in Negril do not have restaurants—there are so many places to eat in the area that it is not necessary, though often you can get someone to deliver breakfast to your hotel room. Negril is popular with independent travellers, but it is still difficult to find beachside accommodation at less than US$40 a night (for a double in season). It is worth bargaining for a reduction, particularly if you are staying more than one or two nights. If you ask around you might be able to get the spare bedroom in a local house for less.

luxury

The best of the traditional 'resort' hotels in Negril is **Swept Away**, PO Box 77, ✆ 957 4040, ✆ 957 4060, UK reservations ✆ 0181 367 5175, US and Canada ✆ 1 800 545 7937, where there are 134 rooms in villas that stand in profuse tropical gardens of palms (coconut palms, Japanese fan palms, sago and date palms, travellers' trees) right on the beach. Each room has a large veranda and is furnished and louvred with stained wood, with cool terracotta tiles on the floor; there are fans and air-conditioning, but no TVs. You can enjoy the full range of body-beautiful activities, from aerobics in the sports complex to beauty treatments in the salon with a spa. There are watersports on the beach and evening entertainment. Heterosexual couples only. **Grand Lido**, PO Box 88, ✆ 957 4010, ✆ 957 4317, UK reservations ✆ 01749 677200, US ✆ 1 800 859 *SUPER*, has taken the all-inclusive concept upmarket, packaging sheer luxury, with 24-hour room service and champagne at the flick of a finger. It still has the brisk air and the constant activity and entertainment of the all-inclusive and it is quite a large resort, with 200 rooms set on excellent beaches; as always with Superclubs, there is a nudist area (well tucked away). The grounds are lovely and the rooms very comfortable: all have TVs, fan-ventilation and air-conditioning; many have an excellent view of the magnificent sweep of Bloody Bay. There is plenty to keep you busy: a beauty parlour, watersports and jacuzzis, nine bars, a games room, a library and afternoon tea. Jackets are required in one of the à la carte restaurants (but they can lend you one if you forgot yours).

very expensive

The most original of the all-inclusive hotels at the top end of the beach is **Hedonism II**, PO Box 25, ✆ 957 4201, ✆ 957 4289, UK reservations ✆ 01749 677200, US ✆ 1 800 859 *SUPER*. It calls itself the naughtiest club in town and has been offering an adult playground now for over 15 years, with the slogan 'Be Wicked for a Week!' The resort allows couples and groups, but encourages singles in an endless catalogue of hedonistic activities: bar open 19 hours a day, nudes and prudes beaches, watersports, diving, trapeze and juggling instruction, wet T-shirt competitions, body-painting lessons (yours or somebody else's), singalong piano bar, drink and dance till you drop (or find a partner), mirrors on the bedroom ceiling, breakfast served until late—and then it all begins again. There is an à la carte restaurant for the evening. You may be put in a room with a stranger if you arrive as a single. It's pricey but a riot for a weekend or a couple of days during a trip around the island.

Poinciana Beach Resort, PO Box 44, ✆ 957 4256, ✆ 957 4229, US reservations ✆ 1 800 468 6728, has been set up with families in mind as well as the usual Caribbean couples. The 130 rooms are in blocks closely ranged on the seafront around the central pool and dining area. Daytime activities include watersports and visits to the exercise room; there's a children's programme and evening entertainment.

expensive

The best of the more traditional (non all-inclusive, non-resort) hotels on the beach side of town is the unusual **Negril Cabins** Resort, PO Box 118, ✆ 957 4350, ✆ 957 4381, 50 African-looking cabins on stilts set in superb lawns and tropical gardens. There is a meandering pool with a swim-up bar and an easygoing atmosphere about the central areas. The rooms, some louvred and fan-ventilated, others with air-conditioning and TV, each have a balcony and make very comfortable retreats. There's tennis and a fitness centre, and the beach is just 5 minutes' walk away.

Seasplash Resort, PO Box 123, ✆ 957 4041, ✆ 957 4049, is a small and friendly self-catering resort at the top end of the beach. The 16 suites are situated in modern blocks in a narrow garden, well decorated and spacious, with all the modern comforts: full kitchens, TVs and balconies. There's a restaurant and beach bar, with watersports right outside.

But the most stylish of the small hotels in Negril are really the ones on the cliffs, where you will find palm-thatched wooden cabins with louvres and ceiling fans, set in charming and abundant jungle-like gardens, with magnificent views over the cliffs to the sea. **Tensing Pen Village**, PO Box 13, ✆ 957 4417, ✆ 957 0161, US reservations ✆ 216 546 9000, has 12 very quiet and secluded rooms, in stone and wooden cottages or cabins, on paths that meander through wonderful greenery of sea grape and bougainvillea, right on the cliff edge. Rooms are fan-ventilated with ice-chests, four-posters and louvred French windows giving onto a balcony; no TVs. Tensing Pen was opened in 1975, and takes its name from Sherpa Tensing, the first man to climb Everest. The charming central house, under a huge fig tree, has a library, sitting area and a small kitchen.

Catcha Falling Star, PO Box 22, ✆ 957 0390, is a similar hideaway on the cliffs, a few one- and two-bedroom cottages linked by stone-lined, sandy paths in a garden of crotons and sea grape and flamboyant trees. There are hammocks on the cool verandas and a jacuzzi in the garden; rooms are louvred and screened. It's comfortable and peaceful, set around a central house and small gym. Breakfast (no other meals) is served right on the spectacular cliffs.

The oddly named **Nirvana on the Beach**, ✆ 957 4314, ✉ 957 9196, US reservations ✆ 716 789 5955, ✉ 789 4753, takes the small-is-beautiful concept to the beach. It is a peaceful and private enclave on its own strip of sand. There are suites and wooden cottages scattered around a pretty sifted-sand garden; rooms are very comfortable, fan-ventilated, with full kitchens, some with four-posters. **Whistling Bird**, ✆ 957 4403, US reservations ✆ 303 442 0722, is also a collection of cottages dotted around an 'intensive' garden on the beach. Rooms have pretty décor and louvred windows.

Banana Shout, PO Box 4, ✆ 957 4007, back on the cliffs, also has real charm—rooms overlook the sea or the tropical profusion of a garden, where hummingbirds flit around the lily ponds. There are 10 rooms in villas and cottages, with dark wooden furniture, screens and louvres, and decorated with Haitian art. All rooms are fan ventilated and have kitchens (there is no restaurant, though breakfast can be ordered). Simply walk down the steps cut in the cliffs for a swim.

The 12 villas and two studios of the **Rock House**, PO Box 24, ✆/✉ 957 4373, in a garden setting on the cliffs, have a wonderfully relaxed atmosphere. Accommodation is very comfortable with four-posters and muslin netting, outdoor showers with hot and cold water, and a slightly surreal pool-bar down on the cliffs.

inexpensive

Not far from the centre of town, at the beginning of the cliffs, **Heart Beat**, PO Box 95, ✆ 957 4329, ✉ 957 0069, has some thatch-roofed cabins and 'tree houses' on stilts in slightly ragged gardens of palm and sea almond.

Chippewa Village, ✆/✉ 957 4676, has just a few wooden cabins with fans, louvres, hot and cold water and a mini-component stereo; some rooms have views of the morass. Continental breakfast is included.

You can also try **Errol's On the Beach**, ✆ 957 3312, where there are eight simple rooms in small clapboard houses, with fans or air-conditioning; there's a restaurant and bar.

cheap

Just south of Negril Lighthouse there are cabins, cottages and tent sites at **Lighthouse Park**, ✆ 957 4490; the tent sites are very cheap.

Addis Kokeb, PO Box 78, Somerset Avenue, ✆ 957 4485, is a guest house on the cliffs, in its own stony garden with trees and cactus and aloe plants. There are a couple of simple cottages, and communal rooms that serve as a gathering point in the wooden main house, with kitchen and library. Some rooms share baths.

There are a number of places where you can stay cheaply on the beach. The very simple double rooms at **Roots Bamboo**, ✆ 957 4479, have private baths and porches, giving onto the lush beachside garden. There's not much atmosphere, but it has a restaurant and bar, and some very cheap tent sites. And you can find comfortable rooms at a small spot with the unlikely name of **Perseverance Resort**, ✆ 957 4333. They're basic but clean, with some private baths and some fans. Other similar accommodation is available through **Ms Gloria**, ✆ 957 4741, who has just a few plain rooms on the beach, and **B.T.'s Resort**, ✆ 947 4744, across the road from the beach, which offers basic rooms in cabins.

Eating Out

Negril has literally hundreds of restaurants and snack bars along its roadsides. There is no really smart and formal restaurant (except the à la carte restaurants in the all-inclusives—but to go there just for a meal, you would have to buy an evening pass, for two), but there are many beach bars which serve drinks and snacks by day and then turn into lively bars and restaurants by night. A few of the restaurants offer a pick-up service.

moderate

Kuyaba, ✆ 957 4318, is on a meandering wooden deck right on the sand of Negril beach, under a pointed thatch roof. The name means 'heaven' in the Arawak Indian language and, with its candle light and serene seaside ambience, it's about as close as Negril's got. It serves simple fare by day and then in the evening more adventurous cuisine—snapper stuffed with orange and shrimp in a coconut sauce. Take advantage of the free pick-up service.

The restaurant **Red Snapper**, ✆ 957 0100, has several different dining areas, 20 feet above the sea on the cliffs. Start with a cocktail served in a pineapple, while being serenaded by a mento band or a drummer. The kitchen is on view as they grill—a long menu including seafood (some home-smoked) and vegetarian dishes. Crab legs in garlic are followed by conch, or snapper curried in a coconut sauce.

The **Hungry Lion**, ✆ 957 4482, set in a forested tropical courtyard across the road from the cliffs, is a charming and original restaurant, with bright yellow walls and sprays of bougainvillea, benches and tables under a tin roof, and a fountain. Exotic natural foods and juices are a speciality—eggplant parmesan followed by lobster in lemon butter or kingfish in coconut milk—served by hip waiters. It is quite small and popular, so it fills up quickly; get there early. *Dinner only.*

At the far end of town, beyond the lighthouse you will come across the **Lighthouse Inn**, ✆ 957 4052, which sits on a deck beneath trees garlanded with fairy lights. Enjoy the conch or any number of fish steaks, pepper shrimp and other Caribbean combinations including ginger chicken; free pick-up service.

Another restaurant with great Caribbean style, in a wooden building among the trunks of royal palms, is **Paradise Yard Café**, about half a mile inland from the roundabout, on the road to Savanna-la-Mar. You sit at benches and tables on open terraces, in a proper yard of beaten earth, eating foreign and authentic Jamaican food—enchiladas, jambalaya, callaloo alfredo and fricassee, or the speciality, rasta pasta: red (tomatoes), gold (ackee) and green (green peppers).

Happy Bananas is set in a rustic yellow house behind a yellow picket fence not far south of the roundabout. Banana cocktails are served with angels on horseback (banana in bacon), followed by soups and shrimp or snapper, or a vegetarian dish; and to follow—*banane flambée.*

cheap

Two restaurants that are praised for their specialities are **Cosmo's** (most of the way up the beach; *see* p.128) where you are supposed to get the best conch in the town, and **Erica's** (quite a long way down on the cliffs), where you are assured the finest lobster in town (served, among other ways, in butter, lime and garlic).

And for an excellent local meal, you should try the **Three Sisters** restaurant, in an old wooden house that looks a bit like a church about half a mile inland on the Sav road. Real Jamaican dishes (oxtail, brown stew chicken, tripe beans and peppered steak) are presented at tables with bright tablecloths and plastic roses, and served with a tonnage of ground provisions; also juices. *Closed in the evening.* A simpler stopover in the same vein is **Sweet Spice I**, slightly further into town.

Back on the cliffs, **Peewee's** provides unsophisticated, reliable food, rice 'n' peas or a burger with chips. And there are a couple of places which specialize in chicken: at **Chicken Lavish** (they also serve steam fish and curried or sweet and sour chicken), close to the centre of town, you can dine on the covered terrace enclosed by a white picket fence, or order a takeaway; and at the bottom of the West End Road you will find the inimitable **Roy and Felix (Serious Chicken)**, which is set in a colourful bamboo-and-thatch construction at the corner of Summerset Road. Finally, if you want to try out the original Jamaican schoolkids' lunch, then you should go to **Hammonds** for a pattie and a cocobread.

Entertainment and Nightlife

Besides the beach bars (*see* p.128) there plenty of spots on the cliffs, where you can spend the day chilling out until the great highlight of the day, watching the sunset. Traditionally **Rick's** is the popular venue for this pursuit—worth trying once though it does involve buying drinks with tokens and it can get pretty packed, because tourists are bussed in for the event, and you might feel compelled to jump 40 feet into the water below. If you want something a little less crowded, try the **LTU Pub** a couple of hundred yards further on; still lively at times, but with fewer lobster-red tourists and more locals. Another popular daytime hangout is the **Pickled Parrot**, perched on the cliff, a shingle-roofed gazebo and platforms on the cliff-edge with the waves crashing beneath; it offers drinks and simple meals all day long, satellite TV, swings and a waterslide.

The sunset's just as good from the beach. Try **Alfred's Ocean Palace**, which can get particularly lively and **De Buss**, last resting place of a pink and green double decker that washed up here, perhaps in the sixties, and is now decrepit to the point of collapse; there is a bar with occasional live music and a jerk centre.

A number of the hotels have programmes of evening entertainment, including shows, and many of them have discotheques. The all-inclusives are quite well geared up for nightlife; they will sell non-residents an evening pass, which will include drinks, and sometimes food. Check **Hedonism II** for a rumbustious evening of fun.

Negril is known for its music—ask around, or consult the papers or the posters nailed to the telegraph poles, to find out who's playing. The main reggae parks are **Central Park** and **MX3**. For dancing try **Compulsion**, at Plaza de Negril next to the roundabout, or **Close Encounter**, right on the King's Plaza.

East to Savanna-la-Mar

Off the road inland (from the roundabout) there are the ruins of an old plantation house at White Hall. The house itself burned down a while ago, but the view is magnificent. About 10 miles farther on you come to Little London, which used to be known for its population of East Indians, and occasionally you will see obviously Indian faces.

The town of Sav-la-Mar, as it is known, is the capital town of the parish of Westmorland. It is a busy if slightly run-down and lacklustre place. It has always been a port (sugar from Frome used to be exported from here), but its position on the coast has not always been a blessing as it is quite regularly scourged by storms— in 1912, a schooner ended up in Great George Street in the middle of the town.

East to Lucea

Headed north out of Negril, beyond Bloody Bay, the main road passes into country-side and then follows the vagaries of the windswept coastline to Green Island and eventually Lucea, which sits at the head of a huge bay guarded by an old fortress.

Lucea is the capital of Hanover Parish. Among the old colonial buildings left in the town the most noticeable and impressive is the court house, at the heart of the town overlooking the market and bus terminus. It is typically Jamaican Georgian in design, with stone arches on the ground floor, a wooden upper floor and a classical pediment; the clock tower is odd though. The clock itself was sent here by mistake (it should have gone to St Lucia) and so a special tower had to be built for it. The curiosity is the rounded cupola, designed in the shape of a German military helmet by a German plantation owner.

The small **Hanover Museum**, *open Mon–Fri, adm*, is housed in the former work-house and old police station (you can still see evidence of the slave cells), after you pass the parish church on the edge of town, off the road to Negril. It takes a histor-ical view of the area, with some artefacts from as far back as Arawak times: there is a garden with a small *caneye* (an Arawak hut), a *zemi*, a *boucan* (for smoking meat) and a cotton-tree canoe—and inside you will find Jamaican coins (quatties, gills, bobs and bits) and the Hanover weights and measures (each parish had its own), reports of Henry Morgan and Captain Bligh, an orange rinder and other curious domestic utensils such as a floor brush made of a coconut and a kitchen bitch coconut oil lamp.

Built in 1761, **Fort Charlotte** is on the western point of the harbour mouth, with walls 6 feet thick. It is officially closed now and looks a bit sad: there are just a couple of cannon on salt-decayed rollers. From Lucea the main road continues along the coast towards Montego Bay.

South of Lucea, almost lost in the fertile hinterland of Dolphin Head, you will find **Mayfield Falls** (*adm includes lunch*), a series of falls, with 22 bathing pools offering a 'natural jacuzzi' in a charming river-bed which runs through farming country in a magnificent valley surrounded by serrated peaks. You walk up through the bottle-green water beneath luxuriant hanging greenery and amid the sprouts of bamboo, to the highest of the falls, which tumbles about 50 feet. It's famously difficult to find; drive south along Lucea East River and keep asking the way, or take the road leading south from Hopewell and follow the sign.

Mandeville Court House

The Southwest and Mandeville

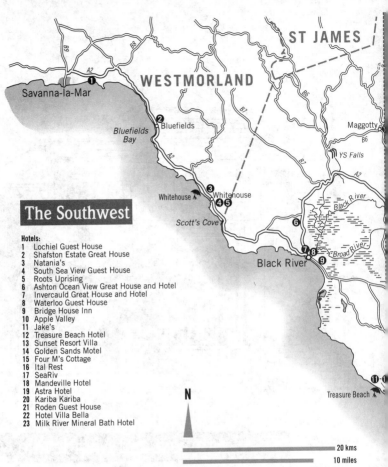

The Southwest

Hotels:
1. Lochiel Guest House
2. Shafston Estate Great House
3. Natania's
4. South Sea View Guest House
5. Roots Uprising
6. Ashton Ocean View Great House and Hotel
7. Invercauld Great House and Hotel
8. Waterloo Guest House
9. Bridge House Inn
10. Apple Valley
11. Jake's
12. Treasure Beach Hotel
13. Sunset Resort Villa
14. Golden Sands Motel
15. Four M's Cottage
16. Ital Rest
17. SeaRiv
18. Mandeville Hotel
19. Astra Hotel
20. Kariba Kariba
21. Roden Guest House
22. Hotel Villa Bella
23. Milk River Mineral Bath Hotel

20 kms
10 miles

The southwest has a natural calm and quiet that speaks of life in Jamaica a generation ago. The Jamaicans themselves like to take a break down here. The plains, ridges and rugged uplands of the southwest show the full drama of Caribbean countryside—in just a few miles the land changes from the broad yellow expanse of the coastal savanna where there is desert-like scrub, and sweeps up to some of Jamaica's most fruitful lands, the fertile cultivated mountains of St Elizabeth Parish. The roadsides here are curtained with sugar-cane standing up to 15 feet high and, in the the hills, tall, shaggy-leafed vines of yams climb their frames next to neat lines of potatoes. The southwest takes in the parishes of St Elizabeth and

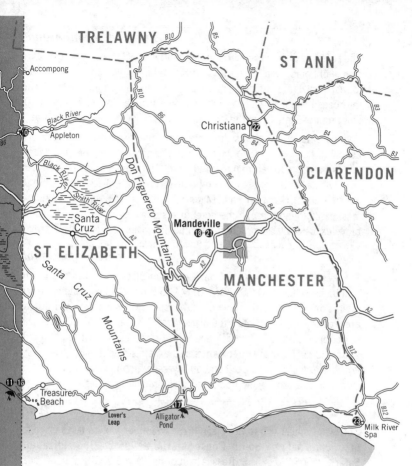

Manchester, and parts of Westmorland. Mandeville, capital of Manchester Parish and one of Jamaica's largest towns, lies 2000 feet up in the mountains. An industrial centre that grew up around the bauxite industry, it has more recently been settled by Jamaicans who, having spent their working lives abroad, have returned to build themselves a home they can retire to. And down on the coast is Black River, the capital of St Elizabeth, with a scattering of small Jamaican settlements either side. Treasure Beach to the southeast is the only 'resort' town in the area; in fact it is a fishing village, encrusted with a few villas and some small hotels and guest houses. It is slow and easy, one of the best bits of Jamaica.

Getting There and Around

The best way to get to and around the southwest of Jamaica is by **car**. It's a couple of hours' drive from Montego Bay to Black River and a touch more to Mandeville (the distances are not that long, but the country is rough and the roads tortuous). The car-hire company **Praise Tours**, ✆ 966 9020, works out of Santa Cruz; the larger firms will deliver a car from Mo Bay.

If you are travelling by **bus** there are some direct services from Montego Bay, Negril and Kingston to the area, but you may have to hop on the local minibus services to get from town to town. The main terminals in the area are Savanna-la-Mar (at the top end of the main street), Black River (close to the fire station), Santa Cruz and Mandeville (on the main square). **Taxis** are most easily found through the hotel foyers or at the bus terminals. Some **bicycles** are available for hire through the Invercauld Hotel in Black River.

Tourist Information

There is a **Jamaica Tourist Board** office in Black River upstairs in the Hendricks Building, ✆ 965 2074/5, 📠 965 2076, the first building to the town side of the metal bridge over the Black River itself. In a **medical emergency** you can contact the Black River Hospital, ✆ 965 2212, on the shorefront or, if you just need to see a doctor, you can call Dr John Brown, ✆ 965 2305. There are three **banks** in the main street of Black River; elsewhere you will depend on the hotel foyers, which may not have a lot of cash. You can also try unofficial exchange through the shops.

Tours

The ever popular trip to the Black River swamp or morass takes up to an hour and a half; try **South Coast Safaris**, ✆ 965 2513, **St Elizabeth Safari**, ✆ 965 2374, or **St Bess Attractions**, ✆ 965 2229, all based near the metal bridge in town. You can take a day trip from the north coast resorts to the Black River swamp and the YS Falls with St Bess Attractions.

Beaches

The beaches along the south coast are mostly made of fine, dark sand; they are quite narrow, but have some lovely spots for swimming and sunbathing. Few of the public beaches along this area of the south coast offer much in the way of watersports, and so you will be dependent on the hotels for the limited snorkelling gear and occasional boat trip. None of the beaches in this area charges an entry fee.

The slender strip of dull sand around **Black River** improves a little towards **Treasure Beach** to the south, where there are three main bays. **Frenchman's Bay** is the nicest, a curved stretch of west-facing brown sand, good for walking; **Calabash Bay** is more of a fishing beach, as is **Great Bay** beach.

To the west of Black River the sand begins to turn lighter in colour. You come to a small but pleasant beach at **Font Hill**, within a wildlife sanctuary and crocodile reserve. There were no changing facilities at the time of writing, but some are planned; apparently the crocodiles won't bother you.

There is also a very natural beach at **Bluefields Bay**, a strip of light sand at the roadside with trees growing all along it. There are a few snack huts here, which are to be moved into a car park set back from the beach.

There are also good spots for **inland bathing** in this area of Jamaica, particularly as you go north into the hills. YS Falls are a justly popular tourist attraction. Or you can try Apple Valley, which is not far off, or Mayfield farther west, where you can climb the bed of a river over a number of waterfalls.

Sports

For the conventional land-based sports, ask at the hotels. A number of them have **tennis** courts and there are **golf** courses in Mandeville and near Negril. There are **horse-riding** stables at **Ashton Great House**, ✆ 965 2036, at Luana just north of Black River (ride through the plantation flatlands or on the beach) and at **Mayfield**, ✆ 965 6209, near Treasure Beach on the road to Lovers' Leap.

Black River

Black River is a faded and rundown Jamaican town, whose past prosperity is evident in the elaborate gingerbread houses now decaying on the waterfront. The town made its wealth (and got its name) exporting dyes, mainly those made from logwood, used for the blue in jeans in the last century. The cut logs would be floated downriver and would bleed their colour, turning the river black. Black River saw its heyday at the end of the last century and was the first town on the island to have electric lighting. By the 1930s, when part of the downtown section was burned, the export trade had declined so badly that there was no money to rebuild. Black River is the capital of the Parish of St Elizabeth. There is no formal centre to the town—it is scattered along the waterfront and on the main road inland—but it does boast some attractive buildings: the yellow-brick Anglican church with a square tower stands at the main crossroads in town; the parish court house, an imposing building with square pillars and triangular pediment is on the seafront. The **Black River** itself flows into the sea right in the town, draining one of Jamaica's three swamps, the Great Morass (the other two are in Negril and at the eastern tip of the island). Cruise upriver and see tendrils hanging like curtains from the extended families of mangrove trees, and great blue herons and jacanas or purple gallinules creeping and strutting around on the pancake lilies (which submerge at night). You have a good chance of seeing a crocodile flop into the water and saunter lazily away. You won't be eaten by one; they are too tame—so tame that they will actually pose for photographs (at least they can be moved around for an optimum shot). The most amenable ones are called Charlie, Freddie, Lester and Big George. Unfortunately there are no manatees left in the Black River area (they can only be seen at Alligator Hole River and at Milk River, a few miles further east).

West from Black River

The drive west from Black River is very attractive; the road snakes intermittently along the coastline and inland, always in the shadow of the huge forested mountains to the north. At Scott's Cove, where there is a travellers' rest stop known for its fried fish and bammy, you cross from St Elizabeth into the Parish of Westmorland.

The road passes through two drowsy little Jamaican towns: White house and then Bluefields, from where Henry Morgan set off to sack Panama in 1670. Bluefields was one of Jamaica's Spanish settlements (then called Oristan), but was so often attacked by pirates and buccaneers that it was abandoned. It was used as a harbour by the navy in the 18th century. Eventually the road comes to **Savanna-la-Mar**.

East of Black River

About 15 miles along the coast to the east of Black River, the town of **Treasure Beach** is a Jamaican gem, a lovely, tranquil retreat ranged along the undeveloped shoreline. It has enough hotels and guest houses to be called a 'resort' town, but only just, and it is completely untouched by the hustle and hurry of north-coast tourism. The Jamaicans themselves go on holiday there. There are a number of good bars and restaurants where you can chill out in between bouts of sunbathing on the beach and then return for more fun in the evening. The lowlands of St Elizabeth are particularly known for their 'brownings', people of light brown skin who are supposedly descended from shipwrecked pirates.

This area, used as grazing land for cattle, is often quite parched and yellow in the dry season. A few miles beyond the town you will find a fantastic view from **Lovers' Leap**, where the cliffs drop a sheer 1600 feet into the sea from the Santa Cruz mountains. The story goes that two slave lovers were chased here by an ardent planter who had eyes for the girl, and they jumped to their death rather than be split up. There is not much here, just a snack bar, a sitting area and a view.

The main road leads out of Black River to the north, skirting the Black River Morass and leading to **Bamboo Avenue**, one of Jamaica's best known sights, a 3-mile tunnel of bamboo which constantly creaks in the breeze. It is a little touristy—you will see minibuses letting out their passengers to gawp for five minutes—but impressive nonetheless. In this area, particularly around the town of Middle Quarter, you will find vendors at the roadside selling plastic bags of 'swims' (shrimps cooked in pepper sauce). Well worth buying; negotiate.

A few miles off the main road to the north you will find one of Jamaica's most beautiful sights. At **YS Falls**, *adm expensive*, the river tumbles over seven falls and into rockpools where you can swim. You ride to them in a tractor-drawn jitney, which is a bit embarrassing, but you can concentrate on the spectacular scenery: where sugar cane and logwood once grew, there are now open fields, used as grazing for Jamaican red poll cattle. There are bars at the reception area on the main road and at the falls themselves. Beyond the falls, visit the **Appleton Estate** sugar factory and distillery, *adm includes rum tasting*. It is set among swathes of cane; during working hours there is a tour of the distillery, which produces 10 million litres of rum each year in the column stills and the oak barrels of the cool storage house. You might be lucky and get a tour of the sugar factory itself.

Just north of here is the Maroon village of **Accompong**, which has a yearly festival on 7 January. Back on the main road east from Black River you pass through the town of Santa Cruz and the mountains that share the name. In times past, these mountains were considered to have the finest climate on the island, particularly recommended for people with pulmonary complaints: 'a dry atmosphere, freighted with ozone, and the ceaseless energy of the breezes'. Before you climb the huge Spur Tree Hill, at Nain, you will pass the plant that processes bauxite into alumina and sends it to the Port Kaiser shipping terminal for export. Close by is the very simple fishing village of **Alligator Pond**, where colourful boats line the shore and you can get an excellent fry fish or lobster with a festival roll.

© (809–)   **Where to Stay**

Black River

moderate

In Black River itself (not on the beach) **Invercauld Great House and Hotel**, PO Box 12, © 965 2750, @ 965 2751, has plenty of old Jamaican style. In the original great house, a very attractive green and white colonial building, there are eight rooms, with dark-stained floorboards, arched doorways and ventilation grilles. Other rooms are in modern buildings beside it. Facilities include a pool and tennis court.

inexpensive

A slightly less splendid, but equally characterful colonial Jamaican house is **Waterloo Guest House**, ✆ 965 2278, where there are five fan-ventilated rooms in the rickety main house (a very attractive wooden building with three eaves of sifferent sizes) and 16 others, with air-conditioning and TVs, in a new block behind. There is a swimming pool. Just to the north of the town you will find the **Ashton Ocean View Great House and Hotel**, PO Box 104 Luana, ✆/✉ 965 2036. It is set in an old estate house which commands a magnificent view over the countryside around. It has been modernized, and painted oddly in white and turquoise, but shades of the old plantation style return in the lacquered wooden floor, the rugs, the wooden interior walls and louvred day-rooms. There are 24 rooms, 11 of these in the tin-roofed main building, which has less atmosphere. Rooms have fans and air-conditioning, phones and TV.

cheap

You can find good rooms amid fertile splendour at **Apple Valley** in Maggotty, ✆ 997 6000, just five simple rooms in a hilltop house by the river, with ideal spots to swim and walk nearby; camping is available. There is a string of fairly characterless but very cheap modern villa hotels on the shore road east out of Black River. You might try the **Bridge House Inn**, which has 14 comfortable rooms, with a breezy modern dining room and a television room upstairs, above its strip of brown sand.

Whitehouse and Bluefields

inexpensive

There are some outstanding **villas** in the Bluefields area (try Mullion Cove and Bluefields Bay Villas), but if you are passing through and only want to stay for a couple of nights, try the excellent guest house at **Natania's**, ✆/✉ 963 5342, US reservations ✆ 1 800 330 2332, just up from Whitehouse. There are 16 rooms with wooden furnishing and louvred windows in a modern wooden house with huge walkaround balconies. It has a small secluded beach; very quiet, but friendly.

cheap

The **South Sea View Guest House**, outside Whitehouse, ✆ 963 5069, ✉ 963 5000, has 8 simple rooms in a modern seafront villa.

In South Sea Park (a collection of modern villas near Whitehouse) there is a good guest house that goes by the unlikely name of **Roots Uprising**, ✆/📠 963 5550—just four rooms with hot and cold water, all meals available and a friendly reception. Other houses in this area may well have spare rooms for hire, so ask around and bargain. **Shafston Estate Great House**, Bluefields PO, ✆ 0997 5076, has a superb setting high on the hills above the town (village) of Bluefields at the end of an impossibly rickety road. There are 10 extremely basic rooms, with shared bathrooms with cold water only, but the place has the unforgettable aura of an old Jamaican estate house and a veranda from which you can admire a hazy horizon that stretches from Whitehouse to Savanna-la-Mar. Not everyone's cup of tea, it's firmly on the backpacker circuit; all inc. **Lochiel Guest House**, ✆ 955 9344, is also set in an old Jamaican estate house just outside the town of Savanna-la-Mar. There are 12 fan-ventilated rooms; some, in the main house, have lumbering old furniture and wooden interiors and others, in a block behind, are a bit more modern. Some rooms share bathrooms but there is hot and cold water. Breakfast is included.

Treasure Beach

expensive

The **Treasure Beach Hotel**, PO Box 5, ✆ 965 2305, 📠 965 2544, is a traditional beachfront resort hotel, with a relaxed atmosphere. There are 36 modern and very comfortable rooms in small blocks ranged along a palm-dotted hillside around a large main block with dining room and bar. They look over the pool and garden and a stretch of brown-sand beach. **Sunset Resort Villa**, Calabash Bay PA, ✆ 965 0143, 📠 965 0555, US reservations ✆ 1 800 786 8452, is set in a modern villa on the clifftop above Calabash Bay. There are 12 rooms, all with private patios, air-conditioning and satellite TV, and a couple with kitchens (but there is also a restaurant serving international cuisine). Palm-thatch gazebos offer the finest view of the sunset. Some *moderate* rooms.

moderate

The most stylish place to stay in the area is **Jake's**, Treasure Beach PA, ✆/📠 965 0552, UK reservations ✆ 0800 614 790, US ✆ 1 800 *OUT POST*, a hip retreat on the cliffs of Treasure Beach, with a superb view across the sea to the sunset. Jake's is quite rustic, with adobe buildings marooned in a sea of tall wild grass, but its colours give it plenty of style. The cottages are painted rich red and mauve, turquoise and tangerine. There are just seven rooms, with muslin nets and fans (anyone who insists on air-conditioning would not be right for this place), and solar-heated water. Behind the tin-roofed gingerbread terrace, with its bar and sitting area, is a scattering of parasols and upturned cable-barrels to eat on; Jamaican fare is adapted a little for the European palate. And just above the sea is a meandering, tile-studded swimming pool with Adirondack chairs strategically positioned for watching the waves. There is a small beach. You will probably need to book in advance in the winter season.

inexpensive

The **Golden Sands Motel**, ✆ 965 0148, ✆ 965 0167, is an ugly concrete construction on the golden-brown sand of Frenchman's Bay. There are three buildings in fact, with 20 simply decorated rooms, some with private kitchens. Cold water is laid on and so, if there are enough people, is a restaurant; it's excellent value with a funny transient crowd.

cheap

Near the Golden Sands Motel is the **Four M's Cottage** on the beach, ✆ 965 2651, ✆ 965 2697, restaurant and kitchens. There are villas for hire in this area and you are often able to find rooms in people's houses by walking around the town and asking: **Ital Rest** has two rooms, and camping space available. There is one place to stay in the area of Alligator Pond, **SeaRiv**, on the road to the Kaiser port, ✆ 962 7265. The building is a modern concrete villa which, if you don't mind the isolation, makes a passable stopover, with reasonable rooms at a good price. Fans and phones, no TVs, and a nice section of dark-sand beach, usually all to yourself.

Eating Out

In Treasure Beach there are a number of restaurants and hotel dining rooms where you can get a reliably good meal. At **Tiffany's**, ✆ 965 0300 (*moderate*), you dine on the roadside terrace or in the pretty, colourful interior. International fare and a cheery atmosphere. An excellent place for breakfast and light lunches goes by the curious name of **Trans Love**, where you sit in a palm-thatched yard a little inland from the Treasure Beach Hotel. They roast their own coffee here, and offer home-baked breads and juices, and then, if you're still sitting there at lunchtime, ackee quiche and baguettes and sandwiches. For something more authentically Jamaican, try the **Fisherman's Bar**; let them know in advance what kind of fish you will want, and they will catch it for you that morning. Otherwise, and elsewhere in the southwest anyway, you are really dependent on hotel dining rooms.

Evenings are pretty quiet altogether, though you may come across an open-air party with a sound system—a Jamaican musical evening. There are a couple of easy bars, open in the daytime, at the mouth of the **Black River**, where the river trips into the swamp start. **Treasure Beach** has a number of hotel bars and restaurants where you can find a drink. Try **Jake's**, which gathers a good crowd of travellers and Jamaicans. Alternatively, visit the **Fisherman's Bar** for a bit of local atmosphere. And if you are in the area of Alligator Pond you can stop at one of the many beachside bars and shacks, the laid-back **Seafood Village** for example, or the slightly more formal **Red Lobster** bar, a little inland at Spring Garden.

In the area of **Bluefields**, at the settlement of Belmont you will find a palm-thatch gazebo called **Pablo's Paradise**, where a bar and some tables are scattered under sea almond trees in a grassy garden on the waterfront. And then there is a collection of good bars at Bluefields beach, where you can get a cooked fish and a beer until late in the night. The bar at the **Casa Mariner** has a deck that stretches out over the shallow water behind the concrete building. Otherwise try the **Sandpiper** in Cave, also set on a deck on the waterfront.

Mandeville

As the 20th century's ultimate rest-cure is to sun ourselves on the finest beach we can find, it is odd to think that a hundred years ago people went to great lengths to get away from them. Mandeville was where they came instead, to the hill station in the mountainous uplands, where the climate was healthier and cooler—this was before the days of malarial prophylaxis, when they wore far too many clothes for the climate and beaches were regarded as degenerate anyway.

Mandeville is the capital of Manchester Parish, and it is set in mountainous uplands at 2000ft, which give it its cooler climate. The town was laid out around a 'village green', with the Georgian court house and the parish church opposite one another across the open square. Nowadays they look oddly aloof among all the chaos of the Jamaican market and the taxi-men touting for business.

In the 1950s the area suddenly became the centre of the Jamaican bauxite industry. And latterly Mandeville has become popular with Jamaicans who have spent their working lives abroad and have decided to return to the island to live. The old town has been encrusted with neat and prosperous-looking suburbs, peopled by the 'English' as they are called (because many of them have been away in the UK for 30 years). It has been dubbed the 'retirement capital of Jamaica'.

There are direct **bus** services from Kingston to Mandeville, but if you are travelling from Montego Bay or the west you will usually be forced to hop through the different towns along the way (Savanna-la-Mar, Black River and Santa Cruz). There are some **car hire** companies in the town. Contact Allen Garfield, 3½ Caledonia Road, ✆ 962 3049, or Candi Car Rental, ✆ 952 3153. And **taxis** are available through the hotels or the taxi association, ✆ 962 2021. Taxi drivers also collect at the bus station on the main square. The Kirk Vine airstrip (KVN) is just south of the town and there are occasional scheduled local **flights** from Kingston and Montego Bay.

Tourist Information

There is no official **tourist information office** in the area, but you will find the Astra Hotel, ✆ 962 3265 in Mandeville a useful source of information about the area. In a **medical emergency**, contact Mandeville hospital, ✆ 962 2067. There are plenty of **banks** in the town, try Caledonia Road just west of the main square. **Shopping** is limited to the 12 malls, but there is not much specifically designed for tourists here.

Sports

Tennis is available through some of the hotels. The **golf** course at the **Manchester Country Club** is the oldest in the Caribbean, with 18 tees that play to nine greens, ✆ 962 2403.

Around the Town

For all the encrustation of suburbs, the 'green' is still the heart of Mandeville. It stands on a hill, dominated at one end by the imperious classical façade of the **court house**, faced with coral stone and ornamented with pillars and a double curving staircase, and at the other by the huge parish church, built in 1816, with tall, arched windows and a wooden interior, its inner walls covered with memorials to local families. The court house is still used as such, but the square has lost its old-colonial feel now. Instead it displays all the vibrant life of any Jamaican town, with constant music, a tangle of power wires, buses and taxis crowding the area, and the spillover from the market. There is a constant confusion of traffic driving around the square (the traffic is as bad in central Mandeville as it is in Kingston, and there are plans to reroute it). In the suburbs that surround the heart of the town—Ingleside, Godfreylands and Caledonia—there are a number of colonial houses and a club where there are tennis courts and a golf course, even a squash court and a full-size snooker table.

There are a number of unlikely sounding but entertaining things to do around Mandeville. **Mrs Stephenson's garden**, *adm*, on the northern outskirts of the town, is interesting even for those who are novices botanically speaking. She has 50 species of orchids as well as the ortanique (a cross-fertilized citrus fruit, named for the *or*ange, *tan*gerine and its un*ique*ness—it was invented by Alcan in the fifties), the stag-horn fern and pig-tailed anthurium. Not far off, at Shooter's Hill, you will find the **Pickapeppa sauce factory** (*visits by arrangement*; ✆ 962 2928), the source of the pungent concoction that the Jamaicans dash liberally on their food. At the **Alcan aluminium factory** you see the rich red Jamaican earth travel three miles on a conveyor belt to eventually become aluminium oxide. Finally **Marshall's Pen** is a peaceful and charming spot, a 200-year-old great house set in gentle hills, once a coffee plantation and now a farm for Jamaican red poll cattle. Bird-watching tours and private visits to the house can be booked through the Astra Hotel if you arrange it in advance.

The area around the town is known as the feeding tree (the Jamaican equivalent of the breadbasket) because of all the cultivation—the north of Manchester is known for growing yam and Irish (rather than sweet) potatoes, and nearby St Elizabeth is also known for its vegetables. You may see the market ladies travelling in trucks to Kingston to sell their produce on Thursday or Friday nights. Local produce is also sold along the roadside: bags of cashews and strings of whatever fruits are in season. The countryside is very beautiful, with orange and green patterning and the occasional huge scar from an open-cast bauxite mine.

On the coast to the southeast of the town, in the sugar-cane flatlands of Clarendon Parish, there is a working spa at Milk River, formerly a popular mineral bath. The waters are supposedly the most radioactive (naturally occurring) in the world and they were known for their efficacy in curing gout and rheumatism. You might be lucky enough to see a manatee or sea cow, a ponderous and extremely endangered herbivore with a body 3 metres long, a skin like a whale and a tail like a beaver, in the waters around this area. There is a working beach at Farquhars, a couple of miles beyond here along a rough road, where you can get a steam fish and bammy among the crowd of food stalls.

✆ (809–)

Where to Stay
moderate

The most comfortable place to stay is the **Mandeville Hotel**, PO Box 78, 4 Hotel Street, ✆ 962 2460, ✆ 962 0700, which is set in its own enclave just off the town square. The building is modern but the hotel has an unhurried air about it. There are 60 well decorated rooms (some of them suites) with TVs, phones and fans, with a bar, the Manchester Arms, downstairs and a pool in the pleasant gardens. In the town of Christiana, in the hills to the north of Mandeville, you will find a nice retreat in the **Hotel Villa Bella**, PO Box 473, ✆/✉ 964 2243. The style of the décor harks back to the fifties; the building is modern, but there is a gracious air of times past in the drawing room and on the veranda, where an old sign says: 'ring twice for ice water, three times for the maid'. There are well kept, comfortable rooms upstairs.

inexpensive

Back in Mandeville, the **Astra Hotel**, PO Box 60, ✆ 962 3265, ✉ 962 1461, is a friendly, family-run hotel just outside the town centre, on Ward Avenue. It has 40 comfortable, clean rooms upstairs in the villa and in modern blocks behind; it's also a good source of information about the area. There are a number of guest houses in the area around Mandeville: some of the villas are built with 6 bedrooms (for the families of the returning residents), which are let out when they are not there. Try **Kariba Kariba** at 39 New Green Road, ✆ 962 3039, where there are five rooms and suites with private bathrooms and a restaurant.

cheap

Ten simple rooms with a shared kitchen can be found at the **Roden Guest House**, down the hill on Wesley Road, ✆ 962 2552. At Milk River on the south coast, the **Milk River Mineral Bath Hotel**, Milk River PO, ✆ 924 9544, ✉ 986 4962, evokes an older Jamaica. The building is a genuine old Jamaican red-tin-roofed affair with gingerbread pickings, louvres, screens and cooling vents; the 23 rooms are authentically decorated and very comfortable, with TVs, phones, fans and Bibles in each. The baths downstairs are free while you are staying at the hotel. It sees mainly a Jamaican crowd who come to take the spa waters, so it is an amusing place.

Eating Out

In Mandeville, the **Hungry Hut** is a good spot for local food—try the curry goat or the stew chicken with ground provisions—as is the **Grove Court**, opposite the court house on the square (*both moderate–cheap*). At the **Angel Food Health Restaurant** (*cheap*) in Mandeville Plaza there are vegetarian dishes and natural juices. You can always take away a chicken from **Tweeties** (*cheap*) next to Texaco Station. If you are travelling through there are a number of places where you can stop over for a genuine Jamaican meal. The **cafés** on Spur Tree Hill have a splendid view. And if you go down to the south coast at Milk River or at Alligator Pond you can get a fish and bammy.

Ocho Rios, St Ann and St Mary

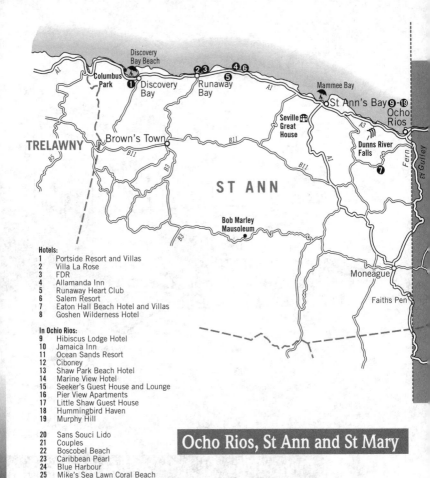

Hotels:

1 Portside Resort and Villas
2 Villa La Rose
3 FDR
4 Allamanda Inn
5 Runaway Heart Club
6 Salem Resort
7 Eaton Hall Beach Hotel and Villas
8 Goshen Wilderness Hotel

In Ochio Rios:

9 Hibiscus Lodge Hotel
10 Jamaica Inn
11 Ocean Sands Resort
12 Ciboney
13 Shaw Park Beach Hotel
14 Marine View Hotel
15 Seeker's Guest House and Lounge
16 Pier View Apartments
17 Little Shaw Guest House
18 Hummingbird Haven
19 Murphy Hill

20 Sans Souci Lido
21 Couples
22 Boscobel Beach
23 Caribbean Pearl
24 Blue Harbour
25 Mike's Sea Lawn Coral Beach

Ocho Rios, St Ann and St Mary

Even 25 years ago the coves of the whiplash coastline around Ocho Rios were almost completely undeveloped and the town itself was nothing more than a tiny fishing village. Nowadays, from an epicentre of skyscrapers in Ocho Rios Bay, the resorts stretch along the northern coastline, offering the full range of tourism, from high-pressure all-inclusive fun-parks to elegant colonial retreats. And Ocho Rios itself will keep you busy daytime and evening with its fair share of sights and a string of restaurants, bars and clubs.

And there are also some off-beat places in this area, where you will find a more tranquil and natural Jamaica. There are a number of

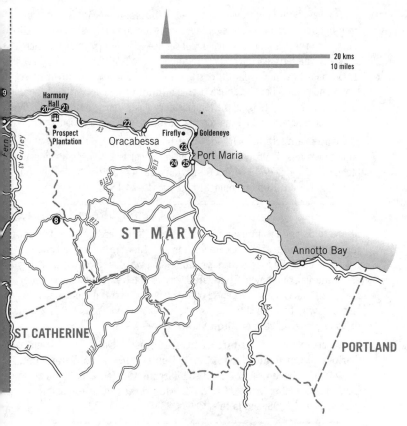

small hotels and villas on the coast that are ideal for a quiet hideaway or for a stopover on a leisurely island tour. Inland there is all the magnificence of the tropical island. St Ann is known as the Garden Parish; St Mary is also stunningly fertile—there are a number of astonishingly exotic botanical gardens around Ocho Rios. And once you have left the developed belt along the coastline, it doesn't take long to reach genuine Jamaican countryside, where you will find steep-sided valleys, watered by numerous falls and rivers.

Getting There

You are quite likely to arrive in Jamaica at Montego Bay airport. Runaway Bay lies an hour and a half east along the coast and Ocho Rios a couple of hours away. Both towns are well served by **buses**: from Mo Bay they run from before dawn until late evening; from Kingston (1½hrs) they run all hours too. There is an occasional direct service to Negril (3½hrs) and there is usually one service a day to Port Antonio (2½hrs), leaving about midday. If you miss this then it is still possible to hop from town to town (Port Maria and Anotto Bay) by **share taxi** and **minibus** and you will get there in the end. In Ocho Rios, all the long-distance buses depart from the roundabout (the junction of the Kingston road with the north coast road).

The closest **airstrip** to Ocho Rios is at Boscobel, which is served by Air Jamaica Express, ✆ 957 4051. If you wish to charter a plane you can contact Tim Air, ✆ 979 1114, or Wings Jamaica, ✆ 923 6573. And if you would prefer a helicopter, contact Helitours, ✆ 974 1525.

Getting Around the Area

Share taxis and local **buses** ply all the roads in the area, departing from the roundabout or the clock tower (for Port Maria). If you are catching transport along the coastal road, say from Runaway Bay, go to the shopping areas and flag one down. There are many private **taxis**, which collect at the hotels, the clock in the centre of town and at the pier if there is a cruise ship in town; if you need to ring for one, contact **Maxi Taxi**, ✆ 974 2971, or **JUTA**, ✆ 974 2292, or **Alton Smith**, ✆ 999 7573.

There are plenty of **car-hire** companies around Ocho Rios. Contact **Caribbean Car Rentals**, ✆ 974 5617, **Don's**, ✆ 974 7726, **Paramount**, ✆ 994 2357, **Island**, ✆ 974 2178 and **Bargain**, ✆ 974 5298. In Runaway Bay, contact **Rising Bird**, ✆ 973 5492. **Motorbikes** are available through **Abe's**, ✆ 974 1008, and **Jake's**, ✆ 974 8838.

Tours

Day trips available from Ocho Rios and Runaway Bay range from the classic **Dunn's River** day trip and the many plantation tours to a visit to the **Bob Marley Mausoleum** in the hills of St Ann; other tours will take you up into the **Blue Mountains** and to the great houses near **Montego Bay** or even to **Negril**. Contact **Jamaica Tours**, ✆ 953 2825, or **Caribic Vacations**, ✆ 974 9106. These tours are usually in buses; you might prefer to hire a taxi driver for the day. The **Touring Society of Jamaica**, ✆ 975 7158, offers picnic trips to the waterfalls and the back country, from Boscobel.

The main **Jamaica Tourist Board office** in Ocho Rios, ✆ 974 2570, ✎ 974 2559, is on Main Street, upstairs in the Ocean Village Shopping Centre close to the main beach. You can also get tourist information from the series of pink and white gazebos dotted around the town: at the entrance to the Jamaica Grande Hotel, at Pineapple Place and opposite the Taj Mahal Shopping Centre.

There is no hospital in Ocho Rios, the closest is in St Ann's Bay about 7 miles west, but there are **emergency** and consultancy services available through Dr Crooks, ✆ 974 6403, also an ambulance service ✆ 999 7425, or Dr Francis, ✆ 974 2429.

For exchange of money there are **banks** and **cambios** all around the town of Ocho Rios, particularly around Main Street. There are almost limitless, dreary shopping malls, many of them duty-free, around Ocho Rios, where you can buy anything from a gold necklace or a Walkman to yet another 'Jamaica Me Crazy' T-shirt. There are a number of craft markets in the town and at Dunn's River Falls.

Beaches

Ocho Rios has plenty of good beaches; the problem is that access to many is limited because there is no route over the private land around them. Some hotels will allow you in on a day pass, otherwise you have to stick to the public beaches. For watersports around Ocho Rios and Runaway Bay you are really dependent on the hotels or on the main public beach in Ocho Rios. All of the beaches and falls below charge a small admission.

The main public beach in Ocho Rios, the **Ocho Rios Bay Beach**, is reached through the Ocean Village Shopping Centre (also called UDC beach after Urban Development Corporation). It is a busy, mile-long curve of excellent sand backed by palms and almond trees and looking out onto the cruise ship pier. Watersports concessions throng the beach, and so you can easily get a jetski, a kayak, or go parasailing; there are also changing rooms and a snack bar.

Jamaica Inn has one of the best beaches on the island, but it is effectively private. However, you can sometimes buy a day pass to other hotel-owned beaches, for example, the small but quiet and charming strip of sand owned by the Shaw Park Beach Hotel in the **White River Bay**, the **Sans Souci**, on a sheltered cove between two headlands, and **Prospect Beach**.

A novel day on the 'beach', but with a more expensive entry charge, can be had high up in the hills at **Irie Beach**, in a charming gulley festooned with greenery on the White River. The river rolls and crashes over falls and down rock sluices for about 150 yards, and finally into a large pool of cool green water, excellent for swimming. Enough light penetrates the gulley for sunbathing and there is a bar and restaurant, serving soups, burgers and salads brought down from the music studio above. Very pretty; follow the signs on the White River Road.

In Oracabessa, near Ian Fleming's house, Goldeneye, there is a small but very stylish suntrap called **James Bond** beach, a short strip of white sand shaded by sea grape trees and backed by a colourful bamboo bar and grill. Ice-cool music hangs in the air; there are sports facilities (snorkelling and jetskis) and changing rooms.

West of the town, beneath the **Dunn's River Falls** complex (*see* p.160), there is a tolerable strip of sand with a snack bar; the water is shallow and pleasant but full of crowds on their way up the falls. **Mammee Bay** has a charming beach, with mounded sand, though the reef right offshore hampers swimming; there's a snack bar, changing facilities and some sports including boating in kayaks and dinghies. You should be able to get a pass from the Mammee Bay Estates. For beaches in the Runaway Bay area, *see* p.169.

Watersports

There are plenty of **day** and **evening cruises** on yachts out of Ocho Rios, including picnic and snorkelling trips, and rum and sunset sails. Contact *Wild Oats*, ✆ 974 7044, a 45-ft yacht, or *Red Stripe*, ✆ 974 2446. **Scuba** diving is well served in this area and the operators will take you out onto the reef which follows the coastline about a mile off-shore. You can expect to see good corals and sponges in spur and groove formations and in 'coral mountains', which rise 50 feet from the sandy bottom, and the wreck of a tug boat, the *Lady Catherine*. Contact **Resort Divers**, ✆ 974 5338, **Sea and Dive**, ✆ 974 5762 or **Garfield**, ✆ 975 4420, or ✆ 995 3700 after hours. **Deep-sea fishing** can be arranged through *Kingfisher II*, at the dock in Ocho Rios Bay, ✆ 979 7140, or **Triple B Charters**, ✆ 974 4243.

Land Sports

Tennis is available in many of the hotels, or you can contact the **Jamaica Grande** resort in the middle of town. There are **golf** courses in Upton, above the White River, to the east of Ocho Rios, ✆ 974 2528, and in Runaway Bay, ✆ 973 2561. For **horseback riding** through the hills of the Garden Parish or a canter through the waves you can contact **Chukka Cove Farm**, ✆ 972 2506, also polo lessons, or **Hooves Ltd**, ✆ 974 6245, in Beecher Town above Ocho Rios. **River rafting** is also possible here if you do not want to go as far as the more traditional places in Port Antonio and Montego Bay. **White River Safaris** offer a ride down the White River in an inner tube or on a raft.

Ocho Rios

Ocho Rios, or Ochee as it is often known, is Jamaica's second tourist town. It lies midway along the island on the north coast, about 70 miles east of Montego Bay and the same distance over the mountains from Kingston. It is a businesslike resort, with two or three cruise ships in the harbour on some days, and tourists in droves. Ocho Rios is not capital of either St Ann's or St Mary Parish (instead it calls itself the cruise ship capital of Jamaica), but it is the biggest and most important town in this area, a centre of transport and tourism with a thriving local life.

The name Ocho Rios looks as though it might derive from 'eight rivers'. There are plenty of rivers about, but the name is in fact a corruption of *las chorreras*, meaning waterfalls or spouts, of which there are also many tumbling off the hills immediately behind the town. (The Battle of Las Chorreras, which took place in the area in 1657, was the Spaniards' final attempt to reclaim the island from the English.) There are also some breathtakingly lush gardens that demonstrate the vigorous fertility of the region in the Shaw Park area.

Ocho Rios developed slowly from a small fortress in the 18th century into a fishing village and then a port serving the estates in the nearby hills—there were nine great houses at the time of emancipation in 1836. Earlier this century it became a shipment port for bauxite; you can see the huge loading works as you leave town to the west.

In the sixties, tourism development began and Ocho Rios exploded into a new life, building like mad and almost completely without plan. It is ranged along a 4- or 5-mile stretch of coastline, beneath some villa estates in the hills behind. The main strip heaves with activity night and day. Ocho Rios not very attractive town and, because it has no heritage (more than about 30 years old), it feels a little soulless at times. That is not to say you don't get a good holiday there, though.

Around the Town

Ocho Rios has no traditional centre—there are no parish buildings on a formal square. The only real monument, near one of the markets, where the taxi drivers gather, is the clock tower.

The other main focus is the roundabout, the meeting point of the roads from Kingston and Montego Bay. ('Round-about' is really an optimistic word for this traffic convention. At the time of writing it was more of an 'anywhere-about' as the cars did not follow any recognizable driving patterns when negotiating it.) Apart from these two points, the town—banks, shopping malls, restaurants, bars, watersports shops, hire car companies—is dispersed along the main drag running east from Ocho Rios Bay beach.

High in Shaw Park above the town, **Coyaba River Garden and Museum**, *adm and guided tours*, is set in a cleft shaded by huge cedar trees. Here you will see makali palms (with fronds shaped like fans) and bauhinia or bullfoot trees, so called because of their cloven leaves; their flower is a complex purple bloom called the poor man's orchid. You will also see *impatiens* (Busy Lizzy), shrimp plants with their erect yellow and white flowers and six or seven species of banana-like ginger lilies. There is also a good museum, which takes a quick view of St Ann's Parish since Arawak times, with some excellent old maps, descriptions of traditional Jamaican architecture, stories of Marcus Garvey and Bob Marley (who were born in the parish) and some quaint colonial pictures and cartoons, including a famous one of a newly arrived planter. The **Shaw Park Botanical Gardens**, *adm*, are laid out over a hillside where two rivers run down into multi-layered lily-ponds. Among the vine-covered arbours, lawns and waterways you will see exotic tropical plants including red shrimp flowers and flame of the forest trees. You will probably hear the 'heartbeat' or ram pump, which uses the downward pressure of the waterflow to pump water up. Further west, the **Enchanted Gardens**, *adm*, are also laid out around some waterfalls and a river: heliconias, ginger lilies and an aviary with over 90 species of birds, including flamingos.

The road south from the roundabout (to Kingston) heads up into the mountains towards Moneague. As it climbs, it passes through **Fern Gully**, an absurdly fertile chasm 3 miles long where the vegetation makes a canopy over the road. Once a river-bed (the stream now diverted), its upper reaches are hung with a tangle of creepers and lianas and many of Jamaica's 500 varieties of fern. The sunlight occasionally penetrates in angled shafts. Until a few years ago the gulley was alive with fireflies at night, but now the petrol fumes have killed them off.

As you leave the town to the west you pass under the gantry of the enormous bauxite shipping station—it was disused but has been working again recently. Next there are two fortresses: the first is nothing more than a couple of cannon hiding behind a defensive wall. The other, nearby, is bigger and more impressive, but it contains the local sewage plant, so don't bother to investigate it.

Dunn's River Falls, *open daily, 8–5, shoes available for hire, adm*, a couple of miles out of the town, is probably Jamaica's most famous sight. It is a series of waterfalls that tumble 600ft down a gulley on the hillside, outstandingly pretty but usually crowded. Make sure you bring a swimming costume and set out early or after closing time to avoid the crowds. Starting from the beach at the bottom, you join a conga of other tourists, holding hands and dicing with death as you edge gingerly up among the terrifying and relentless 3- and 4-foot cascades. It's all a bit of a rigmarole, but, in such an exquisite place, fun nonetheless.

As the endless parade of shops, bars and restaurants and hotels that makes up the town begins to peter out to the east you cross the White River, which marks the border with the Parish of St Mary. Soon you come to the **Prospect Plantation**, *open daily 10.30–3.30, adm*. There are three daily tours of its grounds, where many of Jamaica's plantation crops are set out on view, including cassava, banana, coffee and of course sugar-cane. You will see how unripe ackee was used for soap in old-time Jamaica and taste coconut milk fresh from the tree. Horseback rides into the mountains are available.

Close by is **Harmony Hall**, *open till 6pm*, a turreted estate house built of cut-stone in the 19th century, which has been restored with its tray ceilings and embellished with gingerbread fretwork. Now it is an art gallery and craft shop. Upstairs there are rooms exhibiting the work of artists who have practised in Jamaica, including the Jamaican 'Intuitives', and displays of crafts from around the Caribbean; there are also temporary exhibitions and regular craft fairs. Downstairs there are books and clothes and bamboo furniture, and a café and bar outside.

The next settlement along the coast is Oracabessa, a slightly tatty town on the hill above a harbour that was used as a banana shipment port at the turn of the century. Author Ian Fleming, creator of the character James Bond, lived here from 1946 until his death in 1964, in a house called **Goldeneye** (the name Oracabessa is supposed to derive from the Spanish for 'golden head'). The name James Bond was borrowed from another keen birdwatcher, the author of *The Birds of the West Indies*. Goldeneye is privately owned, but it can be rented as a holiday villa.

Some way inland, after a pleasant ride on a rickety road, is **Sun Valley Plantation,** Ⓒ 995 3075, a working banana plantation. Three tours each weekday, *9, 11, 3, adm*, take you through the life cycle of a banana, from rhizome to hand or bunch and tells of other tropical plants including ackee and nutmeg. Go on a Tuesday or Wednesday, when they are reaping.

A thousand feet up on the hill above Port Maria, Noël Coward's house, **Firefly**, *adm expensive*, has perhaps the finest view in the whole of the Caribbean. (Three hundred years before Coward lived there, the same site was occupied by the buc-caneer Henry Morgan.) The house looks east; on a clear day the panorama takes in the Blue Mountains to the south, and the northern coastline of the island, where successive headlands outreach one another, as far as Port Antonio. The house was completed in 1956 and Coward lived here until he died in 1973. He is buried in the garden under a simple tombstone. There is an excellent tour, starting in his painting room, where there are some of his canvases and his brushes in their bamboo-section water pots. Next there is a 20-minute video of his life and then you see his dining room and music room, with two pianos, record sleeves and musical scores. Upstairs there is the 'Room with a (fantastic) View' and his bedroom. Henry Morgan's old kitchen (supposedly) has been turned into a café and gift shop (complete with T-shirts emblazoned with Noël Coward's paintings). Look out for the occasional concerts and entertainment here.

Back on the coast itself is **Port Maria**, the capital of St Mary Parish, set on a strikingly lovely bay. As you enter the town from the west you pass the old centre of the town, where you will see the attractive old parish church, the war memorial and the old burned-out parish offices (with a dedication to Alexander Bustamante). The modern town is across the river and around the bay. There is not much to interest a visitor there unless you want a pattie and a drink at lunchtime as you pass through. The island offshore takes its name Cabarita from the Spanish word for goat (not from carburettor, as you might be assured). In the early days of Caribbean exploration, there was no reliable supply of food and so sailors would plant fruit trees and leave livestock in case of emergency. For this reason there are a number of places around the Caribbean called Goat Island, Cabrit or Cabarita.

From Port Maria the main road heads south and inland into the hills, re-emerging on the coast at **Annotto Bay** from where it heads into the Parish of Portland and eventually to Port Antonio via the massive and beautiful foothills of the Blue Mountains (*see* p.220). If you are heading across to Kingston on the Castleton Road, which runs out of Annotto Bay, visit the Botanical Gardens (*see* p.222).

✆ *(809–)* **Where to Stay**

There is a real shortage of good regular hotels in this area (but *see* Jamaica Inn, p.164)—it's mostly populated by all-inclusives.

luxury

Another enclave of up-beat Jamaican luxury is the **Sans Souci Lido**, PO Box 103, ✆ 974 2353, 🖷 974 2544, US reservations ✆ 1 800 858 8009, which lies 4 miles east of the town just over the White River. Although Sans Souci is an all-inclusive, the atmosphere is not like a fun-park; there is a calm about the place, and entertainment is more likely to be saxophonists and three-piece ensembles than wet T-shirt competitions. The hotel is large, with 111 rooms in blocks ranged over hillside grounds that run down to a good beach, where most watersports are available. Beneath the main house and open-air dining terrace, there is a spa, offering all the beauty treatments you can imagine, and a work-out area. Twenty-four hour room service.

Couples, PO Box 330, ✆ 974 4271, ✉ 974 4439, US reservations ✆ 1 800 *COUPLES*, UK ✆ 0181 900 1913, is an all-inclusive resort to the east of the town, where you can enjoy an action-packed regime of water-sports, or intensive lazing around on the passable beach and the offshore island, where there is a nudist area, plus other essential activities such as massage and pool volleyball. Everything is arranged in pairs here, from the swimming-pool loungers to the cocktails (the bar is open all day) and the hammocks. And love is in the air, certainly if you follow the example of the lions on the hotel logo; well sex anyway. There are 172 rooms, in large blocks above the sea. Breakfast and lunch are buffets, but dinner is *à deux*, à la carte, in one of the three restaurants: Italian, continental or gourmet (the formal one, in which you must wear a long-sleeved shirt). Lots of evening entertainment, piano bar and floor shows. Heterosexual couples only.

Ciboney, PO Box 728, ✆ 974 1027, ✉ 974 5838, US reservations ✆ 1 800 333 3333, is yet another all-inclusive but with a certain elegant style. There are 289 rooms, all in suites, set on the hillside above a huge mock-colonial plantation house dripping with latticework and louvres. There are tennis courts and squash courts, a spa for manicures, pedicures, water-jet treatments, etc., and if you are feeling hot you can always take a dip in one of the resort's 90 swimming-pools. A regular shuttle takes you down the hill to the beach, where there are watersports. Numerous restaurants include a bright and colourfully decorated 'market place' for light snacks, and some more formal venues for dinner: the Manor dining room, with pineapple-backed chairs and international cuisine, and the Orchid, with a choice of low-calorie light meals. The hotel is large and constantly active, but there are very comfortable rooms and the honeymoon suites are an excellent retreat.

The **Boscobel Beach**, PO Box 63, ✆ 974 3331, ✉ 975 3270 (reservations through Superclubs), is an all-inclusive that caters specifically for families with children. It's a busy hotel with a sociable atmosphere. The kids are divided into age groups and taken off your hands to be put through their paces in arts and crafts and given lessons in Jamaican *patois* while you engage in the more urgent pursuits of tanning and windsurfing on the beach. There are children's play and entertainment areas and a zoo. Adults have their own area in the hotel, with a pool and evening entertainments such as relaxing in the piano bar, and fine-dining. There are 200 rooms in the complex, with arrangements for children and adults in the same room.

very expensive

The **Jamaica Inn**, PO Box 1, ℃ 974 2514, ✉ 974 2449, US reservations ℃ 1 800 243 9240, 2 miles from the centre of the town, is one of Jamaica's most elegant hotels. Its setting is magnificent, enclosed in its own pretty bay, with a fantastic stretch of sand between small headlands. The old white and Wedgwood-blue estate house has a gracious colonial air, echoed in the old plantation style of the columns and balustrades, and louvred doors and fantail coolers above them. Each impeccably decorated room looks out onto the sea from an external living room on its own colonnaded balcony. There is a pool and some watersports (kayaks and sunfish) if you are feeling active, or the library and scrabble if the desire should pass. Just 45 rooms and a certain formality (a jacket and tie are required in the winter season) but friendly: the staff recognize guests who return year after year.

expensive

Ocho Rios also has a number of smaller, more moderately priced properties, which are used by the package companies but which still have a certain individuality and style. The **Shaw Park Beach Hotel**, PO Box 17, ℃ 974 2552, ✉ 974 5042, UK reservations ℃ 0171 581 4094, centres on an Edwardian-style villa, with wooden panelling and solid furniture, that stands above a protected cove with an excellent beach, where a number of watersports (glass-bottomed boat trips, windsurfing, sunfish and scuba) are available. Its 118 rooms and suites are comfortable and modern and all have a balcony or terrace with a view across the sea, air-conditioning and phones; most have TVs. The waterfront terrace provides a lovely setting for dinner; there's evening entertainment and Ocho Rios town is not too far off.

moderate

The **Hibiscus Lodge Hotel**, PO Box 52, ℃ 974 2676, ✉ 974 1874, stands in very pretty gardens on the clifftops in town. The pool, some of the rooms, the dining room and bar (where the chairs are slung from the ceiling) are all set on stepped terraces on the cliffside itself, shaded by tropical greenery and a huge almond tree (from which the restaurant takes its name). It is within walking distance of the centre of town, but it is quite private and has a friendly atmosphere and charming setting. There is snorkelling down below in the daytime, and some entertainment in the evenings. Rooms are comfortable if not luxurious. Another good option in the middle range and excellent value for money is the small **Ocean Sands Resort**, 14 James Avenue, ℃/✉ 974 2605. The hotel is in a simple modern block above its own small strip of sand and shallow water out to the reef, and it has a friendly, quite homey atmosphere. There are 28 pretty pastel-decorated rooms, all with tiled floors, telephones and air-conditioning or a fan (some with balconies), overlooking the pool and the restaurant which sit above the sea on a deck. Some evening entertainment. In the centre of town itself you will find a small number of slightly cheaper rooms at **Pier View Apartments**, PO Box 134, ✆ 974 2607, ▧ 974 1384, a short walk from the Ocho Rios Bay Beach. The rooms are cheaper than the suites and they are set in two modern blocks above a crammed garden. All have TVs, air-conditioning and fans and most have balconies; some suites have kitchens. No pool or dining room, but all the restaurants are close by. Some *inexpensive* rooms.

inexpensive

James Avenue, at the lower end of the market, is a good area to find accommodation. Across the road from Ocean Sands is the **Marine View Hotel**, 9 James Avenue, ✆ 974 5753, ▧ 974 6953. The building is uncompromisingly concrete, with pink, white and grey décor; but the large tiled rooms are available at good rates (the cheapest are the ones with ceiling fans). There is a pool and a restaurant where you can get all meals. And round the corner you can also try **Seeker's Guest House and Lounge**, at no. 25 in a small shopping centre, ✆ 974 5763, where there is a pool bar with heavy reggae and rooms with private baths, but no swimming or restaurant. The **Little Shaw Park Guest House**, ✆ 974 2177, is in an attractive tropical garden high above the town in the residential Shaw Park Estate. There are 10 rooms, most with private baths, and a gazebo outside; you can cater for yourself. Just up from the White River on the main road is the **Hummingbird Haven**, PO Box 95, ✆ 974 5188, ▧ 974 5202, a garden retreat set in 6 acres of forested hillside, just up from the beach. There are a few simple cabins and endless tent-sites. A restaurant is nearby but there are also limited cooking facilities available; it's a friendly stopover for independent travellers.

As you head **east of Oracabessa** and then south towards Port Maria you will find a small hotel popular with independent travellers, the **Caribbean Pearl**, PO Box 127 Port Maria, ✆ 994 2672, ▧ 994 2043. The hotel is set in a modern house on the hillside which has a pool on a terrace out front and an excellent view of the broad sweep of the sea. The eight spacious rooms have tiled floors and nets on the beds, and wooden and wicker furniture. It's quite a sociable place, with a communal area for the TV and other gatherings. Packages include breakfast and dinner. Not far off, perched on the hillside, is **Blue Harbour**, PO Box 50, Port Maria, ✆ 994 2262, US reservations ✆ 505 586 1244, where accommodation is sometimes available when the whole place has not been block booked. This is where the guests of Noël Coward used to stay—he lived here himself until he moved up to Firefly, on the hilltop above. Blue Harbour's 12 comfortable rooms have wonderful views over the bays and coastline.

cheap

In the hills above Ocho Rios, tucked away off the main road south from the town, is **Murphy Hill** guest house, ✆ 922 0440. It nestles under a large and ugly antenna and the rooms are not brilliant, but there is a pool and the view is superb; ring to reserve and make sure to order your meals. Another spot where you will find very basic accommodation (cabins and tent-space) and a serene atmosphere, is **Goshen Wilderness Resort**, lost in the country to the south of Ocho Rios (signed off the White River Road).

Very cheap rooms and camping space are available to the east of Oracabessa, in Port Maria, at **Mike's Sea Lawn Coral Beach**, which offers simple rooms with cold water only, and meals to order. There's some snorkelling down on the reef.

Eating Out

expensive

Ocho Rios boasts few good restaurants outside the hotels. The most pleasant, for its setting high above the lights of Ocho Rios in a charming old 1860s house, is **Evita's**, ✆ 974 2333, which you enter through an arbour of four-poster bedposts. You can dine outside on a vine-hung veranda, or in the attractive wooden interior with its stained-wood floor and louvres. The fare is Italian, including dishes from a classic *fettucine Alfredo* to a *Fra Diavolo*, but there are also some Caribbean–Italian combinations—*pasta escovicha* and *lasagne rastafari*. Perhaps the best known restaurant in town is **The Ruins**, ✆ 974 2442, on da Costa Drive. It gets very crowded, so it's hardly one for a romantic meal *à deux*, but it has a delightful setting: wicker chairs and tables on a deck by a floodlit waterfall beneath huge fig trees, with the sounds of the water and the occasional serenade. The fare is partly international (*coq au vin*, lamb chops in mint sauce) and otherwise Chinese (including the chef's special dish of lotus lily lobster).

The **Almond Tree** restaurant, at the lower end of this price category, also has a very sympathetic setting at the Hibiscus Lodge Hotel, on the main street of Ocho Rios. You dine on a terrace high above the sea, with gingerbread fretwork surrounded by greenery and a huge almond tree. Pumpkin soup is followed by snapper or kingfish in coconut and then a volley of tropical fruit ice creams.

In the garden of the Carib Inn, ☏ 974 0236, on the main strip in Ocho Rios you will find **Minnie's** vegetarian and seafood restaurant. Minnie used to have a very popular health food restaurant in Kingston, but now has brought her brand of Jamican vegetarian food to Ocho Rios: vegetable rundown (tropical vegetables and seasoning including pimento, garlic and onion all boiled together in coconut milk) and various seafood dishes, followed by Minnie's herbal teas and tropical fruit juices, all taken on a veranda that looks out onto a huge, fairy-lit tree.

Many of the bars in the town double up as restaurants and so you can take a drink and look at the menu before you decide whether to eat. A bar with a reliable kitchen goes by the odd-sounding name of **Bibirips**. This tin-roofed TV-bar has a balustraded seating area on the clifftop just behind a car park; the menu is plain and wholesome Jamaican food. You might think that it was just another over-imaginative T-shirt, but in fact there really is a **Hard Rock Café** in Ocho Rios. It offers simple fare, such as grilled fish and shrimp fettuccine, and a long list of cocktails, which you can take around the waterfall, or sip while making use of the pool table.

For something a little more Jamaican you can try one of the two jerk centres. The **Double V** is very touristy and lunch comes complete with MC accompaniment, loud music and embarrassing dancing competitions. A much more low-key spot, also popular with the locals after work is the **Ocho Rios Jerk Centre** near the 'roundabout' to Kingston. There are also plenty of more authentic Jamaican restaurants, all-day diners and bars around the town: **Parkway** Restaurant, on Main Street, is a true West Indian dining room, air-conditioned, with the television playing and tables set with plastic table-mats. Enjoy the Jamaican chicken or a fried rice and shrimp followed by banana cake. In a similar vein is the **Lobster Pot** just down the road. A rather tired interior displays some interesting decorative touches that include plastic roses in curious vases made of heat-stretched Red Stripe bottles, the occasional lobster hanging in a fishing net and a whole picket fence. It serves outstanding Jamaican food: brown stew fish, fricassee chicken and creole shrimps, presented to you with a tonnage of rice 'n' peas and coleslaw. On weekend evenings people sell cooked chicken at the roadside in Ocho Rios.

Entertainment and Nightlife

Ocho Rios has numerous and varied venues for an evening out. A couple of places popular with the Jamaicans are **Bibirips** (*see* p.165) and **The Mug**, which is west of the town near St Ann's Bay. It attracts a fun crowd, particularly on a Wednesday. In the centre of town you will find **Bill's Place** on Main Street, an easygoing upstairs bar with a loud crowd, or you can head for the trusty **Little Pub**, where you can often hear loud rock music and there are shows in the evening. Two other spots are popular with the locals after work: try the **Ocho Rios Jerk Centre** (*see* p.165) or a rasta spot called the **Jungle** near White River. You are advised to be careful in this area.

The hotels offer plenty of entertainment, and many also have discotheques. Outside you will also find a string of bars and clubs. If you want to try out a Jamaican club, head for the **Acropolis** (pronounced Acro-Palace) on Main Street, the **Limelight** at Burger King plaza, or best of all the **Roof Club** on St James's Avenue, an open-air lounge and roof top terrace where you will hear the latest sounds on the Jamaican scene, as well as some more traditional reggae. For something a little more sultry, a dose of Jamaican go-go dancing, you can try the **Wicky-Wacky Club**. There are occasional concerts at the **White River Reggae Park**.

West Of Ocho Rios

The country to the west of Ocho Rios is only developed along the coast: there are a number of small Jamaican towns sprinkled along the coast road, and resorts have clustered around the beaches at Runaway Bay and Discovery Bay. Inland, up in the range of hills that rises soon after you leave the coastal strip, you pass into immensely fertile and beautiful country, where cultivation gives over to forested land and only the occasional orange scar of a bauxite mine interrupts the green of the natural country. It seems a world away from the tourism of the coastline. Among the old stone walls and occasional gate-posts of the mostly defunct plantations you still see people riding donkeys or walking, cutlass in hand, on their way to cultivate their patch. Passers-by are rare enough that sometimes they will simply stop and stare with curiosity. It is easy to break the ice, though: simply wave.

The main concentration of resort hotels is around Runaway Bay, about 20 miles beyond Ocho Rios, but there are other places to stay as you drive the north coast road. You will find a string of good bars and travellers' rest stops, and an endless selection of 'Dunn's River Falls shoe-hire' shops.

It is quite easy to get either way along the north coast to Runaway Bay or Discovery Bay. You leave from the normal **bus** terminals, at the roundabout and the clock tower, and the driver will drop you off where you want. If you are making short journeys along the coast there are plenty of **share taxis** during the day—you simply wave them down like everyone else (but check the fare with a Jamaican beforehand). There is a **car hire** company in Runaway Bay, **Rising Bird**, ✆ 973 5492, but remember that any of the large companies will deliver a car to you from one of the main towns. Most **tour** companies will pick you up from here if you want to go on an organized day trip. Alternatively, if you would prefer to travel independently rather than in a minibus, you can fix a trip with a taxi driver (*see* p.154).

There are no official **tourist information** offices or booths in the Runaway Bay and Discovery Bay area, but you should be able to find out all you need from the hotel lobbies. You will also be dependent on hotels for **banking** and tourist **shopping**.

Beaches and Watersports

Priory Beach is passable and there is a delightful strip of sand in **Salem** (not Paradise Beach, but the one opposite the Shell petrol station). Both of these are undeveloped. **Runaway Bay** has some good sand, mostly taken over by the hotels. Beyond here there is a good public beach that charges an entry fee, at **Puerto Seco** in Discovery Bay. It's lively at the weekends; there is gently shelving sand, which makes for good swimming, a snack bar and changing rooms, but no watersports.

If you would like to do a bit of sailing or windsurfing you are really dependent on the hotels and, as many of these are all-inclusive, this is not easy. Try **Club Caribbean**, ✆ 973 4845, or ask around. Pirate cruise trips depart from Discovery Bay, and also **deep-sea fishing**; contact **Pirate Cruises**, ✆ 973 2007.

Scuba-diving is available through **Jamaqua** at Club Caribbean and through **Reef Divers**, ✆ 973 5636. There are **stables** in Runaway Bay, the **LA Equine Centre**, ✆ 973 2498.

Ocho Rios to Runaway Bay

Travelling west from Ocho Rios on the coast road, the first town you reach is **St Ann's Bay**, capital of the Parish of St Ann. The town is the birthplace of Marcus Garvey, the Jamaican national hero and founder of the UNIA (*see* **History**, p.89) and his statue stands in front of the town library. A mile or so beyond the town you come to the site of Sevilla la Nueva, founded in 1510, the first Spanish settlement on Jamaica. The site, comprising the remains of the fortified governor's house, the church and a sugar mill, is attached to Seville Great House and Heritage Park. **Seville Great House**, built in about 1750 as a plantation house, stands high above the coast and has a magnificent view of the sea; its original wattle and daub walls still exist beneath the plaster. It now houses a museum, **Maima-Seville**, commemorating the many influences that have contributed to Jamaica's heritage (Taino Indian, African and European), with a video presentation and exhibits.

Inland the land rises quickly and becomes farmland. The town of Nine Mile, on the road between Alexandria and Claremont, is famous as the birthplace of Bob Marley. Here, on the hillside you will find the **Bob Marley Mausoleum**, *adm, no video cameras*, where you'll be hustled like mad and told all sorts of tall stories. In **Brown's Town** there is a cut-stone and wood local church standing opposite a classic Caribbean iron market (to which the local farmers bring their produce from the hills around).

Back on the coast road you will come to the resort area of **Runaway Bay**, where there is a small cluster of beach hotels and some easygoing restaurants. There is some dispute as to how Runaway Bay got its name. One theory holds that it was here that the last Spaniards gathered before making a break for Cuba, 90 miles to the north, another that it was a group of African slaves who fled. Either way, they are supposed to have holed up in **Runaway Caves**, *open 9–5, adm*, not far away. The 7 miles of limestone caves have been used by the Arawaks and pirates, runaway slaves or escaping Spaniards, and latterly disco-goers. Among the rather tired stalactites and gooey waterfall limestone formations you will see animals set in stone (rhinos, rabbits and eagles), and there is an underground lake. The caves are firmly on the tourist trail, but merit a visit for a swim in the Green Grotto, and for a look at the extraordinary and alarmingly long snake-like, thigh-thick fig tree roots that have made their way down through the cave roof in search of water.

Discovery Bay is a small settlement with a beach (Puerto Seco). The bay is claimed to be the site of Columbus's arrival in 1494, though many disagree. Just beyond the bay (and the bauxite shipment quay) you come to **Columbus Park**, *adm free*, a museum, with snack bar and craft shops. The exhibits are a little disappointing at first: just a few rather sad old artefacts standing around at the roadside. They repay another look, however, as they are extremely well selected and together give an excellent understanding of Jamaican agricultural and industrial history.

All along this stretch of the coast you will pass rum shops, fruit stalls and places where you can get a beer and a local meal. At the small town of Rio Bueno the road crosses the Rio Bueno River and passes into the Parish of Trelawny.

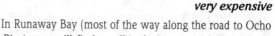

Where to Stay

very expensive

In Runaway Bay (most of the way along the road to Ocho Rios), you will find an all-inclusive resort devoted especially to children at **FDR** (Franklyn D. Resort), PO Box 201, ☎ 973 3067, ✉ 973 3071, a 'giant step for kid kind'. A 'girl Friday' supervises finger painting, tiny tots' computer programming, kiddies' disco technique or simply runs them around until they tire out so that you can busy yourself with more important things like windsurfing and sitting at the pool bar. She also cooks and babysits for you. There is a small, not terribly agreeable beach (at the time of viewing) and the resort has 76 modern, high-pastel suites in a variety of configurations (one-, two- and three-bedroom suites).

If you would like a comfortable stay in a quiet, adults-only resort for a couple of days, try the **Allamanda Inn**, PO Box 65, Runaway Bay, ☎ 973 4030, ✉ 973 5195, where you will find very pretty suites in vine-covered blocks surrounded by a tropical garden. Allamanda is not on the beach, but all the usual facilities are available through a nearby hotel, for the all-inclusive rate.

The **Eaton Hall Beach Hotel and Villas**, PO Box 112, ☎ 973 3503, ✉ 973 2432, US and Canada reservations ☎ 1 800 Jamaica, has an Edwardian atmosphere a little unexpected in the tropics; the main house has dark floors and beams, and even a fireplace in the foyer. It sits on low cliffs, with its 52 rooms and 5 villas ranged to either side in two-storey blocks. The pool and bar stand above the waves, and there is a diminutive but inviting beach (some watersports available), cut into the cliffs. Rooms are comfortable, with four-posters and wooden floors. The package is all-inclusive, but the pace is relaxed.

moderate

Portside Resort and Villas, PO Box 42, Discovery Bay, ☎ 973 2007, ✉ 973 2720, is a small and concentrated cluster of pointy-topped villas in the town overlooking Discovery Bay. They vary in size from one bedroom to five; you can cater for yourself or use the central hotel facilities. The central dining room is right on the waterfront and the resort has its own beach, next to the main Puerto Seco beach. Cooks are available.

The **Runaway HEART Club**, PO Box 98, Runaway Bay, ✆ 973 2671, ✉ 973 2693, in a stately house surrounded by extensive, well-tended gardens a short way in from the coast, has the feel of Old Jamaica. There are just 20 comfortable rooms with balconies, air-conditioning and phones, but no TVs. A shuttle takes you to the beach. The service is energetic and enthusiastic if a little raw, as most of the staff are drawn from the hotel training school next door. It is a quiet and fun place to stay.

inexpensive

The **Salem Resort**, ✆ 973 4256, ✉ 973 5017, has a slightly unfortunate position right on the road in Salem, east of Runaway Bay, but offers comfortable rooms with TVs and balconies in a modern block at reasonable prices; meals are available.

cheap

The **Villa la Rose**, Runaway Bay, ✆ 973 3216, offers outstanding value and a friendly reception. It is set in a modern house and the nine rooms are carpeted and simply decorated. There are ceiling fans and hot and cold water. You can cook for yourself or eat out nearby.

Eating Out

 Eating out is quite limited in this area (outside the hotels, many of which are all-inclusive anyway) and so your best bet is to try the local Jamaican places. In Runaway Bay, the **Seafood Giant** (*moderate*), set in an octagonal gazebo, often has a good mix of tourists and locals, and is known for its fish dishes, fried and steamed.

There is a good **jerk centre** opposite the entrance to the Green Grotto. You will find a few breezy shacks on the waterfront in the area, where you can pick up a fish and bammy. And as you head farther west you will pass the travellers' rest stops; they serve good plain but quite expensive fare. Nightlife is really limited to the hotels, though the occasional concert is staged around the place if you want a real Jamaican experience.

Port Antonio and the Eastern Tip

The eastern tip of Jamaica is the greenest and most fertile part of an overwhelmingly green country. Here, above the banana walks and canefields and the massive river beds and gulleys, the hillsides are rampant with greenery: a restless undergrowth of shrubs and grasses sprouts; overgrowth, blanket-like vines, creep up trees and smother fences. The tree trunks themselves soar out and create a canopy high above, but even they are tangled with lianas and vines. Tree ferns and orchids explode from any convenient anchor—trunks, branches, even telegraph wires. For those unaccustomed to the tropics, all this is astoundingly lovely. Errol Flynn, who lived in this part of Jamaica, declared it more beautiful than any woman he had ever known.

For most of its history, the region has been an agricultural backwater and Port Antonio a dozy town. Suddenly, late in the last century, the banana trade flourished and Port Antonio boomed. Travellers came too: they used the banana boats to escape the northern winter cold, and Port Antonio became the grandfather of Caribbean tourism. The area later enjoyed momentary popularity in the fifties and sixties, when it was visited by the Hollywood crowd.

Many parts of the east are still very simple and undeveloped, where the locals tend their farm plot and wash their clothes in the rivers by hand. It is a friendly place; people wave and greet you wherever you go. There are just a few top- and mid-range hotels here, set in magnificent gardens. Port Antonio and Portland offer beauty and relaxing surroundings unrivalled anywhere else on the island.

History

The Spaniards settled the area of Port Antonio, but it remained undeveloped for a long time after the English took the island in 1655. Pirates used the magnificent coves on the coastline to hide out, and the area was threatened regularly by invading forces from the islands nearby. There was also danger from the Windward Maroons in the mountainous interior, who waged a guerrilla war for nearly a century after the English arrived. Led by Nanny and two other leaders, Quao and Kofi, they made their raids from Nanny Town until it was destroyed by the British in 1734. In 1739 Quao negotiated a peace treaty with the British.

The Parish of Portland was formed in 1723, named after the Duke of Portland, who was governor of the island at the time. To encourage settlers, land grants were made, with tax breaks and incentives such as 'four barrels of beef and 400lbs of biscuit or bread' for each colonist, and 'a barrel of herrings and 400lbs of biscuit or bread' for each slave, so there would be food until the crops ripened.

This fertile region was the original home of one variety of the pineapple. And Captain Bligh (he of the famous mutiny) brought the breadfruit tree to the Botanical Gardens in Bath in St Thomas in 1793. The Society of West Indian Merchants had commissioned him to bring the tree to Jamaica so that its fruit could be used as food for slaves. Bligh also brought the otaheite apple, which bears a red fruit shaped like a pear but with crispy flesh like an apple.

But it was for bananas that the area became best known. This fruit was first exported to Boston in the 1860s by Lorenzo Baker, a sea captain who, delivering a cargo of salted cod and other material, managed to turn a quick profit on a small load of bananas. He founded the Boston Fruit Company, subsequently a part of the United Fruit Company, which shipped bananas to the States from all over the Caribbean and Central America. The trade was so valuable that bananas were known as 'green gold'—bananas were loaded unripe, when they were still green and ripened to yellow during the voyage. At the beginning of this century five million bunches of bananas were exported annually, but the trade was killed in the 1920s by Panama Disease. The UK has imported most of the Jamaican banana crop since the thirties and most American bananas come from the Central American republics.

A by-product of banana trade was the beginning of the 20th century's fastest growing industry—tourism. Visitors poured in on the banana boats to escape the northern winter cold. In the season Port Antonio was the most fashionable place to be, patronized by the likes of Rudyard Kipling and Randolph Hearst. It was even important enough to have an American consulate. The decline of the banana trade in the thirties meant fewer boats and so fewer visitors. In the fifties the film star Errol Flynn took over the remains of the old Titchfield Hotel (by then called the Jamaica Reef) and bought Navy Island in the West Harbour to use as his private home; for a while the glamour returned with his parties, attended by such stars as Bette Davis and Ginger Rogers.

Getting There

Buses serve the coastal road in both directions to Port Antonio, ending up at the terminal on the Eastern Harbour (on Foreshore Road). There is a direct link from Montego Bay, stopping in Ocho Rios at 6–6.30pm and arriving in Port Antonio about 9pm; it leaves again the next morning at 6–7. At other times of the day you will have to make hops on smaller buses or in the **share taxis**. If you are coming to Port Antonio from Kingston you can approach either around the eastern tip (with **K Sons Company**, the red and blue buses; departing from King Street, south of the Parade; other services also go to Morant Bay) or across the mountains, on the Junction road via Castleton. If you intend to pick these buses up along the route, bear in

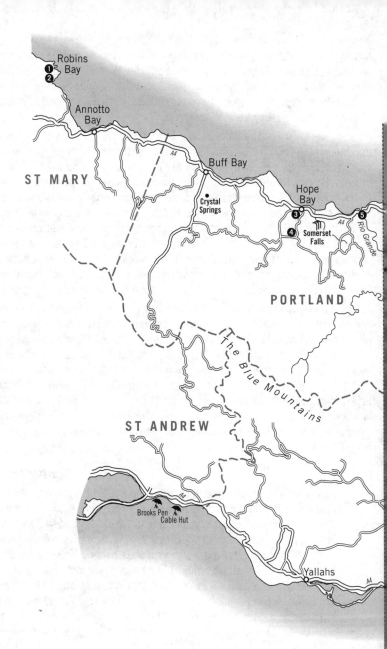

ST MARY

Robins
Bay

Annotto
Bay

Buff Bay

A4

Crystal
Springs

Hope
Bay

Somerset
Falls

Rio Grande

PORTLAND

The Blue Mountains

ST ANDREW

Brooks Pen
Cable Hut

A4

Yallahs

A4

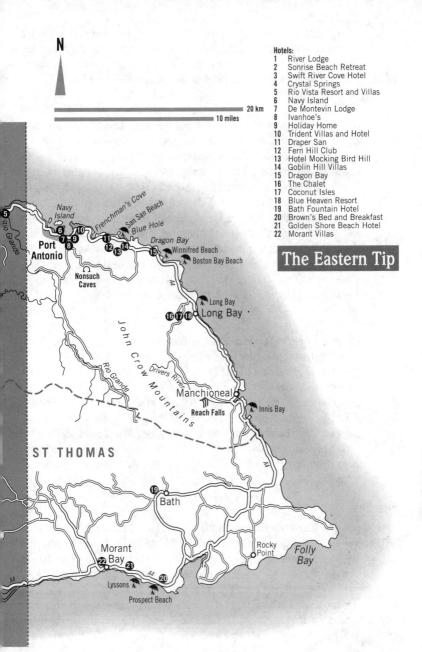

N

20 km
10 miles

The Eastern Tip

Rio Grande

Navy Island

Frenchman's Cove

San San Beach

Blue Hole

Port Antonio

Dragon Bay

Winnifred Beach

Boston Bay Beach

Nonsuch Caves

John Crow Mountains

Rio Grande

Long Bay

Long Bay

Drivers River

Manchioneal

Reach Falls

Innis Bay

ST THOMAS

Bath

Morant Bay

Rocky Point

Folly Bay

Lyssons

Prospect Beach

177

mind that they run early from Kingston to Port Antonio and then late in the afternoon in the opposite direction. Within Portland you can catch local services and share taxis along most roads. To the south there are plenty of services plying the coast road between Kingston and Morant Bay.

Getting Around

Car hire companies in Port Antonio include **Don's Car Rentals**, © 992 2241, at the Trident resort, **Derron's Car Rentals**, © 993 7111, in Drapers and **Eastern Car Rentals**, © 993 3624, in town. For **motorbikes** contact **Portland Bike Rentals**, © 993 3768. If you need a **taxi** in Port Antonio you can contact: **Sunshine Taxi**, © 993 2123, **Koolkats**, © 993 2403, and **JUTA**, © 993 2684. Elsewhere it is best to book one through the lobby of a hotel. The companies above and individual drivers will also take you on a day tour of the area. Alternatively you can contact one of the specialist tour agencies; their tours include trips to Reach Falls, river rafting on the Rio Grande, tours to Kingston, or sights around Ocho Rios such as Dunn's River Falls. Contact: **Adventure Tours**, © 993 3369, **Attractions Link**, © 993 2102, or **JUTA**, © 993 2684.

Tourist Information

There is a helpful **Jamaica Tourist Board office** right in the centre of town, upstairs in the City Centre Plaza on Harbour Street, © 993 3051, ✉ 993 2117. As always the staff in the hotels will help out with queries. In a **medical emergency** there is an accident and emergency room at the General Hospital on Naylor's Hill, © 993 2646, in Port Antonio. For less urgent treatment contact Dr Valenti, © 993 2135. For foreign exchange there are three **banks** right in the centre of Port Antonio; otherwise there are banks in Morant Bay on the south coast and one in Buff Bay. If you wish to go **shopping** you will find boutiques in many of the hotels. For something more ethnic, you can try out the Musgrave market in Port Antonio.

Beaches

The finest beaches in the eastern area, and probably in Jamaica, are close to Port Antonio. There are two good beaches within a shout of the centre of the town: take a boat across to **Navy Island** (*small fee*) and then walk around to the north side of the island. There you will find a small and attractive strip of sand, with shallow water and good snorkelling; also a small bar for drinks. Navy Island has a clothes-optional beach as well, which is secluded but pebbly. **Jamaica Reef** beach (named after an old hotel) on Titchfield Hill, looks over to Navy Island, where there is a narrow strip of sand.

The most exquisite beach on the island is **Frenchman's Cove**, in a charming bay a few miles east of Port Antonio. The sand is good and the cove itself is a bottleneck, shielded from the open water by small headlands that hang with greenery, forming a protected swimming area. But its real attraction is the creek that winds lazily into the corner of the bay from inland, its banks lush with tall trees and sumptuous grass. There is a bar serving food and drinks. **San San** beach is really reserved for the guests of certain hotels around the area. You are permitted onto **Dragon Bay** beach, however, where you will find another protected, bottleneck cove with steep-sided walls and a strip of golden sand. There is a beach bar where you can get lunch and drinks and a watersports shop, **Lady G'Diver**, ✆ 993 9624, that offers scuba-diving, snorkelling (they will take you to Monkey Island, not far off), and boating in kayaks and small sailboats. They also organize trips to Alligator Head, to see the schools of parrotfish and snappers, and excursions to Fairy Hill.

In between San San and Dragon Bay you come to the **Blue Hole** (*see* p.183). **Winnifred Beach**, in the village of Fairy Hill, is also popular as a weekend hangout, with a number of bars. It is approached down a very rough road (turn opposite the Jamaica Crest Resort and then immediately right). A little farther down the coast, **Boston Bay** is best known as the home of jerk; it also has a pleasant ribbon of sand in between headlands which channel the waves in (when they get up, surfers go out there and do their stuff). There is a bar on the beach itself and you can always get a meal at one of the jerk stalls on the main road above.

Beyond Boston Bay the shoreline is composed of cliffs occasionally scooped out by bays. The waves, driven by the prevailing northeasterly winds at the eastern end of the island, can get quite rough, following one another in quick succession and hammering against the shore. But because of the offshore reefs, there are good and safe swimming areas along here. **Long Bay** has a charming mile-long sandy beach— good for walking, but be careful about swimming when the tide is going out. There is a bar, **Fisherman Park**, an easy bamboo affair among the palm trees. **Innis Bay** is a deep bay which collects seaweed when the waves are up but the sand is lovely.

With such a huge rainfall, Portland has amazing **inland water** too. There are a number of well-known falls, including Somerset Falls to the west of Port Antonio and the more attractive Reach Falls in the east, but there are dozens of others which can be found by asking or by taking an organized tour.

Watersports

There are limited watersports in the area, and for them you will be entirely dependent on the hotel concessionaries. For **snorkelling** in the Port Antonio area, try Navy Island, Monkey Island at San San, and Winnifred Beach. The hotels will be able to fix you a sailing trip or a sunset cruise. If you want to go **deep-sea fishing**, Port Antonio is the place to do so; contact *Bonita II,* ✆ 993 3086.

But the area is best known for the **river rafting** on the Rio Grande, ✆ 993 2778, *expensive, be there by 3pm*); this was the place where river rafting was first done for pleasure, early this century. For many years rafts were used for the transportation of bananas down to the sea, where the fruit was loaded onto boats bound for the US. The Rio Grande is a long ride (7 miles, which takes around 2½hrs depending on how long you stop to swim). The trip starts in Berrydale (off the road inland from Port Antonio) and winds down to the coast, ending at the Rafter's Rest restaurant. Tickets are available both at Rafter's Rest and at Berrydale and the company will transport your vehicle to the end of the river. Along the way you can expect to see banana plantations, canefields and the Tunnel of Love, a narrow passage between rock formations. You might even be able to persuade the raftsman to sing the traditional working song, sung by the banana packers as they loaded the boxes onto the ships, and made famous by Harry Belafonte: 'Day-oh, Daylight come and me wanna go home'.

Land Sports

For **hiking** in the forests and valleys around Port Antonio, contact **Valley Hikes**, PO Box 89, Port Antonio, ✆/✉ 993 2543, 999 7529, who arrange a number of guided hikes in the Rio Grande valley, between the Blue Mountains and the John Crow Mountains. Walks vary from day outings to three- or five-day hikes. Along the routes you will pass through plantations (much of the walking is on farmers' trails) and rainforest, and you can expect to see caves, birds and endless waterfalls; guides are local, experienced birders, botanists and herbalists. Valley Hikes is a non-profit-making organization, which also runs a sponsor-a-tree programme: a tree, marked with your name, is planted and maintained for two years along one of the trails (*fee US$10*). Valley Hikes also arranges **horse-riding**. Other stables in the Port Antonio area include the **Bonnie View Hotel**, ✆ 993 2752. A **bicycling** tour with a difference (a specifically downhill tour this one) is arranged by **Blue Mountain Tours**, ✆ 974 7075. The run starts at 5000ft, near the Hardwar Gap, winds down through coffee plantations and the 'rainy forest', into gulleys and over ridges and finishes at a waterfall for a swim. It's all a bit tame and quite expensive, but you get a good view of the Blue Mountains, with brunch along the way.

Port Antonio

Framed by the massive, forested slopes of the John Crow and the Blue Mountains, and set on a charming double harbour, the quiet and faded town of Port Antonio is one of the prettiest on the island. Unlike the major tourist resorts, it has a serene,

unhurried and unhustled atmosphere. Port Antonio was famously described by author Ella Wheeler Wilcox as the 'most exquisite port on earth'.

Port Antonio is the capital of Portland Parish and the largest town in eastern Jamaica, but it is by no means a busy place. Its charming hotels, villas and small guest houses are dispersed along the coast, mainly to the east, tucked in the pretty coves and dotted, stark white against the green, across the fertile hillsides. Port Antonio has a number of fantastic—even grotesque in some cases—modern villas, and a few older houses, now in a state of distressed decay, steadily being reclaimed by the onward march of tropical greenery.

Around the Town

Port Antonio's name derives from an original Spanish name. The bays on which the town sits were called Puerto Anton and Puerto Francisco. For a while under the British the town was renamed Titchfield (after the estate of the Governor, Lord Portland), but now this name is only used to refer to the peninsula between the two bays, which is occasionally called Titchfield Hill.

The most attractive area of the town is on 'the Hill', and much of it was built at the turn of the century. There you will find the classic Caribbean timber-frame and brick houses with large verandas and gingerbread fretwork or cast-iron filigree. Standing on the point and covering the eastern approaches, Fort George was a formidable fortress in the 1730s. Now it is just a few embrasures and some mean-looking cannon on rollers, and has been turned into Titchfield School. The remains of the old Titchfield Hotel are also still visible (most of the original buildings were dismantled and the pieces sold off) in the form of two old swimming pools and a waterslide linking them. In its heyday at the beginning of the century, the Titchfield stood five storeys high with verandas on all sides and had 400 rooms. There was an Italian orchestra to play at mealtimes and a massive ballroom.

Across a narrow channel offshore is one of Jamaica's most charming spots, **Navy Island**. Originally it was called Lynch's Island, but it took the new name from its use by the navy, who built warehouses and defensive positions there (of which nothing remains). The ferry goes on request from West Street, *small fee*, and you can spend the afternoon on the beach or have a drink in the evening. Upstairs in the hotel building you will see posters from Errol Flynn's films and some maps of Navy Island when it was fortified.

The **town centre** of modern Port Antonio is around the war memorial at the head of West Street and here the taxi men and town folk gather to chat; directly opposite you will find Musgrave Market, in a huge red-tin-roofed building. It is always worth a visit, but liveliest on Thursdays and Saturdays. The other main gathering point is Court House Square, just 60 yards away, where there is a clock tower and behind it the court house, a grand imperial building. The view from the Bonnie View Hotel is superb and it is an ideal spot for a late-afternoon drink. Port Antonio is still the main shipping port for bananas and you will see the huge Fyffes and Jamaica Producers banana boats in the western harbour a couple of times a week.

Leaving the town to the west, the main road passes the old railway building and then the town's small industrial estate before it winds along the coast. The **Rio Grande** is Jamaica's largest river (it drains both the Blue Mountains and the John Crow Mountains), but it is best known for river rafting. Here you can enjoy a leisurely ride down the river, punted by a raftsman through the banana plantations and Portland's amazing fecundity (arranged at Rafter's Rest just off the main road, *see* p.186). But as you go down, spare a thought for the apprentice raftsmen who have to haul the rafts the 7 miles back upstream (apparently after five years they get a licence to raft people downstream).

Just south of Port Antonio, on an extremely rough and winding road which climbs into the hills, are **Nonsuch Caves** and **Athenry Gardens**, *open daily 9–5, adm expensive*; neither is that exciting. The caves have a series of chambers (home to a small colony of bats) with limestone stalactite and stalagmite formations in the shape of an owl, a woman with a basket on her head and organ pipes, which really ring. There is an impressive frozen waterfall or flowstone that closely resembles the formations at Dunns River Falls. The gardens have just a few trees including pimento, also called allspice—the reason for the name becomes clear when the guide crushes a leaf for you. There is a magnificent view of the town and the mountains from the building that used to house a restaurant (*now closed*).

If you head due south out of the town, you cross over into the Rio Grande Valley, the area between the Blue Mountains and the John Crow Mountains. Almost at the top of the road is the Maroon settlement of **Moore Town**. This land was granted to the Windward Maroons by the British Crown when they signed the Peace Treaty in 1739. Before this they lived in Nanny Town, far higher in the mountains, which was rediscovered recently. You no longer need the express permission of the

Maroon Colonel to visit Moore Town. Nowadays the inhabitants live a life very similar to all other Jamaicans. Most of their old customs are steadily being forgotten—for example the ceremonies to invoke their ancestors with drum-driven possessions—as is their language, which is descended directly from Coromantee. **Bump Grave**, opposite the school, is really the only 'sight'. It is supposed to contain the remains of Nanny; an inscription describes her as the 'indomitable and skilled chieftainess of the Windward Maroons who founded this town'. The villagers are in the process of building a museum to illustrate the Maroon story. **Nanny Falls** can be found at the end of the road (you have to walk about '30 chains'—a kilometre). **Jupiter Falls**, lost in the densest greenery, and a rockpool where you can swim, are in the next valley.

Port Antonio has not entirely lost the mystique and attraction that it once held for the world's rich and famous travellers. Some still own villas here, which you will see standing out bright white against the green of the hillsides to the east of the town. Leaving Port Antonio to the east, the road passes a ruin at **Folly Point**. Romantic stories circulate about the house: it was built of concrete mixed with seawater which then crumbled; it was a dream home built and abandoned before it was occupied. In fact Folly was lived in early this century and, far from crumbling, the indoor swimming pool is still set with the original Tiffany tiles.

Over the next few miles the road winds past estates with magnificent villas, such as Alligator Head, the point just before San San beach. About mile or so further on you will come to one of Jamaica's most famous sights, the **Blue Hole**, *adm unless you go to the restaurant*, which has been reopened for visits. The Blue Hole is about 100 yards by 50, hung on all sides with greenery. It is 185ft deep (despite rumours of bottomlessness), mainly filled with sea water but fed by a cold river, giving mixed patches of warm and cold water. But the fascination of the Blue Hole is its fantastic colour: between turquoise and azure. The swimming is good here, and there is a bar and restaurant.

The main road continues along the coast and inland, touching tranquil villages and sedate settlements. **Boston Bay** is traditionally the home of jerk (*see* p.60) and the site of the original jerk centres. Long Bay, a sleepy place stretched along a charming beach, did not even have telephones at the time of writing. Manchioneal is a diminutive fishing village, quiet now but the scene of rebellion and executions in the outbreak of 1865, and, just beyond here, at the bridge over the Driver's River you turn inland to **Reach Falls**, *adm*, a couple of miles up into the hills along a road that meanders among the coconut plantations. The falls are spectacular: the water tumbles 25 feet over a steep convex slope into a deep pool of blue-green water surrounded by hanging greenery. You can climb the river gulley for quite a way, *additional charge*, and there are plenty of other pools in which to take a dip (many of them better than Reach Falls themselves).

The hotels around Port Antonio are smaller and more relaxed than those in the main Jamaican resort towns: there are none of the big, all-inclusive-style hotels here. Some places do offer an all-inclusive plan, but they don't go in for the all-day activity and relentless entertainment offered by the big resorts. There is a good range of places to stay, from the opulent hotels and villas to a variety of basic guest houses, and many are set in magnificent gardens. As always, with the smaller hotels, it is worthwhile negotiating the price, particularly if you are staying for a few days.

very expensive

The **Trident Villas and Hotel**, just east of the town, is one of the most sumptuous spots on the island, PO Box 119, © 993 2602, ● 993 2590, UK reservations Windotel © 0171 730 7144, US reservations © 404 237 4608. There are 12 rooms and 14 cottages set neatly in luxuriantly lawned gardens of palms and pine hedges with roaming peacocks and doves, all on a dramatic ledge of pitted volcanic cliffs. The rooms are exquisitely decorated—tiled, with stained wood panelling and solid furniture in the black and white colour scheme that runs throughout the resort. Ventilation is mainly by fan and sea breeze here, though there is air-conditioning, and each room has its own veranda. There is a charming and very private beach in its own protected inlet, and some sports, including windsurfing, dinghy sailing, scuba and tennis; there's some *luxury* accommodation, particularly the magnificent Imperial Suite.

expensive

The **Hotel Mocking Bird Hill**, PO Box 254, © 993 7267, ● 993 7133, stands high on the hillside a few miles to the east of Port Antonio, and has a magnificent view, nearly 180 degrees wide. The stark concrete of the villa belies the relaxed air, and eco-friendly philosophy of the place. The 10 rooms, with locally made bamboo furniture, pretty floral decorations, balconies and hammocks, are set in 6 acres of forest criss-crossed by paths and scattered with benches. The dining room is on a very attractive balcony and offers exceptional home-made fare: jams, mayonnaise and breads, including rye, sunflower, coconut, even cheese breads, baked in their own solar oven. And inventive Jamaican dishes are served with vegetables from Mocking Bird Hill's own organic garden. It is an extremely peaceful spot and you will be looked after well. **Goblin Hill Villas** at San San, © 925 8108, ● 925 6240; reservations 11 East Avenue, Kingston 10,

✆ 925 8108, 🖶 925 6248, US reservations ✆ 1 800 472 1148, has 28 one- and two-bedroom villas in a 12-acre hilltop setting of charming gardens. Goblin Hill is run more as a villa resort than as a hotel and so there is no central restaurant. The villas have maid service and all meals can be provided, though there are full kitchens if you want to look after yourself. The rooms are comfortable and fan ventilated, on a split level or on two floors, all with patios and many with fantastic views, with air-conditioning in the bedrooms and king-size beds. There are no TVs in the villas, but there is a central TV room. Quite a few families come to the resort so there is a children's play area and some activity programmes. There is a charming bar, where you sit on fan-backed wicker chairs, on a stepped deck that twines around a huge fig tree.

If you would prefer to be on the beach itself, **Dragon Bay**, PO Box 176, Port Antonio, ✆ 993 3281, 🖶 993 3284, is set on a very pretty cove. There are 30 rooms, mostly in one- to four-bedroom villa combinations, athough some rooms alone are available, and they stand on a hillside just above the central pool and restaurant. They are furnished with bamboo in a bright white colour scheme, with fans in the main rooms, and air-conditioning in the bedrooms; some have kitchenettes. The beach is pretty and quite busy; watersports are available there including scuba and small sailing boats. There are two restaurants: a thatch-roofed bar on the beach that serves breakfast and lunch, and a more formal dining room on a terrace for dinner. The **Fern Hill Club**, PO Box 26, ✆ 993 3222, 🖶 993 2257, has 31 rooms and suites in villas high on the hill above San San farther east of the town. The appearance is striking—white-painted villas with sharply-pointed shingle roofs stand out starkly against the greenery of the beautifully forested hillside. The brightly decorated rooms have TVs, fans and air-conditioning, plus some jacuzzis, two pools and tennis courts; the beach down below (reached by shuttle) offers watersports. The central great house, with a restaurant serving international and Jamaican fare, has a magnificent view of the coastline and mountains around. Friendly but rather quiet.

The approach to **Navy Island**, PO Box 188, ✆/🖶 993 2667, still retains the romance of Errol Flynn's day. As you chug across the bay, the cottages hide in the greenery and the central house stands tall beneath the royal palms. There are simple, wooden villas open plan within, with two sides of louvres that can be opened like French windows, and broad verandas; all are called by such whimsical names as Fantasy, Frolic and Pinnacle. The dining room stands on wooden stilts high above the water of the bay. Errol

Flynn lives on, swashbuckling still, on the walls of a small gallery, where there are photos and posters from his films, *Robin Hood* and *Dawn Patrol*.

moderate

Across the channel on Titchfield Hill you will find several smaller hotels and guest houses, some of them set in the classic old Jamaican town houses from the turn of the century, built with shingle tiles and cast-iron balconies. **De Montevin Lodge**, PO Box 85, ✆ 993 2604, has 15 rooms in the three storeys of the red-painted brick house; a couple have their own cast-iron filigree balconies. The wooden stairs and door surrounds and large number of pictures of the British Royal Family, create a Jamaican home atmosphere. Rooms have fan ventilation; all meals are available.

inexpensive

Not far away from De Montevin Lodge is **Ivanhoe's** on Queen Street, ✆/✎ 993 3043, where the 15 rooms are in a modern extension, with plush décor, ceiling fans and hot and cold water, attached to a traditional wooden Jamaican house; all meals are available. To the east of Port Antonio you will find a very small and simple guest house, **Draper San**, ✆ 993 7118, which sits in a pretty garden plot on the roadside in Drapers village, within earshot of the waves in the bay below. It's friendly, with just six rooms, a sitting area and kitchen; Italian food is cooked to order.

The **Holiday Home**, ✆ 993 2882, is set in another traditional wooden house on King Street and has nine rooms and a nice balcony where meals are served. The walls are a bit thin; there are some private baths, with cold water only.A few miles to the west of town, **Rio Vista Resort and Villas**, PO Box 4, St Margaret's Bay, ✆ 993 2244, have just a few one- and two-bedroom cottages, with magnificent views over the Rio Grande river valley or over the sea. The rooms are brightly decorated in white and they are fan-ventilated; with satellite TV and maid service.

cheap

Heading east from Port Antonio you come to **Boston Bay**, where villas with rooms to rent are steadily springing up, and then to **Long Bay**, which has become quite a popular stopover on the 'backpack' circuit. Rooms in private houses are available there, though most are not registered with the Tourist Board. There were no telephones in Long Bay at the time of writing, but you can try **The Chalet** and **Coconut Isles**, both in modern buildings just above the beach. **Blue Heaven Resort**, messages via Port Antonio ✆ 993 9847, offers extremely basic rooms in bamboo cottages on a nice creek.

There are not that many places to eat in Port Antonio. If you want to dine out you will have to go to the hotels.

expensive

Trident Villas serves a six-course candle-lit set dinner of very fine West Indian and continental fare in a subdued and elegant setting. The dining room at the Hotel Mockingbird Hill, **Mille Fleurs**, ✆ 993 7267, set on a charming veranda, offers innovative cuisine using the best of the exotic Jamaican fruits and vegetables: carpaccio of tropical fruits or ackee soufflé followed by a soup (combinations such as tomato and sweet potato) and then an ital rundown or chicken in June plum sauce. The three-course menu has a choice for each course (and always includes a vegetarian dish). The **Navy Island Resort** serves a continental dinner in an excellent setting on a deck above the calm water of the bay.

moderate

There is an Italian restaurant (and part-time lingerie shop) in the middle of town, above the War Memorial square, the **Trattoria Romagna**. Its simple and cavernous dining room has a veranda overlooking the activity of the street, where you can enjoy seafood, pasta and pizzas. *Open every day, lunch and dinner.* **Huntress Marina** serves fish and chicken dinners on a rickety palm-thatch deck that overlooks the harbour.

cheap

Numerous local restaurants in Port Antonio will fix you an excellent rice 'n' peas, a curry goat or an escoveitched fish. **Daddy D's** is a popular local diner; brightly painted, with plastic tablecloths and flowers. **Tri-Me** is another excellent stopover for a stew fish or fry chicken. *Closes early.* If you want an ice cream, try **Cream World** on Harbour Street in town. You can pick up a barbecued chicken leg from the people cooking on braziers on the roadside in town, but if you suddenly feel like a jerk (pork or chicken jerk, that is) you can try **Stop Brap Jerk** on the eastern harbour, where there is a concrete deck under the almond tree, and a fine view.

A few miles east of Port Antonio you come to **Boston Bay**, home of jerk. There are three or four centres on either side of the road—**Sufferer's Jerk Centre**, **Mickey's**, **Shaggy's**, and a little down the road, **Fuzzy's**. You sit on open-air terraces amid the barbecues. Chicken and pork, occasionally other meats, are chopped (hacked to bits) to order and served with a festival roll and a beer to wash it all down.

Entertainment and Nightlife

Port Antonio is generally pretty quiet, that's its speciality, but there are some good bars. A place to catch a pleasant daytime drink or a light meal (salads, sandwiches, or burgers) is the **Rafter's Rest**; its curious classical arches look out over the mouth of the Rio Grande. Try the **Admiralty Club** on Navy Island, for a waterfront cocktail, or the **Huntress Marina**. If you want to go dancing, try **Lexus** on West Street, **Blue Jay's Club**, which is a little sultry or, best of all, the **Roof Club** on West Street, a wild and well hip spot, definitely worth checking out.

Around the Eastern Tip into St Thomas

As you pass around the eastern tip of the island you enter the 'rain-shadow' of the Blue Mountains. Since the prevailing trade winds are northeasterly, most of the rainfall drops onto the northern side, giving the south coast a drier climate, with less lush and sometimes even scrubby-looking vegetation. Even so, it is fertile enough for farmers to grow produce for the markets in Kingston and crops for export. The southeastern tip of the island is blanketed with sugar cane; as you drive you will also pass through many plantations, including bananas and tobacco, and, if you go up into the mountains, coffee. The south coast does not have many tourist facilities, but you will find some perfectly acceptable places to stay and to eat if you are driving through.

Beaches

The beaches along the south coast are a little ragged and not that attractive. At **Lyssons Beach** (pronounced 'licence', but quite innocent really), there is a public section with some facilities and vendors at the weekend, and a private area belonging to the University of the West Indies. **Prospect Beach** is tolerable and **Rocky Point**, near the eastern tip of the island, is a reasonable strip of sand in an attractive bay. It is very remote, at the end of a long detour on rough roads through the cane fields; take your own food and water, though there is sometimes a cook-up in the bar that serves the fishermen. The beaches closest to Kingston, **Cable Hut** and **Brook's Pen**, are pebbly. There is not much in the way of watersports along the south coast; swimming is not bad, as the reef protects you from the swell further out, but the water is sometimes a bit murky. There is the occasional **beach bar** in which to drink and watch the waves: in Port Morant Harbour try **Coconut Place**, a gazebo and domino hang-out across the road from the beach, or better still the **Ship Reck Bar**, a bamboo construction with a view of a freighter that foundered on the reef.

The South Coast

Beyond Manchioneal and the Driver's River the road follows the folds and rises of the dramatic eastern coastline, where the sea rolls in huge breakers over a startlingly blue sea. At the town (blink and you'll miss it) of Hector's River you pass from Portland into the Parish of St Thomas. Soon after this the road turns inland and leads past the town of **Bath**, which two centuries ago was Jamaica's favourite holiday resort because of its hot and cold springs. These are still active and it is still possible to bathe at the Bath Fountain Hotel, *small adm.* It is all a little institutional, with white and red tiles and the constant rush of water behind a line of closed doors, but the water itself is pleasantly warm, slightly viscous and oddly buoyant. With a high content of calcium, magnesium and sodium, the water was known the for the treatment of chronic disorders and skin diseases. It is also high in radioactivity. People do drink the waters—there was even an 18th-century theory (presumably not long-lived) that it made you drunk. It is a short walk from the baths to the springs themselves. There are also rooms (*see* **Where to Stay**, below) and a restaurant where you can have lunch, © 982 8410.

Bath also has the second-oldest botanical gardens in the western hemisphere; the only remnants of these gardens now is a cluster of royal palms and a wall opposite the turning to the Bath Fountain Hotel. The town itself is also fairly dilapidated, but you can still see a few attractive old wooden builings which speak of its former prosperity. From here the road heads south through undeveloped, agricultural country and rejoins the coast at Port Morant, where there are oyster farms in the bay.

Morant Bay

Farther along the coast is Morant Bay, the capital of the parish, a quiet and pleasant town with a small central square set on a rise above the coast. Morant Bay was the site of the famous 1865 rebellion: the court house was burned in a clash between the poor farmers and the local militia and subsequently over 400 people were killed by soldiers or executed on the orders of Governor Eyre. Among them were George William Gordon, the champion of the poor in the legislature, and Paul Bogle, the leader of the rebellion. They were both hanged outside the court house itself; at the time of Independence they became Jamaican national heroes.

The town is quiet—certainly in comparison with Kingston. There is a small historical district comprising the court house, in front of which stands a statue of Paul Bogle, the nearby parish church, and the red-roofed iron-market beyond, where the local produce is sold with customary banter. Leaving the town on the main road, you head west, with the coastline to your left and the steadily rising mountains to your right. As you come into St Andrew Parish you enter the domain of Three Finger Jack, a 7-foot-tall outlaw and folk hero who terrorized the area in the early

1780s, who was so notorious that he became the hero of a pantomime performed in London and Kingston. He ran away from the plantation where he was a slave and became a highway robber, killing travellers and soldiers (though he would never harm women) on the road in this area. Plenty is written about his life and the various attempts to end it, in the historical books that you can find around the island. Jack was eventually hunted down and killed by a Maroon named Quashie, and his head was marched to Spanish Town so that Quashie could collect the reward. From here the road continues to Kingston, crossing into St Andrew Parish at Bull Bay, passing the Palisadoes Peninsula and factories and quarries that make scars in the hillsides above the road, and eventually entering the city.

© (869–)

Where to Stay

inexpensive

You could try **Brown's Bed and Breakfast**, on the main road near mile-post 36, © 982 6205, six rooms with shared bathrooms; friendly and very cheap. Alternatively, the **Bath Fountain Hotel**, Bath Post Office, St Thomas, © 982 8410, is up the gulley from the town of Bath. The rooms, upstairs from the baths and sanatorium, are quite simple and a little institutional, but they open off a nice old wooden corridor. Some have private, some shared bathrooms. A useful stopover for travellers heading around the eastern tip of the island. Some *cheap* rooms.

cheap

A number of guest houses and small hotels are opening up along the southern coast of St Thomas, all signed on the roadside as you head east of Morant Bay. In the town itself, the **Morant Villas**, © 982 2422, is officially recommended, but the **Golden Shore Beach Hotel** on Windward Drive, PO Box 8 Lyssons, St Thomas, © 982 9657, has a bit more style for excellent value. It is on a lovely beach, quiet but with the occasional weekend crowd. The rooms are fairly basic but clean, some with air-conditioning, some fans; all rooms have private baths, but some have only cold water. You sleep to the wash of the waves. There is a bar under the palms, with meals available (order by 6pm).

Eating Out

Eating out is really limited to the hotels and local eateries (e.g. **Chef's Seaview Restaurant and Lounge**, just outside Morant Bay), but there are one or two good beach bars overlooking the harbour at Port Morant. Try **Coconut Place**, set in a small gazebo, and the **Ship Reck Bar** (*see* p.189).

West from Port Antonio

Beyond the Rio Grande you pass beneath the massive shoulders of the Blue Mountains. The main road often touches the coast, and it also follows the track of the old railway, which was destroyed in the early eighties in a hurricane. You will still see the pretty old station buildings in some towns. Take one of the side roads that lead inland, up into the Blue Mountains themselves, where you will find spectacular country and the charm of an older, gentler Jamaica. There is not much in the way of tourism infrastructure in this area, just the occasional modern hotel, but you will find some pleasant roadside restaurants and bars, where you can stop off for a drink or a meal. Over the Rio Grande you pass the Port Antonio airport and then come to **Somerset Falls**, *open 10–5, adm*, just off the main road outside Hope Bay. The water runs bottle-green through pleasant gardens and there is a pool where you can take a dip and then a narrow gulley along which you can swim to some falls (or you can ride it in a boat). The falls are really not that exciting; Reach Falls on the other side of Port Antonio are more impressive.

Crystal Springs, *adm*, is a little farther on, a short drive off the main road past a coconut nursery and banana plantations. It's very much a Jamaican weekend concert and picnic park, nice for a short stop. There is a river running through the gardens, an orchid garden, a pool, a restaurant, and guides to show you around; all a little lacklustre. Buff Bay is now a faded parish town, with a church and a few lovely old wooden buildings in decay. Take the turning up to the Hardwar Gap in the Blue Mountains just after the town on the river for a marvellously scenic drive. Soon after Buff Bay on the main road you pass into the Parish of St Mary and then to the town of Annotto Bay, which takes its name from anatto, a dye-product that was used by the Amerindians tribes as a bright red body-paint. And not long after Annotto Bay the road to Kingston turns south via Castleton and the coast road cuts inland, eventually re-emerging on the coast at Port Maria.

✆ (809–)

Where to Stay

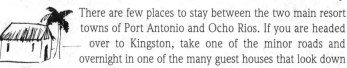

There are few places to stay between the two main resort towns of Port Antonio and Ocho Rios. If you are headed over to Kingston, take one of the minor roads and overnight in one of the many guest houses that look down over the camel-back ridges of the Blue Mountains (*see* p.223).

inexpensive

There is a simple, modern guest house on the scraggy seafront in the Hope Bay area, the **Swift River Cove Hotel**. It has just 10 rooms, with fans and private baths. Slightly inland, in the dramatic setting of huge hills, you will find some very basic accommodation in tin-roofed, timber-framed cabins at

Crystal Springs, ✆ 996 1400; ✆ 929 6280 in Kingston. Hot and cold water is provided in the rooms. There are large open grounds and a central area where you can get all meals. There are two places to stay off the main road in the region of Don Christopher's Point (north of Annotto Bay), a dramatic piece of shoreline. At **Sonrise Beach Retreat**, Robins Bay PO, St Mary, ✆ 999 7169, six cabins are surrounded by palms and wispy pine trees in a sloping lawned garden, above a small central area on the cliffs, with a view stretching down to Annotto Bay, Buff Bay and Orange Bay and beyond to the sunrise. There is a small white-sand beach and good walking around the area, along the coastline and inland to waterfalls. Camping is also available; meals on request. In its former incarnation as Strawberry Fields, Sonrise was a hippy haunt in the seventies. Some say that this is where the Beatles found the name for their song. Some *moderate* rooms.

cheap

Not far off is another very tranquil retreat, **River Lodge**, Robins Bay PO, St Mary, ✆/✉ 995 3003. The five rooms are in the slightly cavernous interior of an old stone building (of unknown origin, though it is unlikely to be a pirate castle, as it is sometimes claimed—because they didn't build them); some rooms share baths, some have open-air showers. The central area with bar and dining room (meals to order) is under thatch. The setting is exceptionally attractive: a valley with a river with freshwater pools for swimming. There are also simple bamboo cabins on the hillside.

Eating out in this area is confined to the places to stay, but there are some cool bars along the coast road. Outside Annotto Bay you might well see people at the roadside selling fruit or small bags of pink 'pepper swims' (shrimps). Do stop and buy some, but negotiate your price.

Kingston to the Blue Mountains

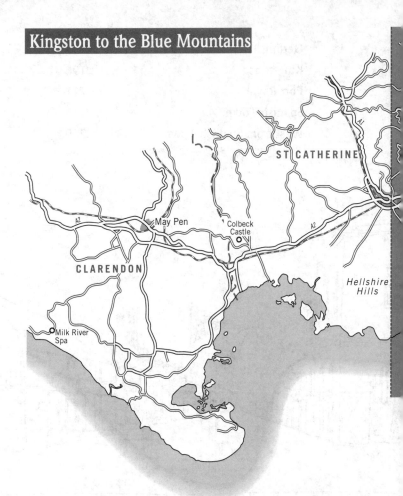

A century ago and more, before tourism switched the emphasis to the north coast, almost all visitors to Jamaica would arrive on the south of the island. Ships would coast beneath the massive peaks of the Blue Mountains and, passing the old buccaneer capital of Port Royal, put in to the magnificent calm of Kingston harbour, one of the largest and finest in the world. Kingston is still the most important city for most Jamaicans, the sprawling, vibrant centre of the island's commercial, political and cultural life. And yet, just a few miles away are some of the calmest and coolest parts of Jamaica, in the Blue Mountains. Here, on the steep cultivated slopes, you will find

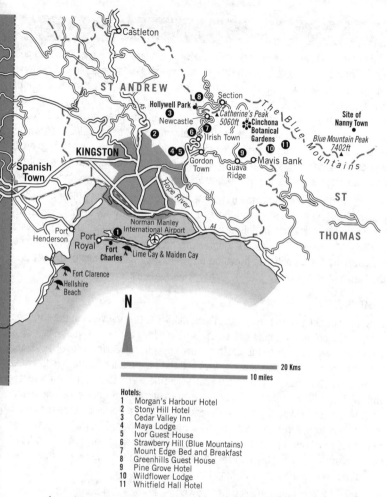

Hotels:
1. Morgan's Harbour Hotel
2. Stony Hill Hotel
3. Cedar Valley Inn
4. Maya Lodge
5. Ivor Guest House
6. Strawberry Hill (Blue Mountains)
7. Mount Edge Bed and Breakfast
8. Greenhills Guest House
9. Pine Grove Hotel
10. Wildflower Lodge
11. Whitfield Hall Hotel

charming and easygoing farming communities. In addition to the world-famous Blue Mountain coffee, farmers grow crops such as cho-cho and lettuce and sell them in the Kingston markets.

This area of the island also has some of Jamaica's most important historical sights. Kingston has surprisingly few, but nearby Spanish Town has a grid of old Jamaican houses built around a square of magnificent Georgian official buildings. And Port Royal, at the tip of the Palisadoes Peninsula, was once so wealthy and illustrious that it was known as the City of Gold and the Treasury of the West Indies.

Kingston

Kingston is the heart of the Jamaicans' Jamaica. It is a large and busy city with a population of around 650,000 which sees all the extremes of Jamaican life. Downtown on the Parade you will find all the excitement and activity of the markets among faded, grand old institutions in the few remaining Victorian buildings. The press is incessant as the busmen shout and the higglers tout their wares; goats wander oblivious and the traffic bobs and weaves; the deafening rap of dancehall is everywhere; an occasional policeman in dark serge trousers and a peaked cap tries to keep order while roving packs of schoolchildren race around him. Close by are some of the island's poorest shanties and 'garrison towns' (which are literally barricaded).

As you head uptown you come to the gleaming air-conditioned offices and shopping malls of New Kingston and, beyond here, set in more spacious grounds, are the walled and fortified villas of the well-to-do on the lower slopes and the ridges of the Blue Mountains. The city is known as the 'corporate area' (the official district of Kingston itself is a small area down on the waterfront and the rest of the city is in the Parish of St Andrew).

History

Kingston has not always been Jamaica's capital. Until the first years of the 18th century, it was an undeveloped stretch of cattle ranches and 'hog styes'. The city of Kingston owes its birth to the death of Port Royal in the earthquake of 1692 and then the fire of 1703. The new city was laid out on a gridiron pattern (still visible between Harbour Street and North Street, and between East and West Streets), and within a few years it had become the commercial centre of the island. Hundreds of ships would put in to Kingston harbour each year and the merchants would look out from scaffold towers or, if they owned town houses, from balustraded lookouts on the roofs, in order to see what ships had come in to trade. Goods would often be shipped from outlying ports on the island, but most merchandise was imported through Kingston.

Kingston quickly outstripped Spanish Town in size. By 1774 there were just over 11000 inhabitants. The Kingston merchants applied to make the city the island's capital in 1754–5; the governor approved, and all the archives were moved to Kingston. But the British king refused to ratify the law and so a couple of years later all the archives had to be moved back again. Eventually Kingston did become the capital of the island in 1872.

Unfortunately, few of the buildings of this era survive. In 1907 the town was comprehensively devastated, firstly by an earthquake, which destroyed the many brick buildings and then by a fire (supposedly fuelled by gas mains ruptured in the quake), which annihilated the wooden ones. About 800 people died. You can see pictures of Kingston before the earthquake (and some shots of the earthquake itself) in old books of postcards and architecture. There were some very attractive old wooden houses with a full streetfront of louvres and others festooned with gingerbread, though Michael Scott of *Tom Cringle's Log* described the actual streets as more like 'dry river-courses than the thoroughfares of a Christian town'. Now it has been completely rebuilt, mostly in concrete, Kingston is not a very attractive city.

The Jamaican Independence celebrations took place in Kingston, at the National Stadium. At midnight on 5 August 1962 the Union Jack was lowered to the strains of a brass band playing tunes such as *Jamaica Farewell*, and the new Jamaican flag was raised in its place.

Getting to Kingston

You can get a direct **bus** connection to Kingston from just about anywhere in Jamaica. Buses arrive and leave from the main bus terminus downtown, a few streets to the west of the Parade, around Princess Street. For Port Antonio, go to the terminal at Half Way Tree and for Morant Bay in the east (and on round the tip of the island and then north into Portland) you should go to King Street, which leads south out of the Parade.

If you do not want to brave the Jamaican bus system, you can always **fly** into Kingston. The city is linked plenty of times each day to all the main towns, on Trans-Jamaica Airways in Kingston, ✆ 923 8680 and 923 9698, 🖷 979 9983. Flights leave from Tinson Pen airport which is in the west of the town, on the Spanish Town Road near Three Mile. If you would like to charter a plane, try Karvin Air, ✆/🖷 978 8405, or call one from the destination you wish to reach (*see* listings in other chapters), and for a **helicopter** contact Helitours in Ocho Rios, ✆ 974 2265, 🖷 974 0306).

Getting Around Kingston

The **buses** in the capital are crowded, hot and chaotic and, with the traffic as it is at present, slow. They will get you almost anywhere, though, if you are happy to put up with all of this. The locals consider them the bane of their lives and any Jamaican who can afford to drives a car.

There are a number of terminals around the town which feed the different areas of the city: downtown at the Parade, Cross Roads, Half Way Tree, Barbican, Papine, at Three Mile and at Duhaney Park. It is possible to get a bus to the Norman Manley International Airport from the Parade and from the terminal at Three Mile. If you want to get to Port Royal you can go by

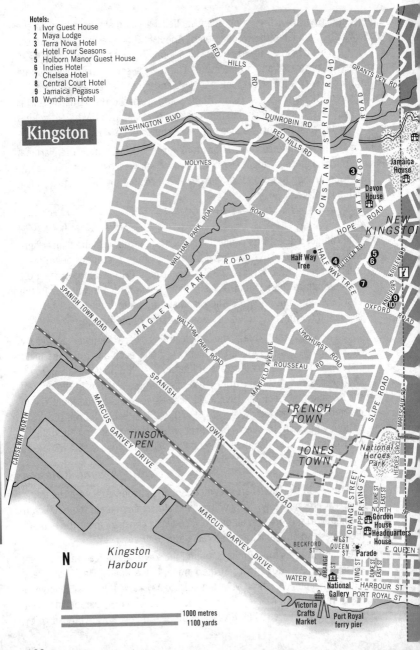

Hotels:
1. Ivor Guest House
2. Maya Lodge
3. Terra Nova Hotel
4. Hotel Four Seasons
5. Holborn Manor Guest House
6. Indies Hotel
7. Chelsea Hotel
8. Central Court Hotel
9. Jamaica Pegasus
10. Wyndham Hotel

Kingston

N

1000 metres
1100 yards

Kingston Harbour

bus (the same one as to the airport), but it is easier to go downtown and to catch the ferry from the waterfront. For Spanish Town you can catch buses from Half Way Tree, on Eastwood Park Road and from Duhaney Park. Transport into the Blue Mountains by bus is limited—services leave from Papine and go occasionally to Irish Town and Red Light below Newcastle and to Gordon Town and Mavis Bank. The (in theory) hourly bus for Jack's Hill leaves from Barbican.

There are plenty of **car hire** companies in Kingston. Contact: **Bargain Rent-a-Car** at 1 Merrick Avenue, Kingston 10, ✆ 968 3617, 🖷 929 4998, airport ✆ 924 8293, US toll free ✆ 1 800 348 5398; **Garmack Car Rentals**, 17 Roosevelt Avenue, Kingston 6, ✆ 978 0278, 🖷 978 0970; **Island Car Rentals**, 17 Antigua Avenue, Kingston 10, ✆ 926 8861, 🖷 926 6987, airport ✆ 924 8075; and **Praise Auto Rentals**, at 72 Half Way Tree Road, Kingston 10, ✆ 929 3580, 🖷 929 3555, US toll free ✆ 1 800 482 9831, Canada toll free ✆ 1 416 396 5540.

Tours

Any number of tours go to Kingston from the tourist towns of the north coast (*see under* relevant towns), or you can make your own arrangement with a taxi driver. Based in Kingston, **Sunventure Tours**, ✆ 960 6685, offers tours of the city and some 'nature' trips including a 'safari' of Port Royal (to the mangroves and to Lime Cay) as well as some hiking excursions to the Blue Mountains and the Cockpit Country.

If you are based in Kingston and wish to explore beyond the area, contact one of town's tour companies. **Galaxy**, ✆ 925 1492, offers a fairly standard menu (river rafting and tours of the major towns on the north coast), and **Jazz-a-Way Tours**, ✆ 929 1052, or ✆ 920 1192, offers some tailor-made trips to less well known parts of Jamaica.

Tourist Information

The main office of the Jamaica Tourist Board is in Kingston, and they have an **information office** in reception: 2 St Lucia Avenue, behind Knutsford Boulevard in New Kingston, ✆ 929 9200, 🖷 929 9375. There is also a desk in the arrivals hall of Kingston Norman Manley airport, ✆ 924 8024.

There are plenty of **banks** around Kingston: the best areas to head for are Knutsford Boulevard in New Kingston and the area of Half Way Tree, or downtown, close to the waterfront. **Post offices** are at Half Way Tree, Cross Roads (at the top of the Slipe Road), in the west on Molynes Road (near the junction of Washington Boulevard), to the east at Liguanea, at the junction of Hope Road and Old Hope Road, and downtown on South Camp

Road. As the capital, Kingston has all the diplomatic representation. Most of the embassies and High Commissions are uptown in the New Kingston area (*see* **Practical A–Z,** p.18).

You should find that your hotel has a doctor on call, if you are in need of **medical advice**. If not, contact the Eureka Medical Centre, © 929 5864, ℗ 929 1836, who run one of a number of air ambulance services on the island, which are affiliated to medical organizations in the States. There are a number of doctors and dentists in Tangerine Place off Half Way Tree Road in New Kingston. Hospitals with accident and emergency departments include the Andrews Memorial Hospital at 27 Hope Road, © 926 7401 (daytime) or © 926 7403 (from 9pm); the University Hospital on the Mona campus, © 927 1620; the Nuttal Memorial Hospital, 6 Caledonia Avenue in Cross Roads, © 926 2139, 926 6210 (at night) and downtown the Kingston Public Hospital on North Street, © 922 0227.

Kingston has a clutch of **shopping** malls in the uptown area; the Island Life Mall on St Lucia Avenue; the New Kingston Shopping Centre on Dominica Drive; the Sovereign Centre in Liguanea; and, on Constant Spring Road, The Springs and the Pavilion Mall. For more regular tourist shopping, try Devon House on Hope Road and the major hotels. The main craft market in Kingston, where you can buy anything from a carving to yet another 'No Problem' T-shirt, is close to the waterfront downtown, just up from the Port Royal ferry terminal. There are some reasonable **bookshops** in Kingston, offering Caribbean books alongside international stock. The best is probably The Book Shop in the Springs Mall on Constant Spring Road, but you can also try the Book Store on Knutsford Boulevard and there are Sangsters bookstores in many of the malls, particularly around New Kingston.

There are some excellent **art galleries** in the New Kingston area. The National Gallery on Orange Street is well worth a look (*see* below). If you would like to buy, you might try the Gallery Pegasus downstairs at the Pegasus Hotel on Knutsford Boulevard or the Frame Centre Gallery in Tangerine Place. The Mutual Life Gallery, in the Mutual Life Building, Oxford Road, is a non profit-making concern that holds an exhibition every month or so of the paintings, sculptures and ceramic work of the Jamaican Artists and Craftsmen's Guild. The Bolivar Gallery and Bookshop, PO Box 413, Kingston 10, © 926 8799, ℗ 968 1874, at 1A Grove Road, just off Half Way Tree Road, exhibits and sells Jamaican art (from stock and temporary exhibitions), furniture, antique prints and maps, and, of course, books.

You'll get the best out of Kingston if you know somebody who lives there—but it is still good to look around the place on your own. The best place to base yourself is really New Kingston, where you will find most of the hotels and guest houses and many of the 'sights'. Be quite cautious at first about getting around town, particularly at night, when it is not a good idea to go out unaccompanied. The atmosphere can be a bit oppressive at times, particularly on the buses, which are worse than they have ever been—the Jamaicans themselves complain about how aggressive and lawless the place is. The easiest way of getting about is to do as the Jamaicans themselves do if they possibly can. Travel by car.

Beaches and Watersports

The closest beaches to Kingston are across the bay to the west. **Fort Clarence**, a strip of light sand backed by sea grape trees, has a couple of bars and a picnic area, and is visited mainly by families at the weekends. There is a small admission charge at Fort Clarence and so many Jamaicans prefer to go a mile or so farther down the coast to **Hellshire Beach**, which sits on a point protected by a reef just offshore. A line of driftwood shacks houses bars and restaurants on the sand. The beach chairs which sit in clusters under the trees are an exercise in Jamaican eccentricity: built of driftwood, they are all 3 feet high and fixed at an impossibly uncomfortable angle. These two beaches are often crowded at the weekends—and people do come here just for the fish or lobster and bammy, which is cooked to order while you chat or take a quick swim. There are no watersports; for these you need to go to the north coast resorts—it's just about possible to make a day trip by bus from Kingston (via Portmore), but quite a trial. Closer to town, but with sparse sand and charging a small admission fee, **Port Henderson** bustles at the weekends, when there is often live music. *See* also **Port Royal**, p.211. There are not many participatory sports on offer around Kingston, but golfers can play at the **Caymanas Park Course** (*green fee*) and those interested in horse-racing can spend an afternoon at **Caymanas Racetrack** (*Wed, Sat and public holidays*). Or you can arrange to to go hiking in the Blue Mountains through **Sense Adventures**, ✆ 927 2097, or **Sunventure Tours**, ✆ 960 6685.

Around the Town

Unlike so many Caribbean towns, which still gravitate around their old harbours, Kingston has entirely lost the romance of the working waterfront. Until 50 years ago almost all visitors would have arrived here on a tender off their ship or seaplane. The famous Myrtle Bank Hotel (opened in 1870 as one of the first tourist hotels in the Caribbean) had gardens that extended right down to the harbour, and was the hub of Kingston social life.

But now that the big passenger liners no longer call (and the freighters put in to the modern docks further west at Port Bustamante), the waterfront is all but dead. The old 'finger' docks which stuck out into the harbour are in decay and just a few characters hang out on Ocean Boulevard, waiting for a quick hustle or the ferry from Port Royal. Since the sixties there has been a gradual shift away from the downtown area as the people and businesses have moved off to New Kingston, and it has become generally run down.

Not far from the waterfront is the **Victoria Crafts Market**, the old red-tin-roofed market building, where the Kingstonians sell their tourist souvenirs: straw hats and wooden carvings, and one or two finer pieces. The **National Gallery**, ✆ 922 1561, *open Mon–Fri, 10–5, adm*, at the foot of Orange Street, has a very impressive display of Intuitive paintings as well as wood carvings by Mallica 'Capo' Reynolds and work by the sculptress Edna Manley. On East Street is the Institute of Jamaica. It is mainly a repository of information and artefacts about Jamaican culture, but it also houses the **National Library**, ✆ 922 0620, *open Mon–Sat, 8.30–4, adm free*, and a natural history museum.

King Street, which was Kingston's main shopping street before the malls grew up in New Kingston, leads from the waterfront up to the **Parade**, the original heart of the town. The Parade is called so because the colonial soldiers would parade here, but it is officially named William Grant Park (after a labour activist prominent in the thirties). The square itself (closed off much of the time) is shaded by trees and it has a number of statues of famous Jamaicans such as Norman Manley and Alexander Bustamante, who used to address the crowds from here during their political meetings. The north side of the Parade is overlooked by the **Ward Theatre**, a white and blue wedding-cake affair which was built after the 1907 earthquake. It is still a working theatre, most loved for the pantomime which plays for about four months each year, starting just after Christmas.

The Parade is also the terminal for Kingston's bus system—chaos. The hawkers tout iced drinks from their handcarts and others walk the aisles with shouts of 'Bag-juice!', 'Box-drink!' and 'Nuts!' or 'Wrigleys!' The busmen practically kidnap you to put you on their bus (your intended destination seems only a secondary consideration). All around the fringes of the square you will also find the main Kingston Market, which spills all over the pavements. Outside the shops of the square and stretching down into King Street, watchmenders, clothes vendors, sweets and cigarette salesmen, music cassette and stationery sellers all tout their wares from countless stalls and from blankets laid out on the pavement. It is mercantile mayhem, *ben dung* plaza at its best. The higglers prefer to lay their wares out on the ground rather than use tables and so you literally have to 'ben dung'. Periodically the higglers, most of whom have come up from the country, are cleared off the street and told to go back into the market buildings and to Princess Street, but they always come back; they prefer it here and trade is better. West of the Parade, past the bus station on Princess Street, are Kingston's poorest shanty towns, or inner city communities as they are

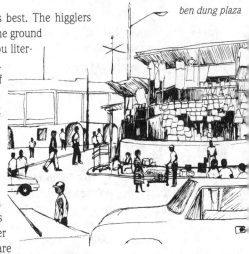

ben dung plaza

known in polite modern parlance. Among them is Trench Town, immortalized by Bob Marley—he lived there when he was an aspiring singer, riding around town on his bicycle selling his latest records. Other 'garrison' towns in this area (because they are literally barrricaded) include Jones Town, Rema, Arnett Gardens (known as the Concrete Jungle) and Tivoli Gardens. These are some of the most depressed areas of Kingston and it would be dangerous to go there as an unaccompanied visitor.

There are a few old houses left in the downtown area of Kingston, most of these in sad disrepair. East of the Parade on Duke Street, however, you will find an excellent example of an 18th-century town house, **Headquarters House**. It is a handsome building with a brick shell, an enclosed, latticework veranda and three triangular eaves. Originally built by a merchant, Thomas Hibbert, it got its name from its one-time use by the military and was the seat of the Jamaican Parliament earlier this century. It is now home of the Jamaica National Heritage Trust.

Across the street is the modern **Gordon House**, the current seat of the Parliament, where the Representatives and Senators sit. Visits can be made by prior arrangement. Not far off on North Street is the modern office of *The Gleaner* newspaper, and further east, on South Camp Road, you will find the Sabina Park cricket stadium, where the international tests are played.

East Street and Duke Street lead up to **National Heroes Park**, dedicated following Independence in 1962. Formerly it was a race-course, which explains its oval shape, and then later it was the George VI Memorial Park. It is still an open park with some grand old buildings and the odd government ministry overlooking it. In the centre is an enclosed area that has monuments to the Jamaican national heroes: Paul Bogle and George William Gordon, champions of the poor in the last century, and to Nanny the Maroon and Sam Sharpe. The graves of Marcus Mosiah Garvey, founder of the UNIA, and those of the fathers of modern Jamaican politics, Norman Manley and Alexander Bustamante, are also there. In the southeastern corner of the square you will also see a statue of Simon Bolívar, *El Libertador*, the hero of South American independence, who stayed in exile in Jamaica.

New Kingston

The buses run from the Parade along Slipe Road towards **New Kingston**, the commercial centre of the modern capital. Knutsford Boulevard is the principal street, and here you will find the businesses and banks. Holborn Road is also something of a centre, with a number of guest houses and restaurants and bars. Nearby Half Way Tree is a gravitational centre of transport and shopping. The old cotton tree is no longer there (and history doesn't relate where it's halfway to), but there is a small park, Nelson Mandela Park, with a clocktower and all the chaos of a Jamaican bus terminal. Constant Spring Road, which leads north from here, is lined with malls and is the main shopping area of uptown Kingston.

On Hope Road at the corner of Waterloo Road you will find the classical **Devon House**, © 929 6602, *tours of house Tues–Sat, 9.30–4.30, adm*, set in its spacious gardens of palms and flowering trees, *gardens open daytime and evenings until about 10pm*. Built in 1881 for Jamaica's first black millionaire, George Stiebel, Devon House is an excellent example of a tropical mansion. The ceilings are high and the doorways wide; some rooms are actually enclosed verandas with louvres that encourage a through breeze. Devon House has been restored to the state of a Jamaican mansion of the 1870s, with some period pieces and some reproductions, and it gives a good idea of the luxury and formality of the time. There is parquet flooring throughout, a Wedgwood-style ceiling in the ballroom with plaster frescoes of cherubs and in the main entrance hall you will see the original wallpaper, with its hand-painted silk panels depicting palm trees and tropical flowers (repainted in 1982). There are games rooms and tea rooms (complete with lockable tea-caddy because tea was expensive at the time) and even a secret gambling room, with removeable stairway, above the ladies' sewing room. Devon House is popular with Jamaicans and tourists alike and so there is a lively, friendly feel to the place; lovers linger and wedding parties have their photographs taken on the mansion steps. There are a couple of cafés and restaurants, the Grog Shoppe in the old stables, and there are trinket shops in the quadrangle, *shops open till 6pm*. Worth a detour for a lunchtime pattie or an ice cream at any time.

As you head up Hope Road you pass a large area of parkland, the site of Jamaica House, built in the 1960s as the residence of the Prime Minister, now just his office, and Kings House, the official residence of the Jamaican Governor General.

You can visit the grounds. Further on you pass the **Bob Marley Museum**, *open Mon–Sat, 9.30–4.30, Wed and Sat afternoons only, adm,* once the Tuff Gong recording studio and later the home of Bob Marley himself. The tour takes you through the house, its walls hung with gold and platinum discs and press clippings, Marley's concert shirts, his Order of Merit: 'Whereas, Bob Marley, International King of Reggae Music...' and the Shot Room, with bullet holes from the attempt on his life and the CIA report on the event. After the tour you are shown 20 minutes of video from his concerts.

Near the top of Old Hope Road are the **Hope Botanical Gardens**, *open daily 8.30–dusk, adm free, tip guides,* which were established in 1881. Set against the impressive backdrop of the Blue Mountains, they are 150 acres of parkland and botanical gardens, vast lawns lined with royal palms, with bandstands, ponds and huge colourful explosions of bougainvillea among the beds of yellow shrimp plants and ixora. They are an excellent retreat from the bustle of downtown Kingston and a favoured spot for Jamaican limers, picnickers and lovers. Guides are available to point out the many exotic and curious plants, such as bottle-brush and pimento (which goes into jerk seasoning). At the top end of the Gardens you will find **Hope Zoo**, *open daily 9–5, small adm,* which has a few lacklustre Jamaican crocodiles (with aerofoil scales and huge and diabolic smiles) and a number of American owls and parrots. There is also a small children's funpark next door.

At the top end of Old Hope Road you come to Papine, close to which is the Mona Campus of the **University of the West Indies**, on the site of an old sugar estate between the hills, where the aqueducts and some of the old buildings stand among the modern lecture halls. Behind here, the main road passes into the Blue Mountains, following the path of the Hope River (*see* p.221).

✆ (809–)

Where to Stay

Most of the hotels are in New Kingston, but if you have a car you might consider the hotels outside the city, in the lower hills of the Blue Mountains.

expensive

The most charming and comfortable hotel in Kingston at the moment is the **Terra Nova Hotel**, 17 Waterloo Road, Kingston 10, ✆ 926 9334, 🖷 929 4933, US and Canada reservations ✆ 1 800 742 4276. It is a 1924 mansion fronted with classical balustrades and white and yellow awnings, set in an expanse of gardens: inside chandeliers hang above the heavy décor and formal wooden furniture and flooring. In this rarefied atmosphere, away from the hustle of town, you are cosseted by staff in black and white formal dress, complete with cummerbunds. There are just 21 rooms in the main house and a newer block, a pool and grill. And the Edwardian elegance of the dining room is the setting for one of Kingston's best formal restaurants for classic international cuisine.

moderate

The **Hotel Four Seasons** is also an Edwardian town house with additions, 18 Ruthven Road, ℂ 929 7655, ℳ 929 5964, US and Canada reservations ℂ 1 800 742 4276. The hotel is quite large, with 79 rooms, some decorated in bright, modern Caribbean style. The interior of the dining room, with its panelled walls and dark, sumptuously thick carpets, is a little unlikely for the Caribbean; you can also eat out on the breezy veranda. There's no pool, but the front desk will arrange for you to go to one. If you are in Kingston on business you might prefer one of the two larger high-rise hotels at the bottom of Knutsford Boulevard: the **Jamaica Pegasus**, ℂ 926 3690, ℳ 929 5855, and the **Wyndham Hotel**, ℂ 926 5430, ℳ 968 4370. They both offer international standards of accommodation and business facilities, and a brisk and busy atmosphere, but little Jamaican character. The **Indies Hotel**, 5 Holborn Road, ℂ 926 2952, ℳ 926 2879, has just 15 rooms in blocks behind a small town house with a pretty foyer with wooden floor and tray ceiling. The rooms, each one with TV, air-conditioning and phones, lead off a peaceful courtyard festooned with golden palm and colourful crotons. They are comfortable though quite basic. All meals are available in the restaurant. Some *inexpensive* rooms.

Close to Kingston, and yet distinctly removed from the bustle of the city is **Ivor Guest House**, Skyline Drive, Jack's Hill, ℂ 927 1460, ℳ 977 0033. There is a magnificent view from the terrace and garden—make your way up there at cocktail time, when the lights from the town are spectacular. Ivor is a small and elegant colonial house offering the sort of gracious hospitality that sits comfortably with the wooden floors, door-frames and the antiques. There are just three-bed rooms: two in the old house itself with four-poster beds, and another in a self-contained cottage. Lunch, afternoon tea, cocktails and dinner are all served (*see* p.208).

cheap

Next door to the Indies Hotel is **Holborn Manor Guest House**, ℂ 926 0296, a popular stopping-off point in town for younger travellers. There are 10 fairly basic but clean rooms with private baths, now gentrified to the point of having telephones and some televisions. There is a friendly atmosphere; home-cooked breakfast is included.

The **Central Court Hotel**, ℂ 929 1026, at the junction of Lady Musgrave Road and Old Hope Road has simpler rooms at very cheap prices, but no other facilities. If you want to be in New Kingston at the cheapest rates of all you might try the **Chelsea Hotel**, just off Half Way Tree Road on Chelsea Avenue, but these rooms are more normally hired out by the hour.

Eating Out

expensive

There are a couple of smart restaurants just outside the town, easily reached by car or taxi. The **Blue Mountain Inn**, ✆ 927 1700, is the most formal and smartest restaurant around Kingston. It sits in a vast cleft in the mountains, on the road to Gordon Town. The interior is dressed up as a drawing room, carpeted in red with black beams and white walls, and there's a magnificent view of the river from here and from the vine-covered terrace, where you can take coffee to the rush of the river water. The menu is international: start with an ackee quiche and follow with lobster bathed in mint and ginger sauce. Jackets are required.

Another very nice spot is **Ivor Guest House** (*see* p.207). There is a nightly changing, four-course set dinner, with three or four choices of main courses. Dishes are mainly international, but they make good use of local ingredients, so you might start with smoked marlin with cream cheese and capers, and follow with a fillet of sea snapper brushed with eskellion, scotch bonnet and spice butter, then top it off with a tropical fruit ice cream.

Guilt Trip, ✆ 977 5130, is laid back and open late, on a terrace with latticework walls and a wooden roof hung with greenery, overlooking a lawn and fountain. The fare is international with a distinctly Jamaican twist: try the pimento-stuffed chicken breast or roasted snapper fillet in a passion fruit cream. And the desserts are magnificent; there is also a bakery on the premises which specializes in cakes, so afternoon tea is particularly popular here. It's difficult to find, and there is no sign: head up Hope Road, turn left (onto Barbican Road) at Matilda's Corner (at Liguanea Plaza). Just a few hundred yards on, down over the bridge, look for the sign for the Orchid Patch on the right; it's in there somewhere.

Another fashionable spot with a lively atmosphere and very fine food is the **Crossings New World Café**, ✆ 978 3547, right next to the petrol station on Old Hope Road where it meets Mountains View Avenue. Menus come in record sleeves and the décor in the dining room upstairs is hip; there are bars downstairs. Exclusively Jamaican ingredients are used in international recipes: lots of pasta and seafood; cho-cho bisque with dill and red pea salad; and conch is a speciality. Serves brunch and dinner.

The **Devonshire** at Devon House is more formal; you dine on verandas overlooking an inner courtyard with a small forest of greenery and a lily pond. Try the roast sucking-pig and Island coconut lobster; lots of steaks if you want them. At **El Dorado** at the Terra Nova Hotel, © 926 9334, on Waterloo Road, in the colonial setting of a neo-classical villa built at the turn of the century, you dine on lobster tail flamed with brandy and grilled chicken with guava sauce.

moderate

Something of the Port Royal of the 1680s still exists in the old brick warehouse building of the **Grog Shoppe** at Devon House—the guests behave rather better now, though. There is an easy mix of visitors and some locals here. After you have tucked into a list of exotic and colourful cocktails (their names taken from some sensational moments in Jamaica's history, including Devon Duppy and the White Witch), you will be served local Jamaican callaloo and hot pot, as well as Blue Mountain burgers and steaks. It's a pleasant spot with tables inside under a ship's figurehead or a fairy-lit mango tree. *Open all day and into the evening.*

Heather's in Haining Road has tables set on a terrace beneath a mango tree. It's popular with expats, who cluster here for a drink and sometimes a plate of food after work: a long menu includes seafood and fish specialities, cottage pie and burgers, and even bangers and mash.

The **Café Central**, in a small concrete garden with tables under the trees around the gazebo bar, is a more easygoing spot, which sees a mix of Jamaicans and expatriates. The cafés courtyard is tucked away at the very end of Central Avenue (off Constant Spring Road). There is a general menu that features stir-fries and sandwiches, but also some tasty cheese dishes including melted cheese sandwiches. *Open for lunch and dinner, Mon–Sat; closed Sun.* The **Hot Pot** is a much more Jamaican affair, set in a courtyard under umbrellas. It serves trusty if odd-sounding Jamaican food in large portions—anything from gungo soup or beef balls to the less worrisome steam fish and fricassee chicken, with a tonnage of rice 'n' peas.

At lunchtime you might try **The Pantry** on Dumfries Road for Jamaican fare: soup and a plate of fried rice or a sandwich. In the evening they serve mackerel rundown, chicken in sweet potato or an ackee pizza. Close by, the **Indies Pub** draws a crowd after work and at lunchtime, when it is popular with New Kingston business people. Simple chicken and fish with chips, or a pizza. Just down Holborn Road you can get a good Jamaican 'roti' from the **Mango Tree Café** in a bamboo- and tin-walled concrete yard. Fast food joints are popular and some of the malls stay open late as people loiter while they eat; try those at Liguanea Mall on Hope Road.

There are a few exclusively **vegetarian** restaurants around Kingston—though a number of places offer a vegetarian dish on their menus. The **Eden Restaurant**, on Eastwood Park Road, just above Half Way Tree, offers lunch and dinner until 8pm. *Closed Sat*—they are Seventh-Day Adventists. You can also get good vegetarian fare among the botanical pandemonium of Jack's Hill (above the city in the mountains) at **Maya Lodge**, ✆ 927 2097 (*see* p.224).

cheap

There are several jerk centres in town. The most popular is the **Chelsea Jerk Centre** on Chelsea Avenue in New Kingston, where you can buy chicken or pork doused in hot pepper sauce. *Closed Sun.* Alternatively try **Peppers** on Upper Waterloo Road. On weekday evenings you can always get a barbecued half-chicken from one of the women cooking on upturned braziers at the roadside, and patties are available around town.

Entertainment and Nightlife

A great place to start any evening in Kingston is on the veranda at **Ivor Guest House** in Jack's Hill. It has a fantastic view across the city as far as Port Royal. Good for a rum punch in old Jamaican surroundings.

Back down in the thick of the town there are plenty of haunts, part bar, part restaurant and sometimes part café too, frequented by Kingstonians. **Heather's** on Haining road is ever popular; close by, **Carlos Café** on Belmont Road gathers a lively crowd of drinkers and diners under its awnings and umbrellas. You might also join the preppy drinkers at **Peppers** on Waterloo Road, or try **Chaser's Café**, on Barbican Road, where an animated bunch hang out drinking and generally make whoopee. A hip crowd gathers to chill out at the **Crossings Café**.

You could try the jazz evening on the last Wednesday in the month, downstairs in the Mutual Life building on Oxford Road—you'll hear anything from Third World to soca jazz. The **Countryside Club** on Eastwood Park Road is a popular venue for late-night drinking and dancing. Discotheques include **Godfather's** on Knutsford Boulevard and **Mirage** at the Sovereign Centre on Hope Road.

It is hard to imagine that the present-day small town of Port Royal was once 'the Treasury of the Indies', the richest and one of the largest cities in the New World. In fact, for over a century the Port Royal buzzed with mercantile activity and military urgency. For many years it was the haunt of the buccaneers, a rabble of sailors who hovered between privateering and outright piracy. Later Port Royal became the most important British naval base in the Caribbean. During one operation in the 18th century Port Royal harbour saw the sails of 124 ships lying at anchor.

The attraction of Port Royal lies mostly in its history and mystery; there is not much to see there at the moment, though there are plans for the beginnings of a restoration programme. However it is pleasant enough for a half-day out from Kingston, and quite a change from the city. Frigate birds cruise overhead and pelicans sit on the gunwhales of the fishing boats. The nicest beaches in the Kingston area are on the cays to the south of Port Royal.

History

Before the arrival of the British in 1655, the area of Port Royal had probably been used as a fishing base by the Arawak Indians—middens and a few Indian artefacts have been found. The Spaniards had called it Cayo de Carena, because they would careen their ships here (to careen a ship was to clean its hull, tipping it on its side in shallow water by weighing down the mast and then scratching off the barnacles and weeds, so that it would sail more quickly).

Port Royal was fortified as soon as the English arrived, in defence against possible Spanish attack from the sea (in the event, the Spaniards attacked overland from the north). Once the point was covered, entry into the harbour was difficult because of the prevailing winds. Initially the area was called Point Cagua or Cagway, but with the restoration of Charles II in England it became known as Port Royal (and the main fortress was named Fort Charles).

The story of Port Royal is inextricably linked with that of the buccaneers. These rogues and sea-dogs had settled in the town after they were thrown out of Tortuga (off the north coast of Haiti). They were possessed by their hatred of the Spaniards and so they made a convenient unofficial navy for the English governor of Jamaica, who granted commissions to the buccaneers in time of war to attack enemy shipping. But in times of peace they were difficult to control and they would go off (often with the tacit blessing of the Jamaican governor and financed by the local merchants) on a little freelance business (more usually called piracy).

Port Royal offered the buccaneers a place to sell the goods they had captured on the seas and, with a tavern for every ten inhabitants, a place for them to retreat to for rest and recreation. Slavers or 'Guineamen' also frequented the harbour, their holds filled with 'black ivory' as the poor slaves were known. The town became a huge and very successful market and a vast bawdy house, described by one visitor as 'one of the lewdest in the Christian World, a sink of all filthiness and a mere Sodom'. Even their own rector described them a 'most Ungodly and Debauched people' (*see* **History**, pp.77–8).

Port Royal also prospered from other kinds of commerce. Manufactured goods were brought out from England, often to be shipped onwards to other islands or smuggled to the planters in the Spanish islands. A large community of artisans and tradesmen grew up around the trade: comb-makers and ivory-turners, pewterers and potters, pipe-makers, sail-makers, chandlers, watermen and wherrymen (who worked the small boats from ship to shore). The inhabitants were fashion conscious and adopted the latest styles from London; one notable cove was seen sporting 'black watered chambles lined with crimson taffety...silk crimson shoes, gloves and a periwig'. Their entertainments were cock-fighting, bull- and bear-baiting, dominoes and billiards. Francis Hanson wrote in 1682:

> *The Town of Port Royal, being as it were the Store House or Treasury of the West Indies, is always a continual Mart or Fair where all sorts of choice Merchandizes are daily imported, not only to furnish the island, but vast quantities are thence again transported to supply the Spaniards, Indians and other nations, who in exchange return us bars and cakes of Gold, wedges and pigs of Silver, Pistoles, Pieces of Eight and several other Coyns of boths mettles, with Store of wrought Plate, Jewels, rich Pearl Necklaces and of Pearl unsorted or undrill'd several Bushels; besides which, we are furnished with the purest and most fine sorts of Dust Gold from Guiney, by the Negro Ships, who first come to Jamaica to deliver their Blacks, and there usually refit and stay to reload three or four Months; in which time (though the Companies Gold may be partly sent home) yet the Merchants, Masters of Ships, and almost every Mariner (having private Cargoes) take occasion to sell or exchange great quantities; some of which our Goldsmiths there work up, who being yet but few grow very wealthy, for almost every House hath a rich Cupboard of Plate, which they carelessly expose, scarce shutting their doors in the night, being in no apprehension for Thieves for want of receivers as aforesaid. And whereas most other Plantations ever did and now do keep their accounts in*

Sugar, or in the proper Commodities of the place, for want of Money, it is otherwise in Jamaica, for in Port Royal there is more plenty of running Cash (proportionably to the number of its inhabitants) than is in London.

The layout of the place and the way of life was much as in an English town of the day. Port Royal's streets were lined with three- and four-storey wooden houses (for which rents were as dear as they were in an expensive London street: £40–60 per annum). There were three markets: one for fruit and vegetables; one for fish; and the third for meat, where anything from veal to turtle was sold. Other food and drink (Port Royal earned its reputation for drinking early on) were shipped from England. As well as the 'taverns, grogg shops and punch houses' there were stocks, a ducking stool and a gallows. The main prison was the Marshallsea and there was a 'house of correction' for 'lazy strumpets'.

The Earthquake

When it came, a few minutes before noon on 7 June 1692, the earthquake seemed like divine retribution; 2000 people died in 3 minutes. There were three shocks 'like the rumbling of a heavily laden cart on gravel', and instantly whole streets of the 'Gilded Hades' slid into the sea. The ships were all forced from their moorings, many of them sinking, and a tidal wave threw one into the ruins of the town. Buildings collapsed as fissures opened up in the earth, engulfing or trapping people half-buried; there are macabre stories about unfortunates being eaten alive by dogs. The tremors were so bad that Fort Charles sank 3 feet and Port Royal became an island once again. Some continued drinking and others started to loot the shops and cut the gold off the dead.

One Lewis Galdy had quite a story to tell: after he was swallowed up by the earth in one shock, he was thrown out again into the sea by the next. He lived to a ripe old age and his story is told on his gravestone, in the Port Royal churchyard. Bodies floated around the harbour and within a couple of days the area had been over-taken by disease, which killed 2000 more. Many of the survivors fled to the mainland to avoid the danger.

The sunken city remained beneath the water in the harbour. 'Wreckers' salvaged what they could at the time of the disaster, but buildings were still visible under the water until the 1880s. Now nothing is really visible as it all has silted up. There have been a number of underwater archaeological expeditions during this century, and endless artefacts have been recovered, among them a pocket-watch whose hands (the hands themselves had decayed but their ghosts were revealed by X-ray) had stuck at 18 minutes to 12, the precise moment of the earthquake.

The merchants rebuilt their town, but in 1703 a fire destroyed it again. It never recovered as a trading town and the last of its inhabitants moved to Kingston. However, it remained an important naval base throughout the next century, during which there was almost constant war in the Caribbean. Despite this, the guns of Port Royal were fired in anger only once, at an escaping pirate who had jumped jail and stolen a ship. He was caught and hanged.

The 18th century was a period of naval heroics and Port Royal was a proving ground for a number of British admirals. Admiral Edward Vernon caused weeks of celebration by winning a wager that he could capture the Spanish stronghold of Porto Bello with only six ships. At the time of the American War of Independence Horatio Nelson was put in charge of Fort Charles (there is a plaque to his memory inside the fort) and Admiral George Rodney cruised the Caribbean waters out of Port Royal, eventually saving the island from capture by the French in 1782 by winning the Battle of the Saints.

By 1816 the pattern of colonial possession around the Caribbean was settled and Port Royal was no longer under threat. The garrison remained for another century, though; the naval flag was finally taken down for good in 1905. As steamships came on the scene in the second half of the 1800s, Port Royal became an important coaling station and ships would put in to the Admiralty Wharf to take on coal, water and other provisions. But this business was eventually eclipsed as air travel became popular, and the seaplane terminal and the airport were opened a little farther up the peninsula.

Getting to Port Royal

A road leads past the Norman Manley Airport along the Palisadoes Peninsula, and occasional **buses** arrive from downtown Kingston; but the easiest way to get to Port Royal is really on the **ferry** from Pier 2 on the Kingston waterfront (and you don't need a vehicle in Port Royal because you can walk everywhere).

The ferry crossing takes about 25 minutes and runs each way seven times a day. As you arrive in Port Royal you will see Gallow's Point, where the pirates were hanged, on the left, now an area of mangroves just to the northeast of the town. Ferries depart from Kingston to Port Royal: 6am, 7am, 10am, 12.30pm, 3pm, 5pm and 7pm; from Port Royal to Kingston: 6.30am, 7.30am, 11.30am, 1pm, 3.30pm, 5.30pm and 7.30pm.

Tours

Bus-borne tours of Port Royal (and Spanish Town) can be arranged through **Destination Tours**, ✆ 929 6368, 929 7865; give them a couple of days' notice. An excellent day out is to take a boat from Port Royal to **Lime Cay** among the reefs to the south of the Palisadoes Peninsula. You will find good reefs (take snorkelling gear) and excellent light sand. As you doze in the sun, cast your mind back 300 years to the time when these islands were used for 'hanging pirates out to dry'—they were put in a wrought-iron cage and left to die of dehydration—a sanguine warning to all sailors as they arrived in the harbour. This might remind you to bring all you need in the way of food and drink because the cays are hot, shadeless and uninhabited. The trip is easily arranged with a fisherman in Port Royal, who will drop you and come to collect you at the appointed time. Nearby, **Maiden Cay** is an inviting strip of sand that only just makes it above the surf.

Around the Town

The town of Port Royal lies at the western end of the Palisadoes Peninsula, the thin, straggly arm of low-lying land that encloses Kingston Harbour. The peninsula, which takes its military-sounding name from trees that gave it the jagged appearance of a palisade, is in fact a series of small islands on a limestone base, joined together by sedimentation. Despite being built in an earthquake zone (the dangers were not understood in the early days), Port Royal was an excellent harbour. In the late 1600s the largest ships could come right up to the shoreline and offload on planks. The coastline is still in flux, with the southern side of the peninsula building up steadily.

Fort Charles (once Fort Cromwell, but renamed after the restored King Charles II), *open daily 10–1 and 2–5, adm*, is the oldest surviving monument of the British occupation in Jamaica. There is a certain empty, drowsy air about the place now, and it is no longer actually on the sea—in 1700 the waves were at its shores and ships tied up to the rings embedded into the fortress wall, but now sedimentation has built up the land around it and left it high and dry a considerable way inland. But with the castellated ramparts, and the cannon still in place (there were 104 of them at the height of its importance), you can still imagine the whistle blasts and cannon salutes of naval activity. Within its walls is a small **Maritime Museum** with a few illuminating descriptions of life during Port Royal's heyday and a number of artefacts that have been recovered during the excavations of the Sunken City itself, including shipwrights' tools and wrist and ankle shackles worn by slaves. Beyond the fort is the **Giddy House**, a Royal Artillery store, which lurched to its present position, at 16 degrees to the vertical, in the earthquake of 1907. Next to it is the Victoria and Albert Battery, which also sunk in the same earthquake.

Not far off is the **Old Naval Hospital**, an early cast-iron section building with a magnificent balcony about a hundred yards long. It dates from 1818 and was constructed to withstand earthquakes and hurricanes, which it did in 1907 and in 1951. Sadly it didn't fare so well during Hurricane Gilbert in 1988 (to be fair, Gilbert was so powerful that the drug-running planes impounded at the international airport nearby were simply tossed into the trees). The Museum of Historical Archaeology which it contained had to be closed and has not been reopened, although there are plans afoot to do so. Port Royal may have lost its influence but it retains its strategic importance, and so next to Fort Charles you will find HMJS *Cagway*, the headquarters of the Jamaican Coastguard (Cagway was an earlier name of Port Royal). Lewis Galdy's tomb can be seen in the graveyard of St Peter's Church. The story of his remarkable good fortune in surviving the earthquake of 1692 is told on the stone. Next to it is the simple grave of three children who died in the earthquake when a wall fell on and buried them; their bodies were only discovered by marine archaeologists this century. They were reburied in 1992.

© *(809–)*

Where to Stay

Port Royal has just one hotel, the **Morgan's Harbour Hotel**, © 924 8464, ✆ 924 8146 (*expensive*), which is built into the old colonial brickwork of Naval Dockyard, a short walk to the east of the town itself. There are 40 air-conditioned and fan-ventilated rooms, decorated with Jamaican wood furniture and set in a shaded, sandy garden with a pool and seafront bar— some rooms have superb views over Kingston and to the hills beyond. There is a marina and some watersports. The hotel is within a shout of the international airport; convenient if you need to take an early flight or have arrived late.

Eating Out

Eating out is limited in Port Royal, though there are a number of simple spots for a lunch or dinner among the many bars. On the waterfront down from the ferry pier you will find the **Fisherman's Cabin**, where you can get any number of seafood and fish dishes, shrimp and lobster included, and other standard Jamaican fare such as curry goat, served with heaped rice 'n' peas or bammy. **Gloria's Rendezvous** is a good stopover for the standard Port Royal meal of fried fish and bammy.

Spanish Town

Spanish Town was the heart of British colonial life for two centuries, capital of the island, social hub and centre of the colonial administration. Now the capital of St Elizabeth Parish, the town lies 12 miles west of Kingston, across some sugar flats

and a morass (a swamp). It is a typical, busy Jamaican town with suburbs rapidly growing around it as a dormitory for Kingston. At the heart of it all, though, is a square of grand tropical Georgian buildings, the finest of its kind in the Caribbean, set in a grid of elegant if rundown colonial homes and warehouses of wood and stone. To arrange a **tour** of Spanish Town, contact the Heritage Trust of Jamaica in Kingston a day or so in advance, © 938 2578.

History

Spanish Town is the oldest continuously occupied town in Jamaica and one of the oldest in the New World. As the name suggests, it was taken over from the Spaniards when the British first arrived. Originally it was called Santiago de la Vega, after the patron Saint of Spain, St James, and it dates from 1523, when the Spaniards moved from Nueva Sevilla on the north coast. It was laid out according to a typical Spanish plan, with a Plaza Mejora, now Parade Square, and a Plaza Menora, where the cathedral is situated.

As the principal town in Jamaica during the whole of the Spanish tenure it was attacked a number of times (by the British adventurers Sir Anthony Shirley and Christopher Newport among others). Whenever an attack was imminent the citizens would hide their money in the countryside nearby and then recover it when the threat had passed. The British invasion of 1655 was expected to be much the same as the others, but, as it turned out, the invaders never left. The Spaniards were forced to flee to the north coast and then to Cuba. The British burned part of the town but then began to settle the area and to rebuild. It took a while to recover and although it was always the senior town and official capital of Jamaica (and seat of the island's governor), for many years it lived in the shadow of Port Royal, which was larger, far more prosperous and housed the office of the deputy governor. The Maroons also hampered its development: they would attack the small settlement, killing planters in their fields and destroying their crops, even coming close enough to burn the town itself.

As well as being a century of wars, the 18th century was a time of great prosperity and Jamaica was Britain's richest colony. In the 1760s, grand official buildings were erected in the main square. The town was also the social hub of British Jamaica for two centuries. The proclamation of the abolition of slavery was read from the steps of King's House in 1838. A small monument in the southeastern corner of the square records all the illustrious moments that were celebrated in Spanish Town and important historical figures associated with the place—Captain Bligh and Admiral Rodney among them.

Historic Spanish Town

The old, historical heart of Spanish Town is **Parade Square**, where you will see some of the finest Georgian buildings anywhere in the former British colonies. It is on the site of the original Spanish Plaza Mejora, but there is nothing left of the Spanish buildings save foundations. Nowadays, with the monumental white balustrades and pediments and the iron railings around the central park, the impression given by Parade Square is a distinctly British one (spiked admittedly by the royal palms and the goats roaming around looking for pickings).

The centrepiece of the square is the **Rodney Memorial**, which stands on the northern side, in its own pillared and dome-topped temple. Sculpted by John Bacon in Greek style (following the then current fashion), it commemorates Admiral George Rodney and was erected following his victory at the Battle of the Saints off Guadeloupe in 1782, a battle which saved the island from almost certain capture and which guaranteed British naval domination of the Caribbean for many years. The memorial was completed in 1801. The two cannon either side were taken from the French flagship, the *Ville de Paris*.

Opposite, on the south side of the square, is the **court house**, which is now nothing more than a shell, following a fire in 1985. Originally it was the site of the Spanish abbey and then of an English chapel, built in a fit of religious fervour following the earthquake in Port Royal in 1692. This building dates from 1819 and had a cupola to reflect that of the Rodney Memorial. On the east side of the square, the colonnaded building with wooden upper storeys and a balcony is the former **House of Assembly**, which was completed 1762. The original assembly room measured 40 by 80 ft, and Jamaica's elected representatives met here until the government of the island was taken over by the British Commonwealth Office in 1866. Now the building houses the Parish Council offices. On the western side of the square stands the **King's House**, *small adm*, also built in 1762, which was the official residence of the island's governor. It was here that the proclamation of the Abolition of Slavery was read on 1 August 1838. This too is no more than a shell. It was burned down to its façade in 1925. Now the overgrown courtyards and stables behind house the exhibits of the Jamaican People's Museum of Craft and Technology, a lacklustre series of exhibits including household utensils, among them a limestone dripstone (for fresh, purified water). There are some interesting illustrations of Jamaican architectural techniques and some early Jamaican postcards—no beaches, but towns and rivers, and one of Tom Cringle's Cotton Tree. There is also a model of the King's House in its heyday.

To the southeast of the main square on Barrett Street you will find the Cathedral Church of St James, head of the Jamaica Diocese and the oldest British Commonwealth Cathedral. It was built in its present form in 1714 (after a hurricane in 1712) on the site of an original Spanish church, but there are commemorative tablets set into the floor which date back to 1662, to the earliest days of British settlement in Jamaica. Among the black and white headstones you will see names such as Beckford, Williams and that of the early Jamaican governor Modyford, whose epitaph reads, 'the Soule and Life of all Jamaica, who made it what it is'. The skull and bones symbol seen on many of the stones was to ward off evil.

These two squares with their rarefied air are surrounded by a gridiron of streets with colonial buildings in varying states of repair—some are complete with sandblasted walls and gingerbread trimmings, others nothing more than a flight of old steps leading to nowhere. The huge military barracks buildings, now the local prison, stand testament to how important the town once was. Traditionally the residential district was east of Parade Square and the commercial area to the west. Beyond here, Spanish Town is now a busy Jamaican town, with markets, shopping malls and some industry. It is also home to the Jamaica Police Academy.

As you cross the Rio Bueno on the route back to Kingston, look left and you will see a pretty, curved cast-iron bridge that spans the gorge, the first of its kind to be erected in the western hemisphere. And beyond here, just off the main road, is the **Arawak Museum**, with a few Arawak artefacts on display. You may be very lucky and find it open.

West from Spanish Town

Beyond Spanish Town in the other direction you can visit the massive ruins of the 17th-century **Colbeck Castle** near Old Harbour. It was supposedly built by a Colonel Colbeck, who arrived in Jamaica as a part of the Penn and Venables expedition in 1655. It looks a bit odd, as it is designed along the lines of a European fortified castle, with a tower at each corner. Odder still, there are no records of it until the late 18th century, but by then it is supposed to be haunted. Beyond here you come to **May Pen**, a busy Jamaican town set around a clocktower. There are many Pens in Jamaica; the name refers to a farmstead where animals were kept. At Toll Gate you take the turning to the south coast, along the Milk River valley and canefields, past a village called Rest, down to the **Milk River Spa**, ✆ 925 9544, where the highest levels of natural radioactivity in the world occur in the water— about 50 times the levels found at Baden-Baden. The water comes out of the ground at 120°F and the spa is popular for its supposed healing powers. And at

Alligator Hole River are some of the few surviving Jamaican manatees. Not far from here, the town of Racecourse has a large East Indian population, who stage very colourful festivals at Divali and Hosay.

Where to Stay and Eating Out

There is nowhere good to stay in Spanish Town. There are rooms on the south coast at the **Milk River Spa**, ℗ 924 9544 (*cheap*), which offers simple accommodation in a charming old wooden house, with a restaurant and the mineral baths themselves and not many tourists. Eating out in Spanish Town is limited to the pattie shops and bars.

Into the Blue Mountains

After the hum and hustle of Kingston, it is a wonderful relief to get into the Blue Mountains. With a climate vaunted as 'a mild, eternal springtime', the Blue Mountains are cooler than the lowlands (Jamaicans actually complain that they are cold at times); the area was used by the colonials as a rest station. The mountains are also extremely beautiful and the views, over Kingston to Port Royal and beyond, are magnificent.

The change of gear is noticeable in the people too. The Blue Mountain communities are gentle and friendly; they are mainly agricultural and they supply the Kingston markets. With the cooler climate they can even grow lettuce. But the mountains are most famous for their coffee, which you will now see covering whole slopes. Blue Mountain coffee is often touted as the finest in the world (*see* p.39).

The beauty of the Blue Mountains alone makes a visit to them a must. Steep camelback ridges furred with a line of pine trees tumble from the string of peaks that make up the central spine of the mountains and tiny settlements cling to the hillsides. The mountains are really more green (more of Jamaica's outrageous growth) than they are blue but, late in the afternoon, as the light begins to fade, you will see the crevices take on a silvery blue, the colour of uninhaled tobacco smoke.

There are great spots for an evening drink or dinner in the Blue Mountains. As you sit on a balcony on the hillside, all the hectic activity of the city is reduced to a tiny, distant roar.

Getting into the Blue Mountains

Just a few main roads lead into the Blue Mountains from Kingston. Two lead up from Papine: one to Irish town and then to Newcastle and the other to Gordon Town and Guava Ridge; irregular **buses** run to these places from the station at Papine, as far as Red Light on the Newcastle Road and to Guava Ridge. The road to Annotto Bay via Castleton (often referred to as the Junction road) is covered by buses from Half Way Tree and Constant Spring.

The Blue Mountains are cut with farm tracks and old mule tracks and it is possible to take excellent **walking tours** in the area; contact **Maya Lodge**, ✆ 927 2097, and **Sunventure Tours**, ✆ 960 6685.

The Mountains

As you leave Papine you enter the Hope River Gulley and the cliffs rise immediately around you. Just after the Blue Mountain Inn the road forks left and winds its way up laboriously, overgrown with grass, for a couple of thousand feet to Irish Town, passing Strawberry Hill and then coming to Red Light (whose name is explained when you consider that there was a large military contingent based around the area for many years). There is an excellent walk down from Red Light to Gordon Town, following the path of the Hope River. Higher up still you come to **Newcastle**, which is still an active military base, its barrack buildings stacked one below the next for a couple of hundred yards down the sloping hillside. The parade ground, about the size of a football pitch, with military badges painted on the wall, is on the only flat piece of land around here. If the soldiers are parading you may find that the traffic is held up for a while.

The road continues to wind up the hill, past the Gap Café (*see* p.222) and then crosses the watershed to the north side at the Hardwar (pronounced hardware) Gap. Here you enter the **Blue Mountain National Park** for a couple of miles, at the pass itself you come to the Hollywell Park Ranger Station and the orientation centre where you can get information about the park. Be prepared for wet weather if you intend to walk in this area; it usually rains and there is mist here every day.

From the Hardwar Gap the road enters the rainforest (the northern side of the mountains are much rainier), which hangs over the road, cutting out any sunlight that has got through the rainclouds, and then leads down to Section. From here it is possible to visit **Cinchona Gardens**, first planted in 1868 to grow cinchona, from which quinine was extracted in order to treat malaria. Gradually it developed into a botanical garden, and you can still see rhododendrons, lilies and orchids. It is difficult to get to, 5000 feet up on a very rough road, but it is a charming and peaceful escape. From Section the road winds down the Buff Bay River Valley until it reaches Buff Bay itself on the north coast. It is a delightful drive and highly recommended if you are crossing the Blue Mountains with time to spare.

The other main road into the Blue Mountains, to Gordon Town, is just as steep and grassy as the Irish Town Road. Gordon Town takes its name from the Gordon

Highlanders who were stationed here at one time. At World's End above Guava Ridge is the **Sangster's Old Jamaica Liqueur Factory**, which merits a quick look. Wonderfully exotic creamy smells hang in the air as the different flavoured rums are put through the blender—passion fruit rum, coconut rum cream, wild orange cream—and then bottled, topped and labelled. There is a shop on the premises where you can buy all these exotic creations.

Beyond the heights of Guava Ridge you come to **Mavis Bank**, *adm*, where, during picking time between September and February, you can visit one of Jamaica's coffee factories. The 'cherry berries' that come in from the fields are thrown into water so that 'floaters' can be removed, the remainder are pulped to take off the flesh. Then they are dried as 'wet parchment' laid out on concrete 'barbecues'. Next they are brought in and husked before being laid aside to rest for a number of weeks. After this they are hulled (another layer of skin is taken off). The resulting 'green beans' are sized and packed in sacks and barrels for export. Some roasting takes place on the premises; the results are ground and tinned.

The **Blue Mountain Peak** itself is Jamaica's highest (7402ft), and a popular climb. The mountains are often lost in cloud and mist in the day and so to get the best chance of a clear view you should aim to reach the peak soon after dawn; most trips set off at 3 or 4 in the morning. If you are lucky, you might be able to see as far as Cuba. On the way down you will first pass through elfin growth, stunted grasses, knee-high trees and lichens, and then into montane woodland, still swirling in cloud, where ferns and orchids sit in the upper branches and trees reach tall to catch the sunlight. You are advised to go with a guide, who can be arranged through one of the many guest houses on the route. The ascent and the walk back can be made in about 7 hours from Abbey Green. The best months to climb the peak are between June and September and in the winter between December and April, though it can be quite cold then. You will need good footwear and some warm and waterproof clothing.

Kingston to Annotto Bay

The A3 road climbs steeply out of Kingston from Constant Spring and Stony Hill and soon picks up the Wag Water valley, which runs all the way across to the north coast. Standing either side of the road at Castleton are some Botanical Gardens that date from 1869, set in 39 acres in the dramatic, incredibly fertile (and pretty wet) Wag Water valley. The plants are marked and there are guides who will explain the 35 palms among the 60ft explosions of bamboo and point out the lair of the trap-door spider (sealed watertight and lined with silk). From here the road follows the river and comes to the north coast near Annotto Bay.

luxury

Just beyond Irish Town on the Irish Town road, scattered over the summit and flanks of a 3100ft hill among the camelback ridges and outrageous greenery of the Blue Mountains, you will find the cottages of **Strawberry Hill**, © 944 8400, © 944 8408, UK reservations © 0800 614 790, US © 1 800 *OUT POST*. The area of Strawberry Hill once belonged to Horace Walpole, Gothic novelist and son of the British Prime Minister, and is named after his estate in London. The hotel, built when the old Great House was destroyed during Hurricane Gilbert in 1988, has been designed in the best romantic old-colonial Jamaican style: the clinker-laid wooden cottages have white louvred windows, tray ceilings, shingle roofs, wooden floors and furniture, and some four-poster beds, with some novel modern touches, including Jamaican dancing scenes and even illustrations from Madonna's *SEX* book in one cottage—and the comforts are modern. There are just 18 rooms (studios up to four-bedroom cottages, some with kitchens), one with facilities for the handicapped. Everywhere there are balconies with stunning views from which you can watch the clouds track through the banana leaves. Well worth a visit.

moderate

Ivor Guest House is a favourite spot, peering down from 2000ft on Skyline Drive in Jack's Hill (*see* pp.207–8).

Another hotel well worth considering if you are arriving on the Castleton Road is the **Stony Hill Hotel**, © 942 2357, which has 27 rooms housed in a string of villas and open-air terraces, scattered along a hillside behind Constant Spring. The exteriors are all hung wth fantastic greenery and the interiors decorated with odd, cubist paintings. It's a little past its prime, but has a calm and quiet atmosphere, a stunning view, and is a good retreat from town. It has a pool and all meals are available.

inexpensive

Higher up into the Blue Mountains, above Guava Ridge off the Mavis Bank Road, you will find the **Pine Grove Hotel**, c/o 62 Duke Street, © 922 8705, © 922 5895, with 14 simply decorated rooms in a block on a hilltop next to the central house, where there is a restaurant and bar, and excellent views both up and down the mountains.

Maya Lodge, PO Box 216, ✆ 927 2097, ✉ 926 0727, near Ivor Guest House, just above Kingston, is lost in the deepest Jamaican fertility at the end of a rickety lane, with 6 cabins, hostel space for 10 and tent sites stretched around a curving hillside from a modern main house. It is a friendly place; guests meet on the thatched veranda which seems almost threatened by the ever-encroaching greenery. Endless information is available on Jamaican wildlife and walking. It gets quite cold on winter evenings, so take a jersey. The menu offers local Jamaican food, strong on vegetarian dishes. Facilities are very basic.

Much higher in the mountains, on an old coffee plantation at 4000ft is **Whitfield Hall Hostel**, contact 8 Armon Crescent, Kingston 6, ✆ 927 0986, another retreat lost in the grandeur of the Jamaican peaks. It's very remote (you need a four-wheel drive to get there, which can be arranged with the number above); meals can be prepared on request, but you can take your own food. No electricity: lighting is by gas lamps. It is a favourite drop-off point for those climbing the Blue Mountain Peak. Not far off is **Wildflower Lodge**, ✆ 926 5874, 929 5394 (*cheap*), which also has beds and provides meals on request. Make sure you book with these last two.

Over the ridge at Hardwar Gap, on the north side, there are other guest houses, including **Greenhills Guest House**, ✆ 997 4087, with very basic rooms off a corridor in a house perched on the hillside above Cedar Valley. Baths are shared; kitchen available. Farther down the hill is the **Cedar Valley Inn**, ✆/✉ 974 0635, set in an old great house and run by a friendly couple, with 6 rooms with shared bathrooms. Guides are available for walking tours, and meals are available. And above Red Light on the road to Newcastle, below the 17 mile post is a small and pleasant place to stay, the **Mount Edge Bed and Breakfast**, ✆ 0991 4292. There are just two rooms, one with a magnificent view right from the pillow, in a stone and wooden house. It offers hot and cold water, use of kitchen (or meals can be prepared), and is very calm and quiet.

In the Blue Mountains you are really dependent on the hotel dining rooms for eating out. High in the mountains, however, on the Kingston side of the Hardwar Gap, beyond Newcastle, is a very pleasant stopover for lunch and afternoon tea, at the **Gap Café**. It provides a magnificent view of Kingston and some superb cakes and coffee, which you take on a balcony with metal garden furniture, while the hummingbirds thrum around you.

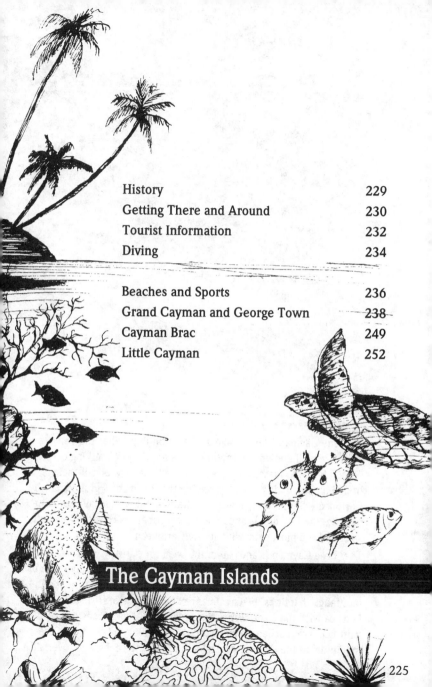

The Cayman Islands

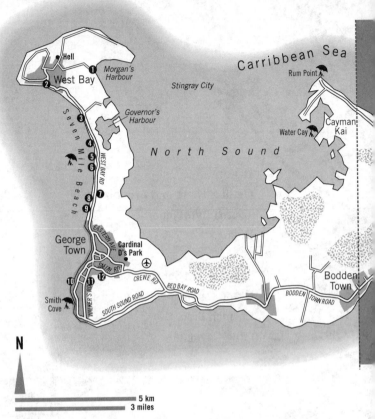

The tiny Cayman Islands have a reputation that belies their size. They are well known internationally as an offshore banking centre, official home to massive corporations, but they are equally celebrated among diving fiends as having the finest coral grounds in the Caribbean. Successfully managed, the two industries have combined to make the Cayman Islands the most prosperous country, for their size, and the most expensive in the Caribbean.

The three Cayman Islands lie in the western Caribbean, to the northwest of Jamaica and south of Cuba, about 500 miles directly south of Miami. They are the coral-encrusted summits of a submarine mountain range that links the Greater Antillean islands of Hispaniola and Jamaica with the Central American mainland. Karst limestone 'cliffrock' was pushed up by tectonic movement and then over the millennia, as the sea rose and fell around it, the peaks were overlaid

North Side Road

Queen's Highway

Queen Elizabeth II
Botanic Park

Frank Sound Road

13

HOTELS
1 Whitehaven Inn
2 Calypso Cove
3 Victoria House
4 Villas of the Galleon
5 Westin Casuarina
6 Holiday Inn
7 Hyatt Regency
8 Beach Club
9 Lacovia
10 Sunset House
11 Erma Eldemire's
12 Adam's
13 Cayman Diving Lodge

with compacted ironshore rock, a now-petrified growth of coral, sand and lagoon mud. Around the islands, the slopes descend in the north to the Bartlett Deep and in the south into the Cayman Trough, at 3500 fathoms, the deepest water in the Caribbean.

The Caymans are in two groups, separated by about 90 miles of sea. In the south is Grand Cayman, with the capital George Town. Its two sister islands, Cayman Brac and Little Cayman, lie to the northeast, separated by the Bogue Channel, which is just 5 miles wide but extremely deep and often very rough. No point on the Caymans rises to more than 140ft. In Grand Cayman the land is so flat that you can see parascenders and the tops of cruise ships towering over George Town from one side of the island to the other. The lack of elevation means that the islands do not have the rainfall of the other Greater Antilles and are less green and luxuriant. There are inland lagoons and mangrove swamps and impenetrable tangles of scrub forest, locally called 'bush'. There is not much wildlife on land, just the ubiquitous Caribbean goat and a few indigenous iguanas (of which there are two different sub-species, one each in Grand and Little Cayman). These two islands also have their own parrots, among the hundreds of other species of birds. Turtles visit the islands, but the marine crocodile, from which the name cayman comes, is no longer seen. There are plenty of other reptiles, though, including lizards, frogs and a freshwater turtle. The marine life is amazing, with a stunning variety of corals, sponges and tropical fish (*see* 'Diving', p.234).

There are about 32,000 people living permanently in the Cayman Islands, two-thirds of whom are native Caymanians. Most live in the towns of Grand Cayman; Cayman Brac has a population of about 1300 and Little Cayman just 70 odd. About half the islanders have a mix of African and European blood, resulting in their distinctive orange-red hair. There is little black–white animosity in the Cayman Islands. Caymanian English is easy to understand once you become attuned to it. If you hear a different, rawer patois, it is probably Jamaican (quite a lot of Jamaicans come to the island to work in the construction industry and as domestics). And Latin-sounding English is spoken by the sizeable Honduran contingent.

Cayman (with the stress on the second syllable), is a Crown Colony of Great Britain, as is evident in the police uniforms, red pillar-boxes and telephone booths, but the USA is the greatest influence nowadays. There are home-delivery pizzas and drive-in takeaways, cheery American restaurants with satellite sports on the tv and dollar tips, and you will see the occasional desperate-looking person power-walking their way along the West Bay road in the midday heat. Grand Cayman has been developed to look a bit like suburban America. It resounds to a roar of rubber on tarmac as the endless procession of American cars cruises by. There is no poverty here and no hustle-factor. At times it feels more like Florida than the West Indies, somehow a little sanitized for the Caribbean.

The Caymans are a sophisticated destination. Even the postcards are sexy and state of the art in design. A holiday here is at least as expensive as one in the USA or Europe, but everything on offer is done well. Seven-Mile beach in Grand Cayman is ideal for an active vacation while the rest of Grand Cayman and the smaller islands of Little Cayman and Cayman Brac offer a slow, gentle pace of life. Among the reams of tourist bumf (and Cayman seems to produce more than anywhere else in all the Caribbean) you can even find details of courses in offshore banking.

History

As Columbus passed Cayman Brac on his fourth voyage in 1503, he saw 'two very small and low islands, full of tortoises, as was the sea all about'. He named the islands the Tortugas after them. Later they came to be known as Los Lagartos, the alligators, but eventually the name Caymanas, after the crocodiles and iguanas on the island, stuck. The first reference to Grand Cayman was by Portuguese explorers in 1526, who called it Cayo Manos.

Initially Little Cayman was most visited. It became a stopover for its reliable supply of fresh water and easily available food—iguanas and turtles (the latter will stay alive for weeks if laid on their backs). Turtlers soon began to arrive; in the season, as many as 40 ships would set out from Kingston. The islands also became a favoured hideout for pirates, who lay in wait for ships sailing the Spanish Main to Cuba. It was not until the invasion of nearby Jamaica in 1655 that the islands were settled permanently. The story goes that two soldiers, Walter and Bowden, came to Grand Cayman; supposedly their names survive in the many Watlers and Boddens on the island to this day.

At the Treaty of Madrid in 1670 the islands were handed to the British, along with Jamaica, by the Spaniards. This did not make the islanders any safer, though; they were still harassed by the Spaniards and roving bands of pirates. The settlers farmed cotton and their own provisions, including yam, plantain and sugar-cane. They continued to capture and farm turtles, which they would keep in 'crawls' (fenced off areas on the shoreline) and sell to ships about to make the transatlantic crossing. In the 18th century turtleshell became fashionable in Europe, where it was used for quills, fans, letter-openers and for inlay work in furniture. The islanders also took what they could find from the ships that foundered on Cayman's treacherous reefs (also saving the lives of many of the shipwreck victims). The wrecks are still happening, though salvage laws are somewhat stricter now.

In 1802 the population on Grand Cayman had climbed to a thousand, of whom just over half were slaves until Emancipation in 1834. A visitor wrote:

> *The inhabitants in general are rather of a turbulent disposition, so much so, that upon one occasion it was necessary to send down a small detachment of Soldiers to assist & support the existing Civil Power.*

Cayman Brac and Little Cayman were only settled permanently in 1833. Their inhabitants lived a poor and simple existence, bartering a few products like rope (from sisal), coconuts and phosphates (from guano) with passing ships. A tradition of boat building grew up on the islands. By the turn of the 20th century there were 5000 Caymanians and, without employment on the islands, the men went to sea to make a living. They were renowned for their seamanship and were in particular demand by National Bulk Carriers of New York.

For three centuries the Cayman Islands were administered as a part of Jamaica, but on 4 June 1960, as the Jamaicans prepared for Independence, the Caymanians seceded, preferring instead to become a Crown Colony directly dependent on the UK. Today the Cayman Islands are administered by the representative of Queen Elizabeth, Governor John Owen MBE, who presides over the eight-strong Executive Council, three of whom are appointed by the governor and five drawn from the 15-person Legislative Assembly. The governor is in charge of defence, foreign affairs, police and internal security. Elections to the Legislative Assembly take place every four years. Since 1994 there has been ministerial government in the islands.

The two pillars of the Cayman economy are tourism (in 1995 there were over a million visitors, two-thirds of whom came by cruise ship) and offshore finance; there is quite a large expatriate community, working in both industries—hotel managers, lawyers, accountants and bankers. The islands are basically tax free (though visitors will find themselves paying a 6 per cent government tax on their hotel room) and the handling of money is made as easy as possible (no direct taxation, laws of confidentiality, absence of exchange controls, teams of lawyers and accountants to handle it all and good communications). The islands are famous for it and they have attracted over 500 banks and 30,000 companies to register on the island, becoming the fifth-largest international financial centre in the world. Many of these companies do not even have an office; they are simply a plaque on the wall.

© (809–)   ***Getting There By Air***

You will probably fly into Grand Cayman; there are a couple of flights direct into Cayman Brac, *see* below, but most people fly from Grand Cayman to the smaller islands—connections can usually be made the same day. The national carrier is Cayman Airways: Grand Cayman © 949 2311; in Cayman Brac reservations © 948 2535, flight information © 948 1221; also US toll free © 1 800 422 9626. There is a departure tax of US$10.

From Europe: There is a twice-weekly direct flight from London on Caledonian Airways, reservations with British Airways, UK © 0345 222111, or © 949 8200 in Cayman. Otherwise connections can be made in Miami.

From the USA: Eight or ten flights daily depart Miami for the Cayman Islands (try Cayman Airways, US ✆ 1 800 422 9626, American Airlines and Northwest). Other direct links from the States, some of them stopping at Miami, include those from Atlanta (three a week on Cayman Airways), Baltimore (twice a week on US Air), Boston, Charlotte and Cleveland (all daily on US Air), Houston (at least daily on Cayman Airways or American Airlines), Indianapolis (daily on America Trans Air), Memphis (daily on Northwest), Oklahoma (three times a week on Cayman Airways), Philadelphia (daily on US Air), Pittsburgh (three times weekly on US Air) and Tampa (five times a week on Cayman Airways and United Airlines). There is an almost daily scheduled service between Cayman Brac and Miami on Cayman Airways.

From Other Caribbean Islands: There are five flights a week to Kingston, Jamaica, on Air Jamaica or on Cayman Airways, some of which stop in Montego Bay. There are occasional chartered flights from Cayman to Cuba.

Getting Between the Islands

Island Air, ✆ 949 0241, fly twice daily, each morning and afternoon, from Grand Cayman to Cayman Brac, ✆ 948 1656, touching Little Cayman, ✆ 948 0021, both on the way there and on the way back. Cayman Airways also have a flight most days to Cayman Brac.

Getting Around Grand Cayman

Buses on Grand Cayman leave from behind the court house in the centre of George Town. There are two routes: green-striped mini-buses head up the West Bay road, departing several times an hour (more frequently during the morning and evening 'rush hour') until late at night; yellow-striped buses head out to the East End once an hour, usually until dusk. Except on the Seven Mile strip, hitching is quite a reliable way to get around.

There is an abundance of **taxis** in Grand Cayman; pick one up on the road or wander into the foyer of the nearest hotel. Fares are fixed by the government: a ride from the airport to George Town costs US$8; to midway up Seven Mile Beach, US$12–14; to West Bay (top of Seven Mile Beach), US$20; to Spanish Cove, US$27; to Bodden Town, US$27; to East End and North Side, US$50; to Water Cay, US$60.

There is a superabundance of **cars** in Cayman, on just a few roads—at times it is difficult to turn right because it takes so long for a gap to appear in the traffic. Driving is on the left and speed limits vary: 25 or 30mph in town and 40 or 50mph on the open road. Traffic proceeds at a stately pace in Cayman, however, which is something of a relief after other Caribbean islands. Rental cars are readily available; you need a local driving licence (issued by the hire firm, price US$5) and must leave a credit card or cheque deposit. You will be offered better rates for a week's hire, and prices are cheaper in summer, but all the firms have roughly similar prices. Rates start at US$30 per day for the smallest car, with charges for insurance and collision damage waiver on top. Contact **Cico Avis**, ✆ 949 2468, **Andy's Rent a Car**, ✆ 949 8111, **Coconut Car Rentals** (good rates), ✆ 949 4037, or **Dollar**, ✆ 949 4790. You can get a jeep through **Soto's 4x4 Jeep Rentals**, ✆ 945 2424.

Scooters and **motorbikes** are widely available, though hoteliers will try to dissuade you from using them because they have to send so many honeymooners home in plaster. Rates are US$25–30 per day, driving licence required. Contact **Cayman Cycle Rentals**, ✆ 947 4021, or **Soto's Scooters**, ✆ 947 4652, both in Coconut Plaza. **Bicycles** are available through the same companies for US$12–15 per day. The only hill on the Cayman Islands is at the eastern end of Cayman Brac, so cycling is easy. Strangely, people seem to cycle on both sides of the road here and so if you are driving or walking, you may find cyclists bearing down on you from unexpected directions.

Tours

Taxi-drivers will happily take you on an island tour, with up to five people in the cab. Reckon on an hourly rate of US$35–40. Bus tours are also available. Typically these are sightseeing tours of West Bay and George Town with shopping time thrown in; they may include a visit to the east end of the island to see the blow holes, botanical gardens and a beach stop at Rum Point for lunch. Some tour companies also include a trip to Stingray City. Contact **Evco Tours**, ✆ 949 2118, **Majestic Tours**, ✆ 949 7773, or **Tropicana Tours**, ✆ 949 0944. For an aerial view of the island, contact **Island Air**, ✆ 949 0241, or **Cayman Helicopters**, ✆ 949 4400.

Tourist Information

UK:	Cayman Islands Department of Tourism, 6 Arlington Street, London SW1A 1RE, ✆ 0171 491 7771, ✉ 0171 409 7773.
Canada:	Earl B. Smith Travel Marketing Consultants, 234 Eglington Avenue East, Suite 306, Toronto, Ontario M4P 1K5, ✆ 416 485 1550, ✉ 416 485 7578.

Germany: Marketing Services International, Johanna-Melber Weg 12, D-60599 Frankfurt, © 069 60 320 94, ✆ 069 62 92 64.

Italy   G & A Martinengo, Via Fratelli, Ruffini 9, 20123 Milano, © 02 4801 2068, ✆ 02 4635 32.

Japan: International Travel Produce Inc., Kawase Building 4th Floor 14–1, 2 Chome Tsukui, Chuo-ku, Tokyo 104, © 03 35456187, ✆ 03 3545 8756.

Spain: Sergat Espana SL, Pau Casals 4, 08021 Barcelona, © 93 414 0210, ✆ 93 201 8657.

USA: 9525 W. Bryn Mawr, Suite 160, Rosemont, **Chicago**, Ill 60018, © 847 678 6446, ✆ 847 678 6675; Two Memorial City Plaza, 820 Gessner, Suite 170, **Houston**, Texas 77024, © 713 461 1317, ✆ 461 7409; 3440 Wilshire Boulevard, Suite 1202, **Los Angeles**, CA 90010, © 213 738 1968, ✆ 738 1829; 6100 Blue Lagoon Drive, Suite 150, **Miami**, FL 33126-2085, © 305 266 2300, ✆ 305 267 2932; 420 Lexington Avenue, Suite 2733, **New York**, NY 10170, © 212 682 5582, ✆ 212 986 5123.

Or you can write to the Cayman Islands Department of Tourism at PO Box 67, George Town, Grand Cayman, British West Indies, © 949 0623, ✆ 949 4053; *open 8.30–5*. There is an information desk at the airport and at the cruise ship terminal when a ship is in town.

The innumerable **tourist magazines** contain advice on everything including extra-curricular banking courses and investment in real estate: *Key to Cayman* (published yearly), *Destination Cayman*, *What's Hot in Cayman* (monthly) and the Cayman Airways in-flight magazine, *Horizons*. The local newspaper is the *Caymanian Compass*, published daily during the week, with a weekend section on Fridays.

In a **medical emergency** the Caymanians are able to care for you well at the hospital on Hospital Road in George Town, © 949 8600, but first try the front desk at your hotel as there may well be a doctor on call.

The emergency **telephone** number for the ambulance is © 555 and for the police © 911. The IDD code for the Caymans is © 809 followed by a seven-digit number. On island and between the Cayman Islands, just dial the seven figures. Public phone boxes are scattered around Cayman; they function with both coins and cards, which can be bought at Cable and Wireless offices and Texaco petrol stations. AT&T USA Direct is available to the USA on © 1 800 872 2881 and MCI Direct on © 1 800 624 1000.

The currency of the Cayman Islands is the Cayman dollar, which is fixed to the US dollar at a rate of CI$1:US$1.25. It comes as a bit of a surprise to find that the greenback is worth only 80 Cayman cents, but business is booming in the Caymans. US dollars are also valid and are accepted everywhere anyway, but you will sometimes get a better price in CI$. Prices are usually quoted in CI$, but sometimes in US$, so you need to be careful.

All major credit cards are accepted around the islands, in the hotels, restaurants and shops, as are traveller's cheques. Tips are 10–15%, usually added to your bill by the restaurants and hotels. **Banks** are open Mon–Thurs 9–2.30 and Fri 9–1 and 2.30–4.30. A couple of banks in town open on Saturday mornings. **Shops** are open 9–5, usually closed on Sundays. There are some duty-free shops, where prices are only quoted in Cayman dollars. The best book shop is the Book Nook: in the Anchorage Centre in town and in the Galleria Plaza about halfway up the West Bay Road.

Diving

Scuba diving in the Cayman Islands is the best in the Caribbean. Cayman is known particularly for its 'walls': the islands are surrounded by a few miles of sand and reefs and then suddenly the sea bed drops almost sheer to 20,000ft. Visibility is superb in the Caymans, often as far as 150ft.

There are caverns, pinnacles and underwater ravines, all of them encrusted with a vast array of corals, sponges and gorgonians: corals like tufts of shaggy white wool, thin tube sponges and vast barrel sponges, the jigsaw patterns of purple seafans standing against the tide, and deep down the fingers of the black corals.

Single damselfish pout and shimmering schools of bar jacks and blue tangs dip and dart in unison in your exhaled bubbles. Camouflaged crabs eye you with suspicion from their hide, and little red and white banded coral shrimps tangle their spindly feet and antennae. Tiny, shy seahorses lunge to find the cover of the coral; starfish flip as they move. At Stingray City in the North Sound, you can cavort with tame rays 5ft across; at Tarpon Alley you will see tarpon and grey reef sharks.

There are reefs on all sides of Grand Cayman, but most popular is the North Wall off the north shore. Cayman Brac is less well known than Grand Cayman, but according to many the diving is better. The main sites are around the West End. In Little Cayman, when the weather is good and the channel is not too rough, the diving is better still at Jackson Bay and Bloody Bay on the north shore. The wall here starts at 18ft below sea level. There are plenty of wrecks off the Caymans, the best known being the *Balboa* off George Town.

The Cayman Islands have strict laws for the protection of their reefs and fish, and there is zoning to encourage regeneration of fish and coral life. Spearfishing and setting traps are prohibited; there are strict rules about anchoring. You are not allowed to take any corals or sponges, dead or alive. However, many of the diving outfits have underwater photography equipment for E6 slide photographs and video, so you can keep them on film at least. If you happen across any buried treasure, then you'll have to work out an agreement with the Cayman government, because all wrecks and hoards officially belong to the Crown.

The first outing is often at 8am in Grand Cayman; there there are so many operators that there is often a race for the good dive-sites. Dive shops usually offer a two-dive outing each morning, which costs from US$60 and a single-tank dive in the afternoon, at about US$45. Night dives cost around US$50. If you need equipment that is charged on top. Divers should have a 'C' card or take a resort course (about US$75), available with most dive shops. There is a decompression chamber on the island, ✆ 949 4324.

There are about 40 dive outfits on the islands—some even specialize in older-guy instructors or blonde-waif instructresses for your maximum diving pleasure. Instruction is available in a number of different languages.

Two large and established operators in **Grand Cayman** are **Fisheye** on Seven Mile Beach, ✆ 947 4209, ✆ 947 4208, and **Bob Soto's Diving Ltd**, ✆ 949 2022, ✆ 949 8731, US toll free ✆ 1 800 BOB SOTO, which has recently won an award for marine conservation. Large operators have all the facilities, but they take out large groups of divers, sometimes on double decker dive boats. However, these crowds are usually broken down into groups of eight or ten, each with a dive-leader. If you would prefer a more personalized trip on a smaller boat you might want to go with one of the smaller operators, who also have the advantage of a certain flexibility—they may well be able to visit a particular dive-site for you. Try **Divers Down**, ✆ 945 1611, on the West Bay Road, **Turtle Reef/Dive Tech**, ✆ 949 1700, ✆ 949 1701, in the West Bay area, next to the turtle farm, and **Dive 'n' Stuff**, ✆ 949 6033, ✆ 945 9207, on the outskirts of George Town. The **Cayman Marine Lab**, ✆/✆ 947 0849, is run by a trained marine biologist who gives a lecture each day in between the dives. Two friendly operators set in slightly out-of-the-way hotels are **Sunset Divers**, ✆ 949 7111, ✆ 949 7101, south of George Town, and the **Cayman Diving Lodge** at the East End, ✆ 947 7555, ✆ 947 7560.

In **Cayman Brac** there are three operators, all based in the southwestern corner of the island either in or close to the hotels. Contact the **Divi Tiara Beach Resort**, ✆ 948 7553, ✆ 948 1316, **Reef Divers** at the Brac Reef Beach Resort, ✆ 948 1323, ✆ 948 1316, and **Brac Aquatics**, ✆ 948 1429.

On **Little Cayman** the dive shops are all attached to the hotels. Contact the **Southern Cross Club**, ✆ 948 1099, ✉ 948 1098, **Pirates Point Resort**, ✆ 948 10101, ✉ 948 1011, and **Reef Divers** at the Little Cayman Beach Resort, ✆ 948 1033, ✉ 948 1040. Many of these hotels offer special diving packages and there are also a number of liveaboard boats based in the Caymans.

For those who do not dive, but who would like to see the colourful reefs, there is always the **Atlantis Submarine**, ✆ 949 7700. The submarine leaves from South Church Street, just down from the museum and trips are quite expensive, starting at about US$55, but the guides are informative and knowledgeable. On some trips, divers outside the sub talk to you through headsets and describe the marine life they are pointing out—find out how groupers cope with the boredom of middle age. You get a deeper tour in the three-man submersibles of **Research Submersibles**, ✆ 949 8296, ✉ 949 8574. They dive the wall down to 800ft; you visit the odd wreck or hang between huge barrel sponges and turtles, with lamps to illuminate the corals as the sunlight fades. Price about US$300 per person.

Beaches

Grand Cayman's **Seven Mile Beach** is one of the world's most famous; its gently shelving sands extend from just north of George Town up the west coast to West Bay. It is the centre of the island's tourism, home to the majority of the hotels, watersports and diving operations. It is marginally less crowded at the northern end, though even here it almost entirely built up; signs on the road indicate paths down to the beach between the hotels. Facing west, Seven Mile Beach has one of the finest views of the sunset anywhere, with a good chance of seeing the Green Flash from one of the beach bars that crowd the strip.

There are a few less busy beaches around the island, interrupting the pitted iron-shore coral that lines most of the rest of the coastline. A favourite with the Caymanians is **Smiths Cove**, a mile or so south of town. Or head for the south coast, where the beaches are protected by fringing reefs. There is a passable public beach, with mounded, steeply sloping sand, sunshades and hammocks, at **Spott's**, not far east of George Town; or go on to the East End (try **Heritage Beach** or **Pirate's Beach**), where isolated suntraps are hidden behind bushes of sea grape at the end of sandy tracks. On the north coast there are a couple of excellent sandy spots with beach bars looking out onto the North Sound. **Rum Point** is set among casuarina pines that roar on the breeze, where the water is clear and shallow for a hundred yards offshore. It is now quite smart and expensive, with a restaurant, a bar and a snack bar as well as a watersports shop. You can reach Rum Point on a ferry from the Hyatt Hotel. Not far off at

Water Cay is another bar on a small beach, **Kaibo**—palms, simple fare, hammocks and picnic tables, and a view over the sand onto the lagoon. The Caymanians ask you not to wander around the town in your bathing costume; nudity and toplessness are illegal but, if you are determined, you may find somewhere right off the beaten track to strip off.

Watersports

All the Cayman Islands have reefs close enough to the shore and shallow enough for excellent **snorkelling**. In Grand Cayman, there are reefs off the south coast and in the northeast, though you should be careful of the currents here. Some of the best snorkelling is at Cemetery Beach at the northern end of Seven Mile Beach, Eden Rock and Devil's Grotto south of George Town and at Soto's Reef.

Windsurfers and small sailing boats can be hired at many of the hotels and watersports shops along Seven Mile Beach. The best winds, though, are out at the East End, where you will find **Cayman Windsurf** at Morritt's Tortuga Club, © 947 7492. General operators include **Sailboards Caribbean**, © 949 1068, which has a MISTRAL concessionary and **Don Foster's Dive** at the Holiday Inn, © 947 4444. All the watersports you can imagine are available in Grand Cayman; you can take a bird's-eye view over the island by parasail, or test out your biking skills on a jetski or, if you're feeling energetic, you can go waterskiing. More stately options include an outing in a pedalo or a glass-bottomed boat. You can even take a high-speed ride around the bay on an inflatable banana.

Yacht tours can also be arranged through the watersports shops and the many small boat operators. Typically they include snorkelling and lunch or a sunset cruise, and some of them make a visit to Stingray City (*see* below). Catamarans include *Cockatoo*, © 949 7884, based at Parrots Landing and Fantasea Tours' *Don't Even Ask*, © 949 2182. You can get an afternoon of rum-soaked fun and tee-ree-ree, unlimited fruit punch, dancing and walking the plank, on the mock-pirate boat *Jolly Roger*, © 949 5577. The (nearly) tall ship *Nancy*, © 949 8988, a very attractive wooden schooner (top sail gaff-rigged), offers slightly less raucous daytime and sunset trips. Most companies offer transport to and from your hotel.

A trip to **Stingray City** is the ultimate in tourist junkets, but entertaining nonetheless. In fact there are two stingray cities: both are sandy sections of sea bed in the North Sound—one lies in 15 feet of water and the other rises to within 3 feet of the surface. The stingrays were first attracted here when fishermen came to clean their catch and threw the fish innards into the water. Now they know they will be offered food and so they are friendly to humans. Stand in the water and you will see the grey shadows cruise by on the bottom of the sea, first circling and then touching you; some pass between your legs, or flare their wings against you as they sniff for food, while others will actually fold their wings around you. The guides lift them out of the water to show you their mouths, or to wear one as a hat. Trips can be arranged with any of the general watersports operators, or through one of the local (and cheaper) companies that work out of Coconut Plaza. For some reason they are all called Ebanks, but you can choose from: **Captain Marvin**, *✆* 947 4590, **Frank's**, *✆* 947 5491 or **C+G**, *✆* 947 4049, from US$25 per person.

Deep-sea fishing, casting for tuna and wahoo or 6ft marlin, is another popular day out on the high seas, and the Caymans have a host of sleek vessels. Rates are US$600–700 for a full day for six people, US$350–400 for a half-day. Try **Capt. Crosby Ebanks**, *✆* 947 4049, near George Town and **Black Princess Charters**, *✆* 949 3821. Also try **Cayman Sunset**, *✆* 949 3666, in Morgan's Harbour.

Land Sports

On land, the most popular sport is **tennis**. There are plenty of courts around. If there is none at your hotel, you can arrange through the front desk to play elsewhere. **Golfers** will find a couple of courses on Grand Cayman. With such low-lying, sandy land, you might expect a links course, and this can be played at Safehaven on the West Bay Road; 18 holes and par 71, *✆* 949 5988. The course at the **Hyatt Regency Hotel**, *✆* 949 8020, can be played as a 9-hole full-length course or an 18-hole course with par-3 holes (using the same fairways and greens; played on alternate days of the week). You can also play a third course, designed for the short-hitting Cayman ball. Book well in advance. There is even mini-golf—on West Bay Road, by the Hyatt Hotel.

The Cayman Islands National Trust arranges a number of **walking** tours around the island: George Town, West Bay and Bodden Town. They also have a guided tour of the bush in the middle of the island, the **Mastic Trail**, *✆* 949 0121. If you would like to take a horseback ride along the beach, contact **Nicki's Beach Rides**, *✆* 947 5839, mobile 916 3530 (*expensive*).

Grand Cayman and George Town

The Cayman Islands' capital is on a broad bay in the southwest of Grand Cayman. The nucleus is almost entirely a modern town, with streets of smart glass-fronted offices and air-conditioned shopping malls, but there are a number of very pretty timber buildings from old-time Cayman dotted around. Nothing remains of the 'Hogstyes' that gave the town its original name, before it was called after King George III at the beginning of the 19th century. The remains of the town's original defense, Fort George, just a few waist-high walls, lie on the shore just north of the cruise ship terminal and main dock. Close by is the Emslie Memorial Church, built in the 1920s on the site of an earlier church.

Inland you come to the main square, a small park with lawns and trees surrounded by a cluster of official buildings. A statue of James Manoah Bodden, Cayman's first national hero, stands in the park. The Legislative Assembly building, a curious modern affair with echoes seemingly of Mexican Indian architecture, stands opposite the court house, an equally modern construction of glass and concrete. Both were built in the 1970s. Perhaps the prettiest building is the public library, which stands on the eastern side of the square; across from here is yet another shop. To the south of the square, the post office, built in 1939, has a covered walkway and a curved façade. To the east of the town centre is a small area which looks a bit more like the rest of the West Indies, where you will find local restaurants and the odd goat meandering around mowing the grass.

Back on the waterfront, just down from the cruise ship dock, the **Cayman Islands National Museum**, *open Mon–Fri 9.30–5.30, Sat 10–4*, is set in the Old Courts Building, one of the island's finest traditional buildings. Built some time in the middle of the last century, with a solid lower storey and a wooden upper, it has served variously as post office, jail and library as well as the court house. The excellent museum has various displays showing the natural history and cultural heritage of the islands: geological exhibits include unique Cayman stones; there are displays of seafaring life; fragments of wattle and daub structures; tiny coins called quotties; also an audio-visual presentation.

Leaving the town centre you soon arrive in the suburbs, modern concrete houses enclosed within chain-link fences, with satellite dishes sitting in the garden. Scattered among them are a few older houses, invariably neat, with wraparound verandas where bench seats hang from the ceiling on chains, set in yards full of pretty blooms surrounded by white picket fences. The graveyards on Cayman are also very well kept: the tombstones (which must be built up on the ground because the rock is too hard to dig into) are usually painted white and adorned with flowers.

West Bay Road runs north straight out of the town, tracking behind the tourist development on Seven Mile Beach, to the old settlement of West Bay. Seven Mile Beach is not actually 7 miles long (more like 5½). Either side of the road there are shopping malls, restaurants and bars dotted among the endless hotels and condominium complexes.

Many of the Caymanians themselves live in West Bay—their ancestors moved to this area when they were emancipated in the 1830s. It is jokingly referred to as the 'Republic of West Bay'. **Hell** is a small moonscape surrounded by mangrove and the occasional frangipani. It looks like petrified cake-mix, a series of grey pinnacles whipped up by some diabolic chef. In fact it is limestone 'cliff-rock' that has been eroded unevenly (through former wave action), leaving a pitted and scarred stony mess. It is called Hell because the sharp points appear like the flames of hell turned to stone. You can send a postcard from the postbox , which will be stamped 'Hell'.

At the northwestern point you will come to the **Turtle Farm**, *open daily 8.30–5, adm*, a farm and research station that breeds the green sea turtles. You can see almost the whole life-cycle of the turtle in the farm. They start as eggs, white and very slightly larger than ping-pong balls; these hatch after about 60 days of incubation in a heated room. Hatchlings are put into tanks, where thousands of nippers scrabble over one another. Gradually they are transferred through the series of tanks as they increase in size, about a foot across at one year, 80lbs in weight by the time they are five years old. They can grow as large as 6–7ft long and reach 200–600lbs. A small percentage of the turtles are released into the wild each year, but most only make it into soup. They are butchered at four or five years old.

Unfortunately it is not possible to see the most interesting part of the turtle's life cycle, the very beginning, when the female turtles crawl up onto the beach to lay their eggs. It usually happens at night and so all you see are their tractor-like tracks in the sand next morning. They select their spot and dig a body-pit with front and back flippers, and then an egg chamber shaped like a flask, carefully scooping up the sand with their rear flippers, which they can use as delicately as a pair of hands. They lay about a hundred eggs and then cover them again before crawling back to the sea. Females each lay an average of five times between May and October. The sex of turtle hatchlings depends on the temperature in the nest—a particularly hot spring will bring more females and a cold one more males.

Other rarer and endangered turtles, including loggerheads, hawksbills and ridleys, are also on view in the farm and there is a small menagerie of iguanas and alligators. In the café an excellent series of displays illustrates Cayman history and the use of turtleshell across the ages. It was used as far back as Roman times; from the Renaissance it was used in Europe as decorative inlay on furniture and in combs, fans and brushes. It was even thought to ward off disease and so made into linings for bathtubs.

In the eastern part of George Town is a small wildlife park, **Cardinal D's Park**, *adm*. There is a walkway past a lagoon and through some gardens where you will see indigenous Cayman birds and animals as well as some from overseas: emus, American wild turkeys, toucans, parrots, macaws and the Cayman blue iguana. Great for children—buy a bag of feed and the ducks, turtles and fish race over.

If you head out of George Town to the east you come to Bodden Town, the island's only other town, and the first capital. Out in the country you will see the cattle grazing and their constant companions, the cattle egrets. A road loops around the shoreline at the east end of the island and among the scrub you may see the rare Cayman iguana. Along the southern shore, look out for the blow-holes cut into the ironshore, which blow like a whale with each incoming wave.

In the heart of the Cayman scrub, off the road linking the north and south shores, you will find the **Elizabeth II Botanic Park**, *adm*. There is a visitors' centre, from which lead a number of walks. A mile-long trail cuts through the Cayman bush (Cactus County, Bull Thatch Bend and Epiphyte Woodland), where you will see iguana habitat, water holes with buttonwood trees, and plants (with informative labels) such as agave and 'duppy bush', so called because its leaves shimmer in the moonlight, and Cayman's various epiphytes and orchids. Look out for the Little Cayman habitat, with a selection of cacti endemic to that island. There is also a traditional Caymanian house, with a small veranda, sloping roof, wattle and daub 'cookroom' (a separate building to prevent a fire in the main house), herb garden, fruit orchard and provision ground. A number of floral gardens feature plants from the other Greater Antillean islands.

Festivals

The big event in the Caymanian calendar is **Pirates Week** in October, a swashbuckling affair of fake eye-patches and tee-ree-ree. Choreographed invasions amuse the tourists, but the evenings are enjoyed by tourists and locals alike in the bar, ✆ 949 5078.

There is also a carnival, **Batanabo**, held over a weekend in March or April each year, in which the islanders and visitors dress in theme costume and shuffle-step through the streets of George Town to steel bands and loud soca music. **Million Dollar Month** (June) is a month-long fishing competition, in which you might just hook the US$25,000 prize money for catching the largest blue marlin of the competition—a number of prize specimens are on view around the island, including a 584lb fish at the airport, ✆ 949 5587. There are a couple of other **fishing tournaments** over the year. **Aviation Week** in June sees any number of aircraft arriving from Miami. There is also a **windsurfing competition** (January) and a couple of **regattas** (one in October). Keep in touch through the tourism publications.

✆ (809–)

Where to Stay

The majority of the hotels are along the 5 miles of Seven Mile Beach to the north of George Town; they range from simple but quite expensive guest houses to the height of luxury. Many offer diving packages. There is very little cheap accommodation in Cayman so you might prefer to stay in a self-catering or 'efficiency' apartment, in one of the many condominium complexes (these have some common facilities such as watersports and a pool, but no restaurant or bar). There are also plenty of villas for rent: contact **Cayman Villas**, PO Box 681, ℃ 947 4144, @ 949 7471, US toll free ℃ 1 800 235 5888, or **Hospitality World**, PO Box 30123, ℃ 949 8098, @ 949 7054, US toll free ℃ 1 800 232 1034, or you can book through your nearest Department of Tourism Reservations Office. All hotels add a government tax of 10% and usually a service charge of 10% and hotel room rates are usually listed in US$.

luxury

The **Hyatt Regency Hotel** on West Bay Road, PO Box 1698, ℃ 949 1234, @ 949 8528, US toll free ℃ 1 800 223 1234, is the most luxurious place to stay on the island. It is large (236 rooms) modern and very neat, decorated in plush Caribbean pastel, with echoes of the colonial era in its mock-classical columns and tall Georgian windows. The atmosphere is quite up-beat, with a dip and sip bar, watersports across the road on the beach and low-calorie *cuisine naturelle* in one of the four restaurants.

You can stay in similar extravagance but right on the sand at an excellent part of the beach, in the **Westin Casuarina Resort**, ℃ 945 3800, @ 949 5825, US reservations ℃ 1 800 WESTIN 1. It has 343 rooms ranged on five floors, north and south wings dressed in mock-classical airs and graces (including a cloistered walkway to the restaurants), pointed in a shade of light blue that matches the Caymanian sea. There is an attractive pool, surrounded by profuse greenery, above the beach where all the watersports are on offer. Rooms, cool and carpeted, have all the requisites for modern Caribbean luxury—tvs, air-conditioning and fans, coffee-makers and mini-bars; most have balconies.

very expensive

The nicest of the big, factory-style hotels right on the beach is the **Holiday Inn**, PO Box 904, ℃ 947 4444, @ 947 4213, US toll free ℃ 1 800 421 9999. The four storeys of rooms stand above a central pool area with palms and palm-thatch parasols, from where it is a short hop to the sea and the watersports. Lively in the evenings.

Unlike the pastel palaces, the **Beach Club Hotel and Dive Resort**, PO Box 903, ℃ 949 8100, @ 947 5167, has a low-key, more West Indian atmosphere, with that classic Caribbean beach club feel. The 41 rooms look down from balconies or give straight on to the sands of Seven Mile

Beach; in the middle stands the central house, with the restaurant and bar set on an attractive, breezy brick-pillared terrace, with its superb view of the sunset. Rooms are comfortable but not sybaritic, with telephone, air-conditioning and tv. There are watersports facilities and waitress service on the beach for hotel guests.

Condominium complexes vary much less in price than the hotels; the eminently comfortable **Lacovia Condominiums**, PO Box 1998, ✆ 949 7599, ✉ 949 0172, occupy an excellent spot on Seven Mile Beach. On offer are 45 apartments in a variety of configurations up to three-bedroomed suites.

expensive

At **Villas of the Galleon**, PO Box 1797, ✆ 947 4433, ✉ 947 4705, there are 74 units, all pleasantly decorated in white and bright pastel, right on the beach; or you could try **Victoria House**, PO Box 636, ✆ 947 4233, ✉ 947 5328, smaller, just 25 rooms, but with a friendly atmosphere.

moderate

There are a number of small, relaxed dive resorts on the island. The **Sunset House Hotel**, PO Box 479, ✆ 949 7111, ✉ 949 7101, US toll free ✆ 1 800 854 4767, is a short distance south of George Town and very popular in the early evening, as the name would suggest. Its blocks of rooms, the pool and restaurant and a palm-thatch bar fringe the ironshore coastline and the reefs begin close by. The 59 comfy rooms are decorated in a combination of styles; all have telephones and air-conditioning, some fans.

If you are happy in the isolated southeast of the island you can try the **Cayman Diving Lodge**, PO Box 11, ✆ 947 7555, ✉ 947 7560, with just 17 rooms and a very easygoing atmosphere, just above the beach. Plenty of sports facilities are available at an all-inclusive rate.

Adam's Guest House on Melmac Avenue, also in the south of town, ✆ 949 2512, ✉ 949 0919, is set in a private house. There are three rooms, an 'efficiency' studio and a two-bedroom apartment.

Of the few reasonably-priced places to stay, the best is **Erma Eldemire's Guest House**, PO Box 482, ✆ 949 5387, ✉ 949 6987, south of George Town, where there are three apartments (with kitchens) and nine simple double rooms; there's a common kitchen for breakfast, a sitting area and a veranda.

In West Bay, close to Morgan's Harbour, is **Whitehaven Inn Guest House**, PO Box 30424, ✆ 949 1064, ✉ 947 4980, just five rooms, with floral carpet and dark-stained wooden furniture. Rooms have fans and air-conditioning, some share baths; bed and breakfast is included. It's a little isolated (a good walk from the beach and the bus route) so you may need some sort of transport. Inexpensive apartments (similar to a condominium) can be found at **Calypso Cove Apartments**, ©/◉ 949 3730.

Eating Out

As Grand Cayman has developed over the last 20 years, so too has a wide range of restaurants—from successful local ventures serving West Indian food, and tiny local Caymanian restaurants in the back streets of George Town, to gourmet establishments with celebrity chefs from the USA, imported dial-a-pizza parlours and burger joints. There are also restaurants specializing in Italian, French, Mexican and Chinese food. Much of the hotel food is imported, but there is generally good local seafood: spiny lobster, conch or turtle (farmed on Grand Cayman). Make sure you reserve tables in winter, when there will be a waiting list of up to three days in the more popular restaurants. Restaurant bills are quite steep in the Caymans and most restaurants except the smaller local ones add a 15% service charge on top. Prices are usually quoted in Cayman dollars. *The price categories used here are: expensive—CI$20 and above; moderate—CI$12–CI$20; cheap—CI$12 and below.*

expensive

A number of restaurants vie for the top spot in Cayman at the moment: **The Grand Old House**, © 949 9333, is in a charming old gingerbread town house on the shoreline south of town. Tables are ranged on the two-tier screened veranda and on the waterfront itself, where they are are hung with fairy lights. Chef Tell Erhardt of US television fame is the inspiration here. The menu is international with some variations on traditional Caribbean themes—citrus-crusted Atlantic salmon on a bed of wilted spinach or sautéed fresh snapper with shallots, mushrooms and a Chardonnay beurre blanc are followed by heavyweight puddings. There is a long wine list of good quality. *Closed Sun.*

Ristorante Pappagallo, © 949 1119, has a spectacular setting on a lagoon in West Bay north of Seven Mile Beach, though the pointed thatch roof is more reminiscent of the South Pacific than the Caribbean. As dusk falls, the mangroves around the lake are lit up—a good setting for a cocktail before you move to the veranda or the air-conditioned dining room to eat.

The restaurant specializes in northern Italian cuisine, with good Caribbean seafood—*agnello alla griglia del ghiottone* (lamb in a rosemary lemon pesto) and tuna in saffron rice, with a creamy roasted garlic and port sauce.

Hemingway's, ✆ 949 1234, at the Hyatt Regency, is another spot for an elegant and intimate meal out, where you dine in a formal dining room or out on the terrace through the French windows. The menu is international: start with Cayman conch fritters in a sweet pepper remoulade followed by grouper stuffed with roasted corn and crab mousse. *Cuisine naturelle* dishes include poached salmon with Sicilian beans. **Lantana's**, at the Caribbean Club on West Bay Road, a little to the south of Hemingway's, serves New American and Caribbean cuisine in a simple and brightly decorated air-conditioned dining room. A long and adventurous menu features a volley of different flavours; start with organic baby greens with goats cheese crumble and follow up with honey-lime basted wahoo with asparagus and wild mushroom risotto.

Smuggler's Cove, ✆ 949 6003, set on the waterfront in town, has tables on a terrace under the sea grape trees: try chicken and shrimps with linguine Bombay, or salmon crusted with almond and walnuts, followed by one of the sumptuous ice creams and puddings. The **Wharf Restaurant**, ✆ 949 2231, on the rocky waterfront, is large and ever popular, its tables scattered between the brightly lit terraces and the covered veranda. Enjoy the Caribbean and international fare, and the tarpon feeding at 9 each evening (though the fish seem happy to swim for you at any time).

If you are driving out of town for the day and would like to linger over a gastronomic treat rather than a light bite, two places are highly reccommended: **Rum Point** (contact through the Hyatt on ✆ 949 1234), is all dressed up with brightly painted fish on the walls, starfish chairbacks and outrageously bright tablecloths. Shrimp cocktail on a citrus-herbed tabouleh and grilled tuna on curried pumpkin are the specialities. At **The Lighthouse**, ✆ 947 2047, you dine on a wooden terrace to the roar of the waves breaking on the reef. There is a long wine list to go with the Italian and seafood menu: *filetto contadina* (a fillet sautéed with wild mushrooms and tomato in a demi-glace sauce) and swordfish *positano*, grilled and laid on a bed of vegetable linguine with tomato coulis. Cheaper alternatives include the nearby **Reef Point**, a local lunch-stop and **The Edge** at Bodden Town.

moderate

Ottmar's, in the Clarion Hotel, ✆ 947 5656, takes its name from its prizewinning chef. The indoor dining area is elegant and plush, with neat table-cloths and candles. The menu features French techniques adapted to Caribbean and American food. Chapultepec is an Aztec-influenced dish of the fish mahi-mahi, or you can plump for red snapper caprice, with banana chutney and fresh mango slices and finish up with mousse Suchard.

The **Whitehall Bay Restaurant**, ✆ 949 8670, perches on a gingerbread deck on the waterfront, with abundant greenery and bright pink décor. It offers the best in simple island fare as well as a few salads—local pepperpot, coconut shrimp, and cracked conch, seasoned and deep fried.

The **Crows Nest**, ✆ 949 9366, just inland from the coast south of George Town, enjoys an equally attractive setting and easygoing atmosphere. You dine on a screened veranda painted in a riot of pinks, oranges and blues, lush with greenery and lit by torches. It serves Caribbean fare and seafood: try the fiery coconut shrimps followed by jerk turkey salad or peppered dolphin with a strawberry sauce, and finish up with a banana toffee pie.

At the **Almond Tree**, ✆ 949 2893, you sit under the eponymous tree (and breadfruit and guinep trees) in a mock-rustic setting evocative of the South Seas, and dine on Caribbean and international fare.

cheap

If you're feeling homesick for a cheery American restaurant, there are plenty of places to go. **Eats** is a traditional American diner in the Cayman Falls Plaza, quite a good place for breakfast or for burgers and pizzas. And there is always the **Texas Lone Star**, serving Tex-Mex food, just outside the entrance to the Hyatt.

Other breakfast haunts where you can sit all day pondering the excesses (alchoholic and probably financial) of the night before include the **Hog Sty Café** in town, which has a brightly painted terrace on the waterfront: burgers, sandwiches and pub grub—even a ploughman's lunch.

For something a little more Caribbean, you can try **Coralita's**, in the centre of town. They offer some of the best basic island fare—fritters and callaloo followed by conch burger or chicken and chips liberally dashed with hot pepper sauce (beware).

Finally, if you feel like a late-night jerk, you can go to the **Breadfruit Tree Garden Café**, set in a pretty garden or **Champion House II**, both offering simple West Indian fare in the backstreets of George Town.

Cayman has recently begun to brew its own beer, Stingray, which is quite dark and bitter for a Caribbean brew, not really what you would expect. However, lighter beers are available— all the American ones and Red Stripe from Jamaica and Carib from Trinidad. The big Caymanian cocktail at the moment is the Mudslide, made with vodka, Kahlua and Bailey's Irish Cream, if you think you can bear it.

There are plenty of bars around the island, some of which enjoy superb waterfront settings. Those on the cliffs to the south of the town tend to be popular with the locals for sundowners after work: try the **Sunset Bar** (at the Sunset House Hotel), with plenty of palm thatch on a walled terrace and an expat crowd; just out of town, sit under parasols on the waterfront terrace of **Paradise Cove**—it can be quite lively at sunset, when there is a happy hour, which attracts a nice mix of locals and tourists. It also has a sandy platform just off the road for a bit of daytime lounging in the sun. Or you could investigate the **Blue Parrot**, south of the Sunset Bar. There are a number of beach bars—one of the best is at the **Beach Club**.

Durty Reid's is an all-American bar in the eastern outskirts of town, with big-screen tv and walls covered with pictures of the US Marines. The sign outside touts it as 'A beanery—warm beer, lousy food, surly help'—but lots of pictures of happy punters are prominently displayed. In Bodden Town you will find **The Edge**, a slightly dark and dingy bar-discotheque with a pool table and juke-box and a terrace over the waterfront. On the north coast on the road to Rum Point is **Apollo 11**, a bar set in a large shed; look out for the huge bar stools, cut from whole tree trunks.

Many of the simpler restaurants in town double as bars and so you can linger as you eat or hop from one to the next as you decide whether to eat. Popular starting points for the evening include **Santiago's**, where you drink under sombreros and ponchos among the standing cacti and other Mexicanalia. Loud music, margaritas and sangria by the jug, fajitas, tacos and seafood chimichanga. Not far off is the **Texas Lone Star**, which can get pretty rowdy in the evening. It is set in a wooden cabin, its walls covered in T-shirts (left by satisfied customers no doubt). Televisions hang from the roof, visible from all angles and playing continuously, so you can catch up on the NFL. The bar is on one side, the eatery on the other; both are popular with a young crowd.

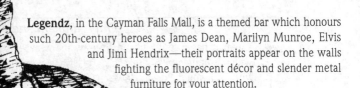

Legendz, in the Cayman Falls Mall, is a themed bar which honours such 20th-century heroes as James Dean, Marilyn Munroe, Elvis and Jimi Hendrix—their portraits appear on the walls fighting the fluorescent décor and slender metal furniture for your attention.

Artifically dark during the day, by night it's lit by the huge bank of spirit bottles which make up the equally large cocktail menu. It attracts an expat crowd of all ages.

You'll have a good night out at the **Holiday Inn**, where there is a comedy club, Coconuts, with artists brought in from abroad. Afterwards you can head outside to the bar on the beach, where you can drink and dance to the resident singer, Barefoot Man, and his band (actually quite fun, and particularly recommended because for once there is no cover charge). There is jazz on Wednesdays at **Casablanca**, a bar-restaurant chequered in black and white, with fifties film stars all over the walls, where you drink Guinness and Victoria bitter, and food is served till midnight; popular with expats. **The Links** at Safehaven also has a jazz happy hour on Fridays.

There are three main nightclubs: **Rumheads 'Niteclub and Sports Bar'** is a big and busy air-conditioned club, where a good mix of young Caymanians, expats and tourists gather. Fluorescent strips and flags surround the central bar, with a dancefloor for the discotheque and band music on one side, and a pool hall on the other; tvs faithfully play the sport above. The music changes nightly, from Caribbean sounds (Wed) to BPM (beats per minute) and high energy dance music; there's a cover charge. **Sharkey's** is a large video dancefloor with disco lights and a bar topped by a huge, fairy-lit model shark. Big nights are: Mon (disco); Fri (80s); Sat (90s). You can avoid the weekend cover charge by drinking early at the **Liquid Lounge** next door; admire the fishy pictures up on screen.

There is something of a circuit when it comes to the bars and clubs in Cayman. This changes from time to time, but at the time of writing the early evening bars were **Santiagos**, the **Lone Star** and **Legendz**. Then you moved on to: **Shakeys** (Mon); **Rumheads** (Tues); jazz at **Casablanca** (Wed); **Rumheads** (Thurs); and **Shakeys** again (Fri and Sat). On Sundays Grand Cayman is dead.

Cayman Brac

Ask a 'Bracker' and you'll be told that success has gone to their heads in Grand Cayman. Cayman Brac, they say, still has the easygoing tranquillity that Grand Cayman had 20 years ago, before there were any hotels along Seven Mile Beach. It is true that Cayman Brac is far quieter and calmer: there are just a couple of hotels and a few villas and none of the buzz or the endless traffic of Cayman.

Cayman Brac is 12 miles long and about a mile wide. It takes its name from its cliff (Brac means cliff in Gaelic), a central core of limestone that extends along the middle of the island. The island gradually rises from the west, achieving a vertiginous 140ft in the northeast, the highest point in the Cayman Islands. There are a number of caves in the limestone, none that exciting. The island is scrub- and cactus-covered, but can be suprisingly lush in the wet season.

Getting There and Around

By air: Island Air, ℭ 948 1656, fly from Grand Cayman to Gerrard Smith International Airport in Cayman Brac twice a day (touching Little Cayman on the way and on the way back) and Cayman Airways, ℭ 949 2311,

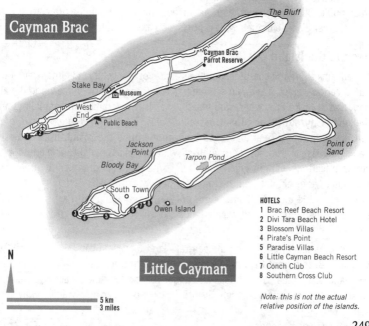

Cayman Brac

The Bluff

Cayman Brac
Parrot Reserve

Stake Bay

Museum

West
End

Public Beach

Jackson
Point

Tarpon Pond

Point of
Sand

Bloody Bay

South Town

Owen Island

Little Cayman

N

5 km
3 miles

HOTELS
1 Brac Reef Beach Resort
2 Divi Tara Beach Hotel
3 Blossom Villas
4 Pirate's Point
5 Paradise Villas
6 Little Cayman Beach Resort
7 Conch Club
8 Southern Cross Club

*Note: this is not the actual
relative position of the islands.*

make the link most days. And there is an international link to Miami, almost daily on Cayman Airways. If you are flying internationally, there is a departure tax of US$10. **Hire cars** are available through Hertz, ✆ 949 1515, Avis, ✆ 948 2847, and at Four D's Car Rental, ✆ 948 1599. Scooters and bicycles can be hired through B&S Motor Venture, ✆ 948 1646, close to the hotels in the southwest of the island. The bus stop signs are for school buses and not for adults. If you stick out your thumb, the few cars that pass will probably pick you up.

Diving

The diving in Cayman Brac is even better than that in Grand Cayman— divers' groups have taken to leaving painted driftwood signs to record their trip and general satisfaction. There are three dive operators on the island, all in the southwest, in or near the hotels: **Dive Tiara**, ✆ 948 1553, **Brac Aquatics**, ✆ 948 1429, and **Reef Divers**, based at the Brac Reef Beach Resort, ✆ 948 1323. If you are not a diver, there is excellent snorkelling opposite the old Buccaneer Inn, close to the airport, and west of there towards Stake Bay.

There are no great **beaches** here. Most of the shoreline is rocky and the only place where there is any sand at all is in the southwest where the hotels are. There is a small public beach, however, with mounded sand and swimming protected by the offshore reef. For the limited **watersports**, you are dependent on the hotels.

Around the Island

A road runs along the coastline, on the stretches of low lying land either side of the raised central 'brac'. The main settlements are at the eastern end, around the airport, and at Stake Bay, where you will find the island administrative buildings and the small **Cayman Brac Museum**, *open daily, 9–12, 2–4, Sun afternoon only*. This has two rooms of artefacts gathered from around the island, from domestic items such as garden tools and 'yobbas' (water storage bowls) to ancient-looking communications paraphernalia and an early ice-making machine driven by kerosene. Other exhibits tell the romantic story of Brac's connection with the sea. There are scale models of ships built on the island, along with sail needles and shears, caulking mallets and wooden 'fids' (for splicing rope) and 'dead-eyes', used to keep the mainstays on the masts taut.

On the brac itself (reached on the central island road) you can take a walk in the **Cayman Brac Parrot Reserve**, on a path cut into the central bush with annotated trees and plants: mango, hemlock and liquorice, and the 'dildo' cactus, covered in spikes. If you are lucky you might disturb a pair of Brac parrots, which will fly away twittering and screeching. Following the track beyond here to the eastern end of the island, past thatch palms and agave (originally used for making rope) and a few small plots of farmed land, you come to the top of the brac itself. There are lighthouses (old and new) and, curiously, two portaloos, at the time of writing anyway. The island's carnival, **Bracchanal**, is held at Mardi Gras (Shrove Tuesday) each year and involves street parades and dancing.

© (809–)

Where to Stay

There are two main hotels on the island, on the southwestern shore, both specialists in diving (packages available), and each with a busy beach-resort atmosphere. The **Divi Tiara Beach Hotel**, © 948 1553, ✆ 948 1316, has 59 rooms in blocks ranged behind the seafront. There is an attractive bar area on a deck under the trees just above the excellent powder-soft sand where hammocks hang among the palms. Facilities include tennis courts, a pool, jacuzzis, watersports and snorkelling (*expensive–moderate*). Not far off is the slightly smaller (40 rooms) and quieter **Brac Reef Beach Resort**, PO Box 56, © 948 7323, US toll free © 1 800 327 3835. Modern, comfortable rooms, with fans, tvs and air-conditioning, are set in blocks that overlook a sandy garden with a tangle of sea grape trees. There is a reasonable beach and some sports—including diving, of course (*moderate*). Other options for accommodation include the condominiums at the **Brac Caribbean Beach Village**, © 948 2265, ✆ 948 1111, US toll free © 1 800 791 7911 (*expensive*), and several houses to rent at **La Esperanza**, PO Box 28, © 948 0531, ✆ 948 0525, in Stake Bay on the north shore (*moderate*).

Eating Out

In the southwestern corner of the island, near the hotels, you can find delicious international fare, moderately priced, in the congenial surroundings of a neat and pretty dining room at the **Coral Isle Club**. Outside the hotels and condominiums there are a couple of easygoing restaurants with a genuine West Indian feel about them, serving home-cooked Caribbean food. Near the turning to West End, **Aunt Sha's Kitchen** is a more local eatery; the dining room is on a terrace dressed in pink, and the constant roar of breakers provides the soundtrack to your meal. Fried kingfish and curried chicken are served with coleslaw or rice 'n' peas. On the north coast you will get an equally good West Indian meal at **La Esperanza**: fish, chicken or shrimp followed by a Key Lime pie. In West Bay you can try **Edd's Place**, for local and international fare, or the **G&M Diner**. For a daytime sandwich or salad, check out **Angie's Ice-Cream and Subs**, close by. There's even a drive-through take-out of all things in Cayman Brac, **Blackie's Seaview** at Tibbett's Turn on the north coast, but it is not often open.

Little Cayman

Five miles west of Cayman Brac is Little Cayman, dozier, more isolated and less developed even than the Brac. It is just 10 miles long, about a mile wide and makes it to a massive 40ft in elevation. The scrub- and mangrove-covered land is relieved by salt-ponds and inland lagoons. At its height, when the island was frequented as a source of fresh water, the population reached 400, but nowadays it is inhabited by just 70 or so, most of whom are involved with the tourism business.

The population of birds is far greater than that of humans and around the ponds on the south coast you will find boobies, ducks and stilts, and flights of magnificent piratical frigatebirds, which puff out their huge red gullets when courting. There are around 2000 iguanas on the island, but unfortunately they have a potentially fatal habit of sunning themselves on the road. Signs at the roadside, with iguanas painted on them, ask you to drive with care.

Life is very easygoing in Little Cayman and the diving is the best in the Cayman Islands. The place is barely developed—electricity reached the island only in 1990; there is only one policeman, one petrol pump and one bank, open only for a few hours a week. They actually had a robbery in 1996, but the word on the streets was that it was an insurance scam. Like the rest of the Cayman Islands, Little Cayman is not far from civilization, but there is still an atmosphere of seclusion and isolation here.

Getting There and Around

For **flights** to Little Cayman, *see* above in Cayman Brac. It is possible to fly direct to Cayman Brac from the States and then make the short hop by Island Air (Little Cayman ✆ 948 0021), which makes two journeys across each day. **Hire cars** are available through McLaughlin Jeeps, ✆ 948 1000, and Paradise Villas, ✆ 948 0001, both of which are within walking distance of the airstrip. All of the hotels seem to have **bicycles** available, and these are quite adequate if you are going to stick to the southwestern corner of the island, where all the hotels are.

There are a number of **dive operators** on the island, each attached to accommodation. Contact the Southern Cross Club, ✆ 948 1099, the Little Cayman Beach Resort, ✆ 948 1033, which has a photographic centre, or Paradise Villas, ✆ 948 0001.

If you are not a diver, there is excellent **snorkelling** on the north shore in Jackson's Bay, directly opposite the road that crosses the island. The beaches around the hotels in the southwest are passable, though there is quite a lot of turtle grass just offshore. There is good sand on Owen Island and a reasonable beach at Point of Sands at the east end of the island looking out to Cayman Brac. The deep-sea fishing off the island is excellent, as is the bone-fishing in the shallow flats; contact the hotels.

Around the Island

The only area in Little Cayman that can be described as a settlement is in the southwest, the cluster of houses that make up the 'Village', as it is usually known. Officially it is called South Town, but this does not imply another town on the island as there is none. Elsewhere, there is just the occasional house or hotel dotted along the shoreline, mainly on the south coast of the island. The grass airstrip is close to the town. It is quite entertaining watching the flights come in and go out. The plane has to cross the main (only) road to get to the terminal building and it is kick-started out of a wheelbarrow.

A road (tarmacked in places, but mostly dirt trail) rings the island just in from the coast. As you head east from the Village you pass between the hotels on the shoreline and the Booby Pond inland, a lagoon fringed with mangrove where boobies and frigatebirds roost and nest. At the western end there is a house with a veranda from which you can view the birds through a telescope. Farther up on the south coast you come to Tarpon Lake, where a boardwalk leads out into the lagoon, through mangroves which have taken nearly 10 years to regenerate after the destruction of Hurricane Gilbert in 1988. The tarpon of the name have been isolated in the lake for centuries and have adapted to their new freshwater surroundings. On the north coast is Bloody Bay: some say it was so called because of the blood on the beach after a conflict between the British and Spaniards but the beach may also have gained its name from whalers who came here to butcher their catch.

© (809–)   *Where to Stay*

The most stylish place to stay on Little Cayman is the **Southern Cross Club**, © 948 1099, ✆ 948 1098, which stands on a sandy stretch of shoreline on the other side of town, nearly opposite Owen Island. There are just 10 spacious rooms, furnished in breezy and bright Caribbean fabrics and louvred for fan-ventilation (there is also air-conditioning), set in double bungalows scattered loosely around the garden. There is a central clubhouse with a freshwater pool and sunning deck. An extremely good place to relax (particularly in the hammocks spread around the grounds), it's very quiet, but sports are available and of course there is a dive shop, with boats that take off from the club's private dock. The plan includes all meals (*expensive*).

Pirate's Point, ✆ 948 1010, ✉ 948 1011, occupies its own small stretch of beach to the west of the Village. Ten rooms are set in cottages (only four of them air-conditioned) in a garden overgrown with sea grape trees, palms and casuarina pines. The central bar and dining room is a little rustic, its walls hung with divers' paraphernalia and driftwood painted with longing messages. It's fun, though, and you will be well looked after in the dining room. Meals are part of the all-inclusive package; some diving and fishing packages are available (*luxury–expensive*).If you'd like a busier, resort-style hotel, then try the **Little Cayman Beach Resort**, ✆ 948 1033, US toll free ✆ 1 800 327 3835, situated on a private stretch of beach just down from the Village. The 32 rooms stand in two-storey blocks either side of the central garden and sitting area. There's a pool and an open-air bar, with steps down on to the passable beach. Rooms are large and comfortable, with air-conditioning, fans and tvs—all the modern comforts. There are the usual sports including diving and fishing, kayaks and sea cycles and a tennis court. There are also eight suites attached to the hotel (*expensive*).

Paradise Villas, PO Box 30, ✆ 948 0001, ✉ 948 0002, on the seafront just close to the airstrip in the Village, are 12 villas built in pink and white wood, with balconies overlooking the sea. The smallish rooms are furnished in pastel tones and have fans and air-conditioning. There's a freshwater pool and watersports (*expensive–moderate*). If you would prefer to stay in an apartment, contact the **Conch Club**, ✆ the Little Cayman Beach Resort, or **Blossom Villas**, ✆ 948 1000, ✉ 948 1001 (*both expensive*).

Eating Out

Each of the hotels has its own dining room and most of them offer a meals-inclusive package. You can also get them to make you a picnic if you are going to take off for the day. The **Hungry Iguana** at Paradise Villas is a gathering place for Little Cayman residents. The main room is part American diner and part bar, with bench seats on one side and a long high bar on the other, serving Caribbean and American lunches and dinners, burgers and salads, fresh catch lightly grilled or blackened, some pizzas, and occasional barbecues under the trees above the beach. There is another dining room at the restaurant, where you can eat gourmet meals flambéed at your table.

Note: page numbers in **bold** indicate main references; *italic* numbers indicate maps.

Index